C000185291

Kate Woodford

Isabel Burt
Lucy Richardson
Nicholas Burt

ORCHARDS COOKERY

Special Thanks

With a very special thanks to our wonderful team who have contributed to the success of Orchards Cookery and to this book:

Rosalie Bomford
Evelyn Yeatman-Biggs
Chris (Bones) Holmes
Jono Seward
Mike Wallis
George Shuttleworth
Andrew Hogg

The school would not have existed if it had not been for the support of Norris and Rosalie Bomford (parents of Isabel and Lucy) who allowed their family home to be used as the location for the cookery school - Thank you!

Published by Orchards Cookery Ltd.
ISBN Number 978-0-9930635-0-3

INTRODUCTION

Orchards Cookery is an award winning cookery school situated in the heart of England, near Stratford-upon-Avon.

The School specialises in training and recruiting Chalet Cooks and also runs Off to University courses, Designer Dinner party courses, Corporate Days and One and Two Day cookery courses.

Orchards Cookery also offers a recruitment service supplying cooks for ski chalets, private parties, shooting, hunting and fishing lodges, holiday villas, yachts etc. and also helps students find placements where they can use their new skills.

The school was set up by two sisters, Isabel Burt and Lucy Richardson (née Bomford), in 2003 in their family home. Isabel's husband Nicholas joined the business in 2008 when he married Isabel and they live in the main house with their children, creating a welcoming family atmosphere for students staying at the school.

Most of the photographs in this book are of food cooked by students during their cookery courses and were photographed by Nicholas Burt.

FOOD ALLERGENS

Allergens (or ingredients that contain or may contain allergens) have been **highlighted in pink** in the list of ingredients in each recipe. This is to help cooks who may have to comply with the EU Food Information for Consumers Regulations, or who are cooking for people with food allergies.

NB Different food manufacturers use varying ingredients in their products so some ingredients highlighted in pink may not in fact contain allergens and vice versa. Cooks must therefore check carefully all food labels and ingredients.

The 14 allergens (as defined by The Food Standards Agency) are listed below with some examples of where they may be found. These have to be disclosed to consumers to comply with The Food Information Legislation 2014 (UK).

Celery - Includes stalks, leaves, seeds, and the root called celeriac. You can find celery in celery salt, salads and some meat products (eg. casseroles), soup and stock cubes.

Cereals containing gluten - Gluten is found in barley, oats and wheat (such as spelt, Khorasan wheat, Kamut) and rye. Also in foods containing flour such as some types of baking powder, batter, breadcrumbs, bread, cakes, couscous, meat products, pasta, pastry, sauces, soup, and fried foods that have been dusted with flour.

Crustaceans - Eg. crab, lobster, prawns and scampi. Shrimp paste is often used in Thai and South East Asian curries and salads.

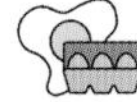

Eggs - Eggs are often found in cakes, mayonnaise, mousses, pasta, quiche, sauces, some meat products and pastries, or foods brushed or glazed with egg.

Fish - Found in fish sauces, relishes, salad dressings, stock cubes, pizzas and Worcestershire sauce.

Lupin - Lupin flour and seeds are used in some types of breads, pastries and even in pasta. It may also be found in other types of flour.

Milk - Milk is the main constituent of butter, cheese, cream, milk powders and yoghurt. It can also be found in foods brushed or glazed with milk and in powdered soups or sauces.

Molluscs - Eg. Squid, land snails, whelks, mussels, oysters and other shellfish. May be found in oyster sauce or fish stews.

Mustard - Eg. Readymade mustards, mustard powder and mustard seeds. Can also be found in breads, curries, marinades, meat products, salad dressings, sauces and soups.

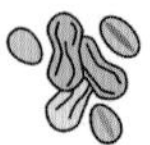

Peanuts - Peanuts are a legume and grow underground. Often used as an ingredient in biscuits, cakes, curries, desserts, sauces (eg. satay sauce) and ground nut oil.

Tree nuts - Eg. cashews, almonds and hazelnuts. Can be found in breads, biscuits, crackers, desserts, nut powders (often used in Asian curries), stir fried dishes, ice cream, marzipan, nut oils and sauces.

Sesame seeds - Can often be found in bread, bread sticks, hummus, tahini and sesame oil.They are sometimes toasted and used in salads.

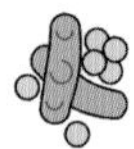

Soya - Often found in bean curd, edamame beans, miso paste, textured soya protein, soya flour, tofu, desserts, ice cream, meat products, sauces and vegetarian products. It is a staple ingredient in oriental foods.

Sulphur dioxide - (sometimes known as sulphites) - Often used in dried fruit such as raisins, dried apricots and prunes. Sometimes in meat products, soft drinks, vegetables, wine and beer.

Orchards Cookery accepts no liability for any mistakes or omissions in the highlighting of food allergens in this book. It is the responsibility of the cook to check all ingredients and manufacturers food labels.

CONTENTS

The asterisk (*) sign in this recipe book indicates that a recipe can be prepared up to that point and continued later.

THE ORCHARDS
SCHOOL OF COOKERY

CANAPÉS

CANAPÉS

CANAPÉS

CANAPÉS

Spicy Savoury Scones

INGREDIENTS ££

225g (8 oz) self raising flour
1 tsp baking powder
¼ tsp salt
Pinch of cayenne pepper
55g (2 oz) butter
2 tsp wholegrain mustard
100g (3¾ oz) cheese, *grated*
4 spring onions, *finely sliced*
1 chilli, *deseeded and finely sliced*
75ml (2½ fl oz) milk *(approx)*
30g (1 oz) cheese, *grated*
(to decorate the top)

METHOD

These are a good base for a canapé when sliced in half.

Preheat the oven to 200°C / 400°F / gas mark 6

1. Mix together the flour, baking powder, salt and a good pinch of cayenne pepper in a bowl.
2. Rub the butter into the flour mixture using your fingertips, until the mixture resembles breadcrumbs.
3. Mix in the mustard, cheese, spring onions and chilli.
4. Make a well in the centre and add most of the milk. Mix together and work into a soft dough with your hands, adding more milk if necessary.
5. Turn out onto a lightly floured chopping board and knead into a shape ready for rolling.
6. Roll out to about 2 cm (¾ inch) thick and use a cutter 4 cm (1½ inch) in diameter to cut out the scones.
7. Scatter the cheese over and bake on a lined baking tray for 8-10 minutes until golden brown. Allow to cool on a cooling rack.

Cut in half and use as a canapé base or serve with soup.

Prawn Filo Cups

INGREDIENTS ££

30g (1 oz) butter
Filo pastry, approx 1 sheet *(leave wrapped up until you use it)*
100g (3½ oz) frozen cooked prawns, *defrosted and dried*
2 tbsp cream cheese
1 tbsp fresh coriander, *chopped*
¼ tsp sugar
½ fresh chilli, *finely chopped*
Fresh parsley, *to garnish*

METHOD

SERVES 8

Preheat the oven to 180°C / 350°F / gas mark 4

1. Melt the butter gently in a saucepan. Using some of the butter, grease, then flour the canapé tin.
2. Open out the pastry and cut into approx 6 cm (2¾ inch) squares *(you will need 24 squares in total)*.
3. Using a pastry brush, coat 12 pieces on both sides with the melted butter. Place one piece in each canapé mould.
4. Coat one side of the remaining pieces of pastry with melted butter and place a second layer into each mould, buttered side up *(place them on top of one another so the corners do not overlap and a star shape is formed)*.
5. Bake for about 7 minutes until crisp and golden brown. *
6. To make the filling, mix together the cream cheese, coriander, sugar, chilli and black pepper and gently stir in the prawns. *
7. Divide the filling between the pastry cups and top each one with a tiny head of parsley.

Mozzarella, Ham & Pesto Crostinis

INGREDIENTS ££

3 slices of white bread, *toasted*
Tomato purée
Mozzarella cheese, *thinly sliced*
Ham, *sliced*
Pesto

METHOD

SERVES 8

Preheat the oven to 180°C / 350°F / gas mark 4

1. Spread a very thin layer of tomato purée over the toast, followed by a slice of ham.
2. Top with mozzarella and a little pesto *(the cheese must completely cover the ham, otherwise it will curl up).*
3. Bake in the oven for 15-20 minutes until the cheese has melted.
4. Remove the crusts and cut into bite size pieces.

Smoked Salmon / Boursin Cheese Spinach Whirls

INGREDIENTS ££

Smoked Salmon Filling

Crème fraîche
English mustard
Smoked salmon trimmings
Lemon juice

Boursin Cheese Filling

Boursin cheese
Cream
Wafer thin sliced ham

Crêpes

30g (1 oz) frozen spinach, *thawed*
1 egg
85g (3 oz) plain flour
150ml (5 fl oz / ¼ pt) milk

METHOD

SERVES 8

1. Squeeze the water out of the spinach, then put all the crêpe ingredients into a food processor. Blend until smooth *(if you need to thin out the batter add a little more milk).*
2. To cook the crêpes, warm some vegetable oil in a small frying pan and spoon in a little of the batter, tilting the pan so it covers the base evenly. Cook for a minute or two and then turn to cook the other side *(you may need to add a little more oil to the pan. Notice that one side of the pancake is greener in colour).*
3. Allow to cool, then place the greener side, face down, ready for filling:
   a) **Smoked salmon filling:** dot lightly with mustard. Spread a thin layer of crème fraîche over it followed by a layer of smoked salmon and a drizzle of lemon juice.
   b) **Boursin cheese filling:** mix together the boursin with a little cream to make a spreadable paste. Spread a layer over the crêpes, followed by a layer of ham.
4. Tightly roll each crêpe, wrap each one in cling film and chill. *
5. To serve, remove the cling film, slice into 1 cm (⅜ inch) rounds and arrange on a plate.

Leek & Sweetcorn Fritters

INGREDIENTS ££

Dip
1-2 tsp wholegrain mustard
4 tbsp natural yoghurt
1 tsp clear honey
1 tbsp fresh chives, *chopped*

Batter Mix
100g (3½ oz) plain flour
1 egg
150ml (5 fl oz / ¼ pt) milk
1 tsp baking powder

3 tbsp olive oil
2 leeks, *finely chopped*
100g (3½ oz) sweetcorn *(small tin), drained*

METHOD

SERVES 8

1. **To make the dip**, mix all ingredients together and chill. *
2. Fry the leeks in 1 tbsp of oil until soft, remove from the heat, stir in the sweetcorn and allow to cool. *
3. **To make the batter**, sieve the flour into a bowl and make a well in the centre, add the egg, milk, baking powder, salt and pepper and beat together.
4. Add the leek and sweetcorn mixture. *
5. Heat the remaining oil in a frying pan, drop small rounds of the mixture into it, cook for a couple of minutes then turn to brown the other side.

Serve warm with the chilled dip.

Mexican Nachos

INGREDIENTS ££

Guacamole
2 large tomatoes
2 medium avocados
1 garlic clove, *crushed*
¼ onion
½ tsp chilli powder
Dash of tabasco
Lemon juice, *dash*

Tortilla chips
Cheese, *grated*
Soured cream
Jar of salsa

METHOD

SERVES 8

Preheat the oven to 180°C / 350°F / gas mark 4

1. **To make the guacamole**, quarter the tomatoes, remove the core and seeds and dice.
2. Blend all the guacamole ingredients *(except for the tomatoes)* in a food processor until smooth. Stir in the tomatoes and season to taste.
3. Empty the bag of tortilla chips on to an ovenproof plate, sprinkle with cheese and bake for 7-10 minutes until the cheese has melted.
4. When the cheese has melted spoon over the guacamole, followed by the salsa and top with soured cream.

Serve immediately.

Endive (Chicory) Spoons with Roquefort & Walnuts

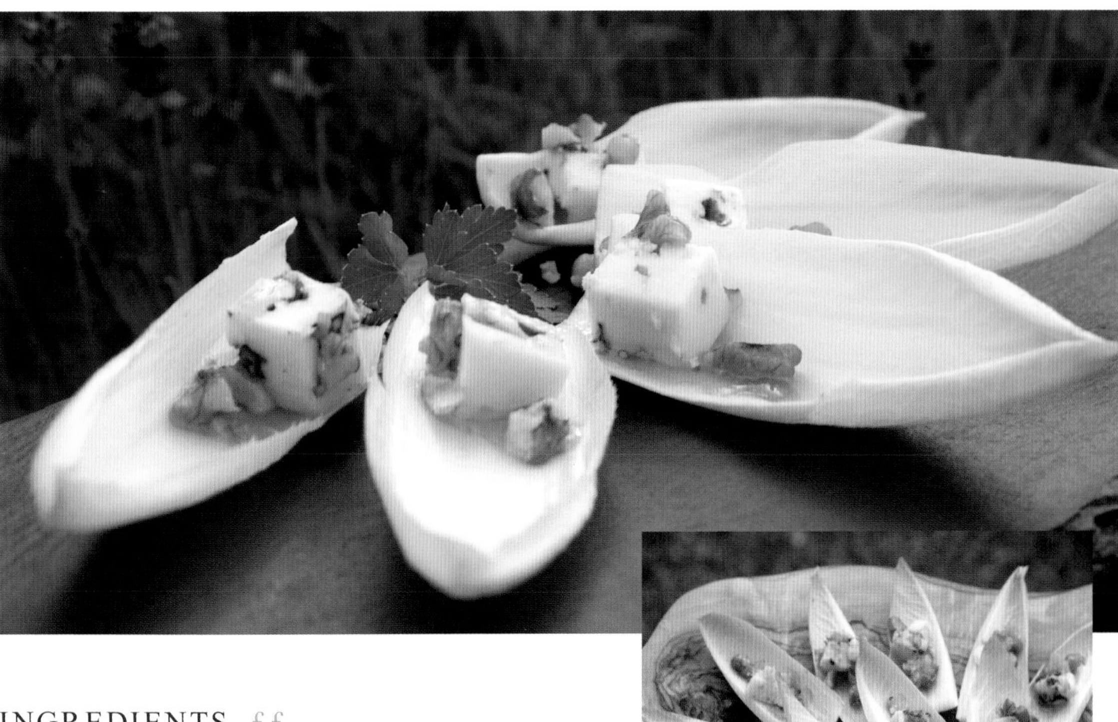

INGREDIENTS ££

Walnut Dressing
1 tbsp wholegrain mustard or Dijon mustard
1 tbsp white wine vinegar
1 tsp sugar
2 tbsp water
2 tbsp walnut oil
2 tbsp olive oil

1 endive *(chicory)*
7g (¼ oz) walnuts, *roughly chopped*
15g (½ oz) Roquefort cheese, *cubed*

METHOD

SERVES 8

1. **To make the dressing**, put the mustard, white wine vinegar, sugar and water into a jam jar and shake to dissolve the sugar. Then add the oils and shake well to combine. Season to taste. *
2. To prepare the endive, trim the bottom and separate the leaves, wash the outer leaves.
3. Arrange the salad leaves on a serving plate, place the cubes of Roquefort on the trimmed end of each leaf, sprinkle with walnuts * and pour a little dressing on to the centre of each leaf.

Catherine Wheels

INGREDIENTS £

Puff pastry, *chilled*
Wafer thin ham
Parmesan cheese, *finely grated*
Wholegrain mustard
Milk, *to glaze*

METHOD

Preheat the oven to 180°C / 350°F / gas mark 4

1. On a sheet of floured baking paper roll the pastry into a rectangle about 3 mm (1/8 inch) thick.
2. Coat the pastry with a very thin layer of mustard.
3. Sprinkle generously with Parmesan and cover with slices of ham.
4. Tightly roll the pastry, wrap in the baking paper and refrigerate *(chilled pastry is easier to work with).* *
5. Slice *(approx 1 cm / 3/8 inch thick)* and place on a lined baking tray *(allow enough space between each canapé as they will expand in the oven).*
6. Glaze with milk and bake for about 20 minutes until golden brown.

Serve warm.

Baby Sweetcorn / Banana wrapped in Bacon

INGREDIENTS ££

8-12 rashers of streaky bacon, *cut in two*
1 banana, *cut in half lengthways and then into pieces 2 cm long*
5 baby sweetcorn, *cut into two*

Variations: you can try lots of other fillings eg. dates or prunes *(known as devils on horseback)*

METHOD

SERVES 8

Preheat the oven to 180°C / 350°F / gas mark 4

1. Wrap the sweetcorn / banana in the bacon. Hold together with a cocktail stick and bake for about 20 minutes until the bacon is crisp.

Egg Nests

INGREDIENTS £

3 eggs
Mayonnaise
Fresh chives *(optional)*

Pastry
170g (6 oz) plain flour
85g (3 oz) butter or margarine
1 small shallot, *blended*
Pinch of salt
Water, *if needed*

METHOD

SERVES 8

Preheat the oven to 180°C / 350°F / gas mark 4

1. **To make the pastry**, blend all the ingredients in a food processor. Gather into a ball *(add water if too dry)*, wrap in cling film and chill in the fridge for 15 minutes *(to make it easier to handle)*.
2. Roll out the pastry and cut to size using a fluted pastry cutter *(the thinner the pastry is rolled the better)*.
3. Place in a greased and then floured canapé tin. Prick the base with a fork and blind bake for about 10 minutes until cooked *(to blind bake, use small paper cases filled with rice or baking beans. Remove paper cases and bake for a further 2 minutes)*.
4. Put the eggs into a saucepan of cold water, bring to the boil and then cook for 6 minutes.
5. Plunge into cold water, * peel and finely chop the eggs.
6. Add a little mayonnaise, season and spoon the mixture into each pastry case.
7. Grind black pepper over the top and decorate with chopped chives.

Serve immediately.

Grapes Rolled in Cream Cheese & Chopped Hazelnuts

INGREDIENTS £££

Grapes, *washed, dried & chilled*
Cream cheese
Hazelnuts, *finely chopped*

METHOD

1. Using your hands, cover each grape with the cream cheese, then place in a small bowl of chopped hazelnuts.
2. Roll the coated grapes in the nuts, arrange on a plate and serve chilled. *

Mini Croque Monsieur

INGREDIENTS £

3 slices of white **bread**, *toasted*
Wholegrain **mustard**
Cheese, *sliced*
Ham, *sliced*

METHOD

SERVES 8

Preheat the oven to 180°C / 350°F / gas mark 4

1. Lightly spread each slice of toast with mustard.
2. Place the ham and then the cheese on the toast * *(the cheese must completely cover the ham, otherwise it will curl up)* and bake for about 15 minutes until golden brown.
3. Remove the crusts and cut into bite size pieces.

Lamb Koftas with Mint & Garlic Dip

INGREDIENTS £££

Lamb Koftas
20g (¾ oz) butter
½ onion, *chopped*
1 garlic clove, *crushed*
250g (9 oz) cooked lamb, *fat and gristle removed*
½ tsp ground cumin
1 tsp ground coriander
1 tbsp fresh mint, *chopped* or 1 tsp mint sauce
1 egg, *beaten*

Mint & Garlic Dip
4 tbsp yoghurt *(crème fraîche can be used)*
2 tsp mint sauce or fresh mint, *chopped*
1 garlic clove, *crushed*

2 tbsp vegetable oil
Fresh parsley or mint, *for garnish*

METHOD

SERVES 8

1. **To make the dip**, combine the ingredients and leave for the flavours to infuse. *
2. Warm the butter in a frying pan and cook the onion and garlic over a gentle heat until soft.
3. Blend the onion and garlic in the food processor with the lamb, cumin, coriander, mint and egg, season.
4. Divide the mixture into 24 portions and roll each into a mini sausage shape. *
5. Warm the vegetable oil in a frying pan and gently brown the koftas, being careful not to break them up.
6. Transfer on to kitchen paper. Put a cocktail stick into the end of each one, so the cocktail sticks lie flat and transfer to a presentation plate.
7. Garnish with mint or parsley and serve immediately with the dip.

Chilli & Honey / Mango & Sesame / Honey & Mustard Roasted Cocktail Sausages

INGREDIENTS ££

16-24 cocktail sausages

Mango & Sesame Seed Glaze
2-3 tbsp mango chutney
1 tbsp sesame seeds

Honey & Mustard Glaze
2-4 tbsp honey
2-3 tbsp wholegrain mustard

Chilli & Honey Glaze
1 fresh chilli, *deseeded & finely chopped*
3 tbsp honey

METHOD

SERVES 8

Preheat the oven to 180°C / 350°F / gas mark 4

1. Place the sausages on a baking tray, prick with a fork and bake for 20-25 minutes until slightly browned *(if using pre-cooked sausages, start at stage 2).*
2. Pour off any excess fat then spoon over the glaze. * Bake for a further 10 minutes until sticky and golden brown.

Serve warm with cocktail sticks.

Sautéed Beef Fillet with Horseradish Sauce on Mini Yorkshire Puddings

INGREDIENTS £££

Batter Mix - makes 18 Yorkshire puddings
55g (2 oz) plain **flour**
1 **egg**
150ml (5 fl oz / ¼ pt) **milk**
Lard
130g (4¾ oz) beef fillet
Flat leaf parsley, *for garnishing*

Horseradish Cream
2 tbsp **crème fraîche**
1 tbsp **horseradish sauce**

METHOD

SERVES 8

Preheat the oven to 200°C / 400°F / gas mark 6

1. **To make the mini Yorkshire puddings**, beat the batter mix ingredients in a bowl, add a pinch of salt and leave to stand for 1 hour. *
2. Coat each well of a canapé tin with a little lard and put the tin in the oven to warm for about 5 minutes.
3. Transfer the batter mix into a jug.
4. Remove the canapé tin from the oven and pour a little of the mixture into each well *(the mixture should not come more than half way up the sides of each well, otherwise they will be too big).*
5. Bake for 7-10 minutes and then turn out on to a cooling rack. *
6. Fry the fillet in butter for a couple of minutes on each side *(so that it is still rare in the middle)*, then finely slice.
7. Combine the crème fraîche and horseradish sauce and, just before serving, spoon a little of the mixture into each Yorkshire pudding.
8. Top with slices of beef, dust with black pepper, garnish with flat leaf parsley and serve immediately.

Peppadew (Sweet Piquanté Peppers) Toasties

INGREDIENTS ££

250g (9 oz) **cream cheese**
8 Peppadews, *well drained*
3 slices of white **bread**
Fresh parsley

METHOD

SERVES 8

Preheat the oven to 180°C / 350°F / gas mark 4

1. Blend the cream cheese and Peppadews in a food processor and season to taste. *
2. **To make Melba toast**, lightly toast the bread in a toaster and allow to cool.
3. Remove the crusts and slide the knife through the middle of the piece of toast *(place your hand flat on top of the slice of toast with your fingers on full stretch. Start cutting from a corner and once you have reached the middle, rotate the piece of toast until you have sliced straight through).*
4. Cut the toast into eight pieces *(Union Jack cut),* place on a lined baking tray, toasted side down and bake for 4-5 minutes. *
5. Allow to cool, * then spoon the Peppadew mixture on to the centre of each piece of melba toast.
6. Top with parsley and serve immediately.

Cocktail Sausages with a Barbecue Dip

INGREDIENTS ££

24 cocktail sausages

Barbecue Dip
1 tbsp olive oil
½ onion, *chopped*
½ garlic clove, *crushed*
2 tbsp red wine
½ tsp soft brown sugar
¼ tsp chilli powder
Dash of Tabasco
1 tbsp Worcestershire sauce
1 tbsp tomato ketchup

METHOD

SERVES 8

Preheat the oven to 180°C / 350°F / gas mark 4

1. Place the sausages on a baking tray, prick with a fork and bake for 30-35 minutes *(if using pre-cooked sausages, bake for 10-15 minutes).*
2. **To make the barbecue dip**, warm the oil in a frying pan and cook the onion and garlic until soft, add the rest of the ingredients, bring to the boil and simmer 1-2 minutes until it has thickened.
3. Serve the sausages warm with the barbecue dip.

Mediterranean Toasties

INGREDIENTS £

3 slices of white bread
Olives, *sliced*
Baby tomatoes, *sliced*
Fresh chives

Hummus (or use readymade hummus)
200g (7 oz) ½ tin chickpeas, *drained & crushed*
½ tbsp tahini
1 garlic clove, *crushed*
2 tbsp olive oil
½ tbsp water
½ tsp marmite *(or ½ tsp cumin)*
½ lemon, *juiced*

METHOD

SERVES 8

Preheat the oven to 180°C / 350°F / gas mark 4

1. **To make the hummus** *(if not using readymade)*, put all the ingredients *(except for the lemon juice)* in a food processor and blend until smooth. Season and add a little of the lemon juice to taste. *
2. **To make the Melba toast**, lightly toast the bread in a toaster and allow to cool.
3. Remove the crusts and slide the knife through the middle of the piece of toast *(place your hand flat on top of the slice of toast with your fingers on full stretch. Start cutting from a corner and once you have reached the middle, rotate the piece of toast until you have sliced straight through).*
4. Cut the toast into eight pieces *(Union Jack cut),* place on a lined baking tray, toasted side down and bake for 4-5 minutes.
5. Allow to cool, then spoon the hummus on to the centre of each piece of melba toast.
6. Top with olives, tomato and chives.

Black Olive & Goats' Cheese / Stilton & Red Currant Pastry Bites

INGREDIENTS ££

Puff pastry, *chilled*
Black olives
Goats' cheese / **Stilton cheese**
Red currant jelly
Egg or **milk**, *to glaze*

METHOD

Preheat the oven to 180°C / 350°F / gas mark 4

1. To make the pastry cases, roll out the pastry and cut into approximately 3 cm (1¼ inch) squares. About ½ cm (¼ inch) in from the edge of the squares score a smaller square *(the outside area of the puff pastry will rise when baked).*
2. Stab the central area with a fork *(to prevent it from rising).* Cut the cheese into pieces and arrange within the central square *(if the cheese is positioned on the outer edge of the puff pastry it will prevent the pastry from rising).* Top with olives / red currant jelly. *
3. Glaze the pastry and bake for 15-20 minutes until the cheese has melted and the pastry is golden.

Smoked Salmon Blinis

INGREDIENTS £

Blinis
60g (2 oz) plain flour
½ tsp baking powder
½ egg
75ml (2½ fl oz) milk
2 tsp fresh parsley, *chopped*

Vegetable oil, *for frying*

Smoked salmon topping
10g (¾ oz) smoked salmon, *roughly chopped*
110g (4 oz) cream cheese
20g (¾ oz) shelled prawns
Fresh dill, *chopped (optional)*
½ tsp lemon juice

Garnish
20 shelled prawns, *sliced open through tail*
Lemon zest
Caviar *(lumpfish roe)*
Fresh flat leaf parsley

METHOD

MAKES APPROX 20

1. **To make the blinis**, whisk the flour, baking powder, egg and milk together in a bowl, stir in the parsley and season with salt and pepper.
2. Warm a little vegetable oil in a non-stick frying pan over a medium heat and pour about 1 tsp of the blini mixture into the frying pan *(each blinis should be approximately 3 cm / 1¼ inch in diameter).*
3. After a few minutes turn the blinis to lightly brown the other side. Add more oil to the pan as required.
4. Transfer to kitchen paper and allow to cool. *
5. **To make the salmon topping**, put all the topping ingredients in a food processor to combine *(blend just enough to combine the mixture, do not blend until smooth).* Season to taste.
6. Transfer the mixture into a piping bag with a star shaped nozzle and pipe the topping on to the blinis.
7. Garnish each one with a prawn, lemon zest, a little caviar and fresh parsley.

Mini Pizza Bites

INGREDIENTS £

3 slices of white **bread**
Tomato purée
Wafer thin ham, *finely chopped*
Cheese, *sliced*
Dried oregano

METHOD

SERVES 8

Preheat the oven to 180°C / 350°F / gas mark 4

1. Toast the bread and spread with tomato purée.
2. Cover with ham and cheese, sprinkle with oregano and bake for about 15 minutes until golden brown.
3. Cut into rounds using a pastry cutter or remove the crusts and cut into bite size pieces.

Caviar Toasties

INGREDIENTS £££

Finely sliced **bread** or mini **cheese biscuits**
Cream cheese
Caviar *(lumpfish roe)*

METHOD

1. Toast the bread, then cut into rounds using a small plain pastry cutter. *
2. Allow to cool, then roughly spread with cream cheese.
3. Spoon a small amount of caviar on the top and serve immediately.

Quail Egg & Caviar Nests

INGREDIENTS ££

3 slices of white bread
6 quail eggs
Mayonnaise
Caviar *(lumpfish roe)*
Fresh parsley

METHOD

MAKES 12

Preheat the oven to 180°C / 350°F / gas mark 4

1. **To make the nests**, cut the crusts off the white bread and roll it out as thin and as square as you can.
2. Butter one side of the bread and using a 5 cm (2 inch) round cutter, cut five circles out of each slice.
3. To shape the nests, place the discs in a canapé tin, butter side face down and bake for 8-10 minutes until crisp and golden in colour. Remove the baskets and allow to cool on a cooling rack. *
4. Put the eggs into a saucepan of cold water, bring to the boil and then cook for 6 minutes.
5. Plunge into cold water * peel and cut into halves.
6. Spoon a little mayonnaise into each nest, place the eggs on top, yolk side up, followed by a tiny helping of caviar and a tiny bit of parsley.

Serve immediately.

Tiger Prawn & Ginger Cakes with Thai Sauce

INGREDIENTS £££

Fish Cakes
100g (3½ oz) cod, *skinned and roughly chopped*
110g (4 oz) raw tiger prawns *(approx 16), roughly chopped*
½ garlic clove, *crushed*
½ tbsp fresh coriander, *chopped*
¼ red chilli, *finely chopped*
¼ tbsp fresh ginger, *finely chopped*

½ tbsp olive oil

Thai Sauce
50ml (1¾ oz) water
50g (2 oz) sugar
½ garlic clove, *crushed*
½ tsp fresh ginger, *finely chopped*
¼ red chilli, *finely chopped*

METHOD

SERVES 8

Preheat the oven to 200°C / 400°F / gas mark 6

1. **To make the fish cakes**, blend all the ingredients and some seasoning in a food processer so that it is just combined *(do not blend until smooth).*
2. Shape the mixture into 16 cakes, and fry in hot oil for a couple of minutes on each side to brown.
3. Place on a lined baking tray * and bake for approximately 5 minutes to reheat.
4. **To make the Thai sauce**, heat the sugar and water in a saucepan until the sugar has dissolved. Then add the rest of the ingredients and simmer for 5 minutes. Allow to cool.

Serve the fish cakes warm with the sauce in a little bowl.

Chicken Satay

INGREDIENTS £££

Satay Sauce
4 tbsp peanut butter
4 tbsp coconut milk
½ tsp soy sauce
½ tsp fresh ginger, *grated*
¼ tsp fresh chilli, *finely chopped*

15g (½ oz) butter
8 chicken tenderloins, *cut into large bite size pieces*

METHOD

SERVES 8

1. **To make the sauce**, combine all the ingredients and pour into a small serving bowl. *
2. Warm the butter in a small frying pan and cook the tenderloins over a medium heat until golden.
3. Put each piece of chicken on a cocktail stick, arrange on a serving plate with the satay sauce and serve immediately.

Cheese & Onion Crostinis

INGREDIENTS £

4 slices of white bread
Paprika

Topping version 1
¼ red onion, *finely chopped*
4 tbsp mayonnaise
20g (4 tbsp) Parmesan, *finely grated*

Topping version 2
¼ red onion, *finely chopped*
4 tbsp cream cheese
30g (2 oz) Cheddar, *finely grated*

METHOD

MAKES 20

Preheat the oven to 180°C / 350°F / gas mark 4

1. Use a 4 cm (1½ inch) plain pastry cutter to cut 5 small circles out of each slice of bread.
2. Choose your topping and mix the ingredients in a small bowl.
3. Season and spread the mixture over each circle, completely covering the top.
4. Sprinkle with paprika and bake in the oven for 12-15 minutes until golden brown.

Serve warm.

Cucumber Cups filled with Salmon Mayonnaise & topped with a Soft Boiled Quail Egg

INGREDIENTS £££

8 x 2½ cm (1 inch) thick slices of cucumber
4 quail **eggs**
30g (1 oz) leftover cooked **salmon**, *flaked*
2 tsp **mayonnaise**
Dash of lemon juice

METHOD

MAKES 8

1. Remove the skin of the cucumber slices by using a crinkled pastry cutter that is slightly smaller than the diameter of the cucumber.
2. Using a melon baller carefully scoop out some of the seeds to make space for the filling *(be careful not to go through the bottom).*
3. Cook the quail eggs for 2½ minutes in a saucepan of boiling water, then plunge into cold water to cool.
4. Mix together the salmon, mayonnaise, seasoning and a dash of lemon juice to taste.
5. Peel the eggs in cold water, then cut in half, lengthways.
6. Dry the well of the cucumber cups with kitchen paper and carefully spoon the salmon mixture into the centre. Top with the egg and season.

Sautéed Chorizo with Avocado Mousse & Feta Cubes

INGREDIENTS £££

Raw chorizo, *cut into 8 slices diagonally (½ cm / ¼ inch thick)*
½ avocado
2 tsp double cream
30g (1 oz) feta cheese, *cut into 8 cubes (½ cm / ⅜ inch)*

METHOD

SERVES 8

1. Fry the chorizo in a dry, hot frying pan until crispy *(for approximately 1½ - 2 minutes on each side)* then transfer on to kitchen paper to remove any excess fat. Allow to cool.
2. Peel and mash the avocado with the double cream. Season *(if not serving straight away add a little lemon juice to stop the avocado from going brown)*.
3. Spoon some avocado on each slice of chorizo, top with feta and serve immediately.

Mini Ham, Egg & Chips

INGREDIENTS ££

8 quails eggs
1 large potato
1 slice of ham
Vegetable oil

METHOD

MAKES 8

1. Prepare the raw quail eggs by carefully cutting off the tops of the shells with a serrated knife. Put the eggs back in the packaging until needed.
2. Cut the ham into very thin strips and arrange on 8 presentation spoons.
3. Thinly slice the potato and then cut into very thin strips. Roughly pat dry with kitchen paper.
4. Heat 5 cm (2 inch) of vegetable oil in a saucepan to 150°C and shallow fry the potato strips until golden and crispy *(be very careful not to get the oil get too hot or it will catch fire)*. Using a draining spoon, put the chips onto a plate with a layer of kitchen paper on it to absorb the excess fat. Keep warm in the oven until you need them.
5. Warm some vegetable oil in a frying pan and fry the eggs over a low heat *(pour the eggs out of their shells into the frying pan)*.
6. When the eggs are cooked transfer them to a chopping board and cut out the centre with a pastry cutter that is just bigger than the size of the yolk.
7. Arrange the chips on top of the ham, place the fried egg on top, season with salt and pepper and serve immediately.

Cucumber & Smoked Salmon Rolls filled with Chive Cream Cheese

INGREDIENTS ££

1/3 cucumber
2 fresh chives, *finely chopped*
30g (1 oz) cream cheese
30g (1 oz) smoked salmon

METHOD

SERVES 4

1. Use a potato peeler to slice the cucumber into ribbons lengthways about 8-10 cm (3-4 inch) long. *(Discard the first couple of slices - you need 4 nice ribbons preferably with seeds in)* and then pat dry using kitchen paper.
2. Mix the chives and cream cheese together and season to taste.
3. Spread some cream cheese mixture over each slice of cucumber.
4. Cut the salmon to roughly the same size as the cucumber slices and place on top of the cream cheese.
5. Roll up each slice and hold in place with a cocktail stick.

Sushi

INGREDIENTS £££

Sushi Rice
125g (4½ oz) sushi rice
165ml (5½ oz) water
1 tbsp rice vinegar
½ tbsp sugar
¼ tsp salt

Dipping Sauce
25ml soy sauce
¼ tsp lime juice
2 drops fish sauce
¼ tsp wasabi paste

Filling Suggestions to Mix & Match:
Tomato & avocado
Smoked salmon & cucumber
Carrot
Leftover cooked salmon
Crab sticks
Smoked mackerel
Tinned tuna

2 sheets of nori
Pickled root ginger slices
Wasabi paste

METHOD

SERVES 8

1. Wash the rice really well and put it in to a small saucepan. Add the measured amount of water, bring to the boil and simmer for 10 minutes with the lid on.
2. Remove from the heat and leave to stand for 25-30 minutes. DO NOT remove the lid. *
3. Mix together the rice vinegar, sugar and salt and stir into the rice.
4. **To make the dipping sauce**, mix all the ingredients together using a coil whisk.
5. Tear off an A4 size piece of cling film *(or use a sushi mat if you have one)* and place 1 sheet of nori on top of it. Wet your fingers and spread half of the rice over the nori, leaving a 1 cm (½ inch) space at the top and bottom *(the rice should be less than 1 cm / ½ inch thick)*.
6. About half of the way up from the bottom, lay your filling along the rice from right to left.
7. Roll up very tightly from the bottom, twist the ends of the cling film to hold it in place and chill.
8. Remove the cling film and cut into 1-2 cm (½ - ¾ inch) thick slices.

Serve with the dipping sauce, pickled ginger and wasabi paste.

Broad Bean, Mint & Pecorino Pesto

INGREDIENTS £££

750g (1 lb 11 oz) broad beans, frozen or (320g / 11 oz) peeled weight
2 tbsp lemon juice
7 tbsp olive oil
170g (6 oz) **pecorino cheese**, *finely grated*
4 tbsp fresh mint, *finely chopped*
2 tbsp fresh basil, *finely chopped*

1 garlic clove, *crushed*
Tortillas, **melba toast** or French **bread**

METHOD

SERVES 8

1. Add the broad beans to a pan of boiling water and cook for 4 minutes.
2. Drain, then plunge into cold water.
3. Remove and discard the skin of the beans *(tear the skin with your nail and squeeze out the inside)* collecting the insides in a large bowl.
4. Add the lemon juice and olive oil and mash together.
5. Stir in the other ingredients and season to taste.

Serve on tortilla *(cut the tortillas like a cake into 16 segments and bake in the oven for 8 minutes until slightly brown)*, melba toast or slices of toasted French bread.

Courgette Fritters with Garlic & Rosemary Dip

INGREDIENTS ££

Garlic & Rosemary Dip
3 large garlic cloves
3 tbsp mayonnaise
3-4 tsp milk
3 small sprigs of fresh rosemary, *finely chopped*

2 courgettes
155g (5 oz) seasoned flour
2 eggs, *beaten*
2-3 tbsp vegetable oil

METHOD

SERVES 8

Preheat the oven to 180°C / 350°F / gas mark 4

1. **To make the dip**, roast the whole garlic cloves *(no need to peel)* for about 10-15 minutes, until soft.
2. Squeeze out the garlic from the shell *(discard the shell)*, crush and mix together with the mayonnaise, milk and rosemary. Leave for at least 2 hours for the flavours to infuse. * Season to taste just before serving.
3. Cut the courgettes into approximately 5 cm (2 inch) batons, place in a colander and sprinkle generously with salt. Put a small plate on top, weigh it down and leave for 1 hour. *(The salt draws out liquid, removing bitterness).*
4. Toss the courgettes in a bowl of seasoned flour. Remove the courgettes, shake off the excess flour and toss in beaten egg.
5. Gently place them into a frying pan of hot oil and shallow fry until golden in colour.
6. Place on kitchen paper to absorb the excess fat and then arrange on a plate with the dip. Serve immediately.

French Omelette Spirals

INGREDIENTS £

30g (1 oz) butter
3 eggs
1 tbsp fresh chives, *chopped*
Wholegrain mustard
Wafer thin ham

METHOD

SERVES 8

1. Break one egg into a bowl, season and beat with a fork. Stir in a third of the chives.
2. Melt a third of the butter in a frying pan, add the egg mixture and tilt the pan to spread the egg evenly.
3. Lightly brown both sides and allow to cool. Repeat stages 1-3 to make two more omelettes.
4. Spread a thin layer of mustard over one side of each omelette, followed by a slice of ham.
5. Tightly roll up each omelette, wrap in cling film and refrigerate.

To serve, remove the cling film, slice into $1\frac{1}{2}$ cm ($\frac{5}{8}$ inch) rounds and arrange on a plate.

Stuffed Baby Tomatoes with Boursin Cheese & Chives

INGREDIENTS ££

12 baby tomatoes
Boursin cheese
Cream
Fresh chives, *for decoration*

METHOD

MAKES 12

1. Halve the tomatoes *(in the same way as you cut a grapefruit - cutting across the core, rather than through it)* and remove the centre using the end of a teaspoon.
2. Mix together the boursin and a drop of cream to make a paste.
3. Using a piping bag, fill the tomatoes with the mixture.

Decorate with chives and chill. *

Caesar Salad Paniers

INGREDIENTS £

3 slices of white bread
Butter
½ baby gem lettuce, *very finely chopped*
15g (½ oz) Parmesan, *grated*
Parmesan shavings, *for decoration*

Caesar Dressing
½ egg
1 anchovy
½ garlic clove, *peeled*
½ lime, *juiced*
¼ tsp English mustard powder
¼ tsp Worcestershire sauce
75ml (2½ fl oz) olive oil

METHOD

SERVES 8

Preheat the oven to 180°C / 350°F / gas mark 4

1. **To make the baskets**, cut the crusts off the bread and roll it out as thin and as square as you can.
2. Butter one side of the bread and using a 5 cm (2 inch) round cutter, cut 4-5 circles out of each slice.
3. To shape the baskets, place the discs in a canapé tin, butter side down and bake for 8-10 minutes until crisp and golden in colour. Remove the baskets and allow to cool on a cooling rack. *
4. **To make the dressing**, blend the egg, anchovies, garlic, lime juice, mustard powder and Worcestershire sauce in the small bowl of a food processor until smooth.
5. While the food processor is running, slowly pour the olive oil though the feeding tube *(if you add the oil too quickly the dressing will be very runny).* *
6. Mix the lettuce with the grated Parmesan, black pepper and dressing, add a little dressing at a time and taste as you go along to get the right proportions.
7. Place a spoonful of salad in each basket and top with Parmesan shavings. Serve immediately.

Elderflower Cordial

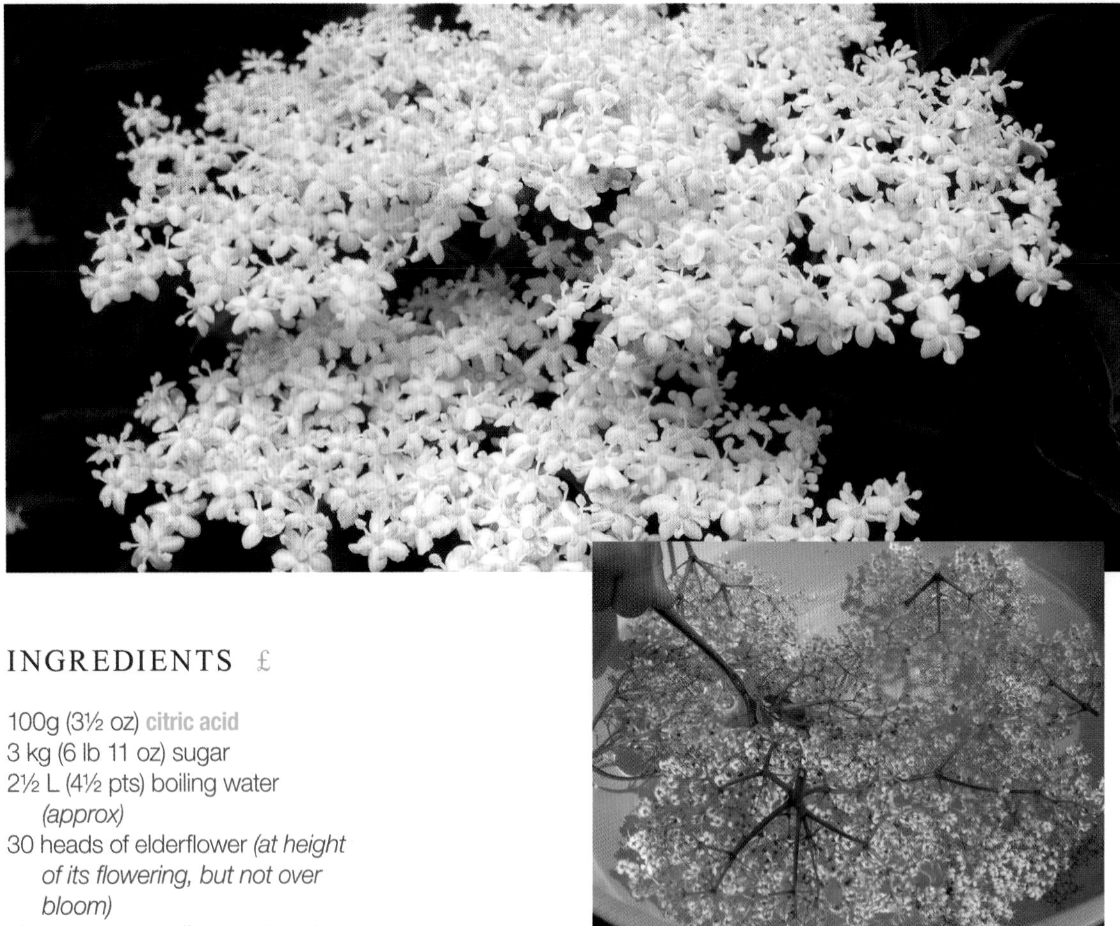

INGREDIENTS £

100g (3½ oz) citric acid
3 kg (6 lb 11 oz) sugar
2½ L (4½ pts) boiling water *(approx)*
30 heads of elderflower *(at height of its flowering, but not over bloom)*
½ Camden tablet *(from a chemist, it is used for making beer), crushed*

METHOD

1. Put the citric acid, sugar and boiling water into a very large bowl and set aside to allow the sugar to dissolve, it will take a long time *(stir occasionally)*.
2. Add the elderflower, cover and leave to infuse for a few days, stirring morning and evening.
3. Strain the mixture through a muslin, add the Camden tablet and bottle in sterilised bottles. Store in a cool place.

To serve, dilute with water, approximately 1 part cordial to 8 parts water.

Nutty about Nuts

INGREDIENTS ££

Olive oil
100g (3½ oz) mixed **nuts**
2-3 tbsp soft brown sugar
¼ tsp dried rosemary
Pinch of salt

METHOD

SERVES 8

1. Heat a dash of oil in a pan, add all ingredients and cook until the sugar has just melted.
2. Spread out on baking paper to cool slightly and serve warm.

German Peppered Salami & Stuffed Olives

£££

The simplest of all our canapés, but equally delicious and great if you are pushed for time.

A good variety of Salami and stuffed olives can be bought from most supermarkets. One of our favourites is finely sliced German Peppered Salami served with green olives stuffed with red pepper.

Arrange the salami slices on a plate in a circle overlapping one another and pile the olives in the centre. Cover until serving. *

Mulled Wine

INGREDIENTS £

125g (4½ oz) sugar
2 cinnamon sticks
1 orange, *skin and pith removed and sliced*
1 lemon, *skin and pith removed and sliced*
4 cloves
250ml (9 fl oz) water
1 bottle of cheap **red wine**

METHOD

SERVES 4-6

1. Put the sugar, cinnamon sticks, fruit, cloves and water in a pan, bring to the boil and then remove from the heat. Add the wine and leave to infuse *(the longer the better)*. *
2. To serve, bring up to temperature, taste and adjust sweetness if necessary.

Serve with a slice of fruit in each glass.

Dips & Crudités

INGREDIENTS ££

Crudités: Carrots, cucumber, red peppers, cauliflower, cut into small stick like pieces

Bread Sticks

Crisps

Tortilla Crisps
Tortillas
Olive oil
Chilli powder or paprika

Melba Toast
Slices of **bread**

METHOD

Tortillas Crisps

Preheat the oven to 180°C / 350°F / gas mark 4

1. Cut the tortillas like a cake into 16 segments, brush in oil and sprinkle very lightly with chilli powder or paprika.
2. Bake in the oven for 8 minutes until slightly brown. Allow to cool. *

Melba Toast

Preheat the oven to 180°C / 350°F / gas mark 4

1. Lightly toast the bread in a toaster and allow to cool.
2. Remove the crusts and slide the knife through the middle of the piece of toast *(place your hand flat on top of the slice of toast with your fingers on full stretch. Start cutting from a corner and once you have reached the middle, rotate the piece of toast until you have sliced straight through).*
3. Cut the toast into eight pieces *(Union Jack cut),* place on a lined baking tray, toasted side down and bake for 4-5 minutes. * Allow to cool. *

Dips Selection

If making the dips in advance taste before serving as the flavours will have continued to infuse.

Aubergine Dip

INGREDIENTS ££

1 large aubergine, *quartered*
Olive oil
200g (7 oz) **cream cheese**
1 tbsp tomato purée
1½ tbsp fresh basil, *chopped*
1 garlic clove, *crushed*

METHOD

SERVES 8

Preheat the oven to 180°C / 350°F / gas mark 4.

1. Drizzle the aubergine in olive oil and roast in the oven for about 30-45 minutes until it is soft.
2. Blend in a food processor with the rest of the ingredients. Season to taste and allow to cool. *

Avocado Dip

INGREDIENTS ££

1 large or 2 small avocados
1-2 tbsp lemon juice

METHOD

SERVES 8

1. Blend the avocado in a food processor with the lemon juice and season to taste. * *(If you are caught out with a bad avocado, discard the bad bits and add a little cream or crème fraîche).*

Honey & Mustard Dip

INGREDIENTS £

1 tbsp wholegrain **mustard**
4 tbsp natural **yoghurt**
1 tsp clear honey
1 tbsp fresh chives, *chopped*

METHOD

SERVES 8

1. Mix all ingredients together and chill. *

Herb Dip

INGREDIENTS ££ | **METHOD** | SERVES 8

150g (5¼ oz) mayonnaise
3-4 tbsp fresh mixed herbs
(eg. basil, parsley, chives, mint)
Milk

1. Mix all the ingredients together, chill and allow to marinate for about 2 hours. *
2. Taste before serving. *(A little milk can be added to get the right consistency).*

Pesto Dip

INGREDIENTS £ | **METHOD** | SERVES 8

1 small pot of yoghurt *(mayonnaise or crème fraîche can be used)*
2 tbsp pesto

1. Mix all ingredients together and chill. *

Red Pepper Hummus

INGREDIENTS ££ | **METHOD**

½ large red pepper, *deseeded and roughly chopped*
½ tbsp olive oil
120g (4¼ oz) chickpeas, *drained* (use ½ 400g tin)
½ tbsp tahini
1 garlic clove, *crushed*
2½ tbsp lemon juice
½ tbsp water
½ tsp marmite

1. Put the red pepper into a small saucepan, drizzle in olive oil and cook over a low heat until soft.
2. Put all the ingredients into a food processor and blend until smooth. Season to taste with lots of salt and pepper. *

Barbecue Dip

INGREDIENTS £

1 tbsp olive oil
½ onion, *finely chopped*
½ garlic clove, *crushed*
2 tbsp **red wine**
½ tsp soft brown sugar
¼ tsp chilli powder
Dash of Tabasco
1 tbsp **Worcestershire sauce**
1 tbsp **tomato ketchup**

METHOD

SERVES 8

1. Warm the oil in a frying pan and cook the onion and garlic until soft.
2. Add the rest of the ingredients, bring to the boil and simmer for 1-2 minutes until thickened.

Oyster Dip

INGREDIENTS ££

85g (3 oz) tin of smoked **oysters**, *drained*
200g (7 oz) **cream cheese**
1 tsp lemon juice

METHOD

SERVES 8

1. Blend all the ingredients in a food processor and season with pepper to taste.

Tapenade

INGREDIENTS ££

50g (1¾ oz) black olives
5 capers
1 **anchovy** fillet
½ garlic clove, *peeled & crushed*
½ tsp Dijon **mustard**
1 tbsp olive oil
½ tbsp fresh mint
½ tbsp fresh parsley
½ tbsp fresh basil
½ tbsp lemon juice

METHOD

SERVES 8

1. Put all the ingredients in the mini bowl of a food processor and pulse until almost smooth.

Pea Guacamole

INGREDIENTS £

110g (4 oz) frozen peas
⅛ small onion, *finely grated*
½ garlic clove, *crushed*
¼ red chilli, *deseeded and chopped*
½ lime, *juiced*
1 tbsp fresh coriander, *chopped*
1 tbsp **crème fraîche**
Tabasco, *few drops (optional)*

METHOD

SERVES 8

1. Cook the peas in boiling water for 3-4 minutes until tender. Drain and allow to cool slightly.
2. Blend the peas and the rest of the ingredients in the food processor *(except for the tabasco and some of the chilli which you need for decoration)*. Do not make the mixture completely smooth.
3. Season and add a few drops of tabasco and transfer to a presentation dish. Allow to cool. *
4. Sprinkle the remaining chilli on top of the guacamole.

Hummus

INGREDIENTS £

200g (7 oz) chickpeas, *drained & crushed*
½ tbsp **tahini**
1 garlic clove, *crushed*
2 tbsp olive oil
½ tbsp water
½ tsp **marmite** *(or ½ tsp cumin)*
½ lemon, *juiced*

METHOD

SERVES 8

1. Put all the ingredients *(except for the lemon juice)* in a food processor and blend until smooth. Season and add a little of the lemon juice to taste. *

Peppadew Dip

INGREDIENTS ££

250g (9 oz) cream cheese
8 sweet piquanté peppers (Peppadews), *well drained*
Fresh parsley

METHOD

SERVES 8

1. Blend the cream cheese and Peppadews in a food processor and season to taste. *

Serve as a dip or put on melba toast.

Beetroot & Walnut Hummus

INGREDIENTS £

100g (3½ oz) cooked beetroot
½ tbsp malt vinegar
25g (1 oz) walnuts
½ tsp cumin seeds
½ slice of white stale bread, *crusts removed*
½ tbsp tahini
1 small garlic clove, *crushed*
½ lemon, *juiced*

METHOD

SERVES 8

Preheat the oven to 180°C / 350°F / gas mark 4

1. Cook the beetroot in water and the vinegar for 1 hour, or until soft. Peel then cut into chunks and check the weight.
2. Toast the walnuts in the oven for 5-7 minutes. Allow to cool
3. Warm a small frying pan and dry-fry the cumin seeds, shaking the pan constantly, until they darken and release their aroma *(this takes approximately 1 minute).*
4. Put all the ingredients in a food processor *(not the vinegar as you have already used this)* and blend until smooth. Season to taste.

STARTERS

STARTERS

STARTERS

STARTERS

Soups

Celeriac & Potato Soup with Crispy Bacon

INGREDIENTS ££

30g (1 oz) butter
½ onion, *chopped*
1 garlic clove, *sliced*
2 leeks, *washed and sliced*
600g (1 lb 6 oz) potato, *peeled and roughly chopped*
300g (10½ oz) celeriac *(peeled weight), roughly chopped*
1 tsp lemon juice
1.1 L (40 fl oz / 2 pts) chicken stock
60ml (2 fl oz) cream

Garnish
6 slices of bacon, *chopped*
Olive oil
4 tbsp fresh chives, *roughly chopped*
French bread, *sliced*
30g (1 oz) butter

METHOD

SERVES 8

1. Melt the butter in a large saucepan, add the onion and garlic and cook over a gentle heat for 5 minutes.
2. Add the leeks and continue to cook until the leeks and onion are soft.
3. Add the potato, celeriac, lemon juice and stock and season with pepper and lots of salt. Bring to the boil and simmer *(with no lid)* for 15 minutes, or until the celeriac is really soft.
4. Add the cream and blend until smooth, then pour the soup through a sieve. Check the seasoning.
5. Fry the bacon in 1 tbsp olive oil until really crisp and dry on kitchen paper.
6. Blend the chives and 6 tbsp of olive oil in a food processor.
7. Fry the French bread in butter over a gentle heat until golden *(use a little more butter if needed).*
8. Garnish the soup with the crispy bacon, chive oil and French bread.

Curried Parsnip Soup

INGREDIENTS ££

80g (2½ oz) butter
4 onions, *chopped*
10 curry leaves, *crushed*
3 tsp yellow mustard seeds
2 tsp turmeric
6 tsp Korma curry paste
8 large parsnips, *peeled (1.150g / 2 lb 9 oz peeled weight)*
290ml (10 fl oz / ½ pt) coconut milk
1 red chilli or few drops Tabasco *(optional)*
4 tbsp fresh coriander leaves

METHOD

SERVES 8

1. Melt the butter in a large saucepan, add the onion, curry leaves, mustard seeds, turmeric and korma paste and cook over a low heat until the onions are soft.
2. Chop the parsnips into about 2 cm (¾ inch) chunks, add them to the saucepan and cook for a further 5 minutes.
3. Add just enough water to cover the parsnips, bring to the boil and simmer for 30 minutes, or until the parsnips are tender.
4. Add the coconut milk and chilli *(deseeded and finely chopped)* or Tabasco and blend until smooth, adjusting the consistency with water if it is too thick. Season to taste *(immediately wash any light coloured plastic utensils or equipment used as the turmeric will discolour it)*. *
5. Divide the coriander leaves between the soup bowls and pour the hot soup over them.

Scallops Wrapped in Parma Ham on Black Pudding with Apple Purée

INGREDIENTS £££

8 slices of Parma ham
24 scallops
Olive oil
24 thin slices of black pudding
15g (½ oz) butter
½ lemon
Sprigs of fresh dill or parsley

Apple Purée
2 Bramley apples, *cored, peeled and chopped*
2 tsp lemon juice
2 tbsp water

Chive Oil
1 tbsp fresh chives, *chopped*
4 tbsp olive oil

METHOD

SERVES 8

1. **To make the apple purée**, cook the apples in the lemon juice and water until soft, then blend in the mini bowl of the food processor.
2. **To make the chive oil**, blend together the chives and olive oil. *
3. Cut each slice of ham into 3, lengthways. Roll each strip around the outside of a scallop and secure the ends with a cocktail stick.
4. Warm about ½ tbsp olive oil in a frying pan and fry the black pudding for about 2-3 minutes on each side, until crispy, then remove from the pan and keep warm.
5. **To cook the scallops** warm 4 tbsp of olive oil in two frying pans *(2 tbsp in each pan if you have two, so that all the scallops are ready at the same time)*. When the oil is really hot fry 12 scallops in each pan for 1 minute 15 seconds on each side. For the last 15 seconds of cooking add half the butter to each pan, along with a large squeeze of lemon juice. Serve immediately.

To plate, put a small amount of hot apple purée on each slice of black pudding and top each one with a scallop. Drizzle the plate with the chive oil and garnish with a sprig of dill or parsley.

Scallops with Beetroot & Apple Purée & Chive Oil

INGREDIENTS £££

Beetroot Purée
1 tbsp malt vinegar
½ tbsp olive oil
400g (14 oz) beetroot

Apple Purée
2 Bramley apples, *cored, peeled and chopped*
2 tsp lemon juice
2 tbsp water

Chive Oil
1 tbsp fresh chives, *chopped*
4 tbsp olive oil

24 scallops
4 tbsp olive oil
30g (1 oz) butter
Lemon juice

METHOD

SERVES 8

1. **To make the beetroot purée**, cook the beetroot, with the skin on, in water with the vinegar for about 30 minutes until soft. Peel, then blend with the olive oil in the mini bowl of the food processor. Season to taste.
2. **To make the apple purée**, cook the apples with the lemon juice and water until soft, then blend in the mini bowl of the food processor.
3. **To make the chive oil**, blend together the chives and olive oil. *
4. Warm the beetroot purée and the apple purée so that they are ready for serving.
5. **To cook the scallops**, warm 4 tbsp of olive oil in two frying pans *(2 tbsp in each pan if you have two, so that all the scallops are ready at the same time).* When the oil is really hot fry 12 scallops in each pan for 1 minute and 15 seconds on each side. For the last 15 seconds of cooking add half the butter to each pan, along with a large squeeze of lemon juice. Serve immediately.

To plate, serve the scallops on a bed of beetroot, spoon over the butter from the frying pan, top with some apple purée and drizzle with chive oil.

Pheasant & Chestnut Terrine with Spiced Winter Apple Chutney

INGREDIENTS £££

Terrine
20 rashers of streaky bacon
15g (½ oz) butter
½ onion, *finely chopped*
1 garlic clove, *crushed*
250g (9 oz) sausage meat
6 roasted chestnuts
2 pheasant thighs, *boned*
2 pheasant breasts, *sliced*

Spiced Winter Apple Chutney
(makes several jars)
1 kg cooking apples, *peeled, cored and diced*
1 onion, *finely diced*
1 cinnamon stick
4 cloves
2 star anise
380g (13¼ oz) Demerara sugar
230ml (8 fl oz) malt vinegar
180ml (6 fl oz) cider

METHOD

SERVES 8

Preheat the oven to 180°C / 350°F / gas mark 4

1. **To make the chutney**, place all the ingredients in a large saucepan and simmer gently *(uncovered)* for about an hour *(stirring occasionally)* until it has reduced to a chutney consistency.
2. Remove from the heat and allow to cool slightly, then remove the star anise and cinnamon stick.
3. Wash the jars and lids and warm the jars in the oven for about 5 minutes, then fill each jar with the chutney.
4. Allow to cool, then place circles of waxed paper *(wax-side down)* on top of the chutney, secure with a lid and label.
5. **To make the terrine**, stretch 16 slices of bacon with the back of a knife *(keep the other 4 to use later)* and line a loaf tin so that the bacon hangs over the sides of the tin.
6. Melt butter in a large frying pan and cook the onion and garlic over a gentle heat until soft.
7. Roughly chop the remaining bacon then put it into a food processor. Add the sausage meat, chestnuts and pheasant thighs and blend until roughly chopped.
8. Add it to the onion mixture and season to taste.
9. Put half the mixture into the loaf tin and press into place.
10. Arrange the slices of pheasant on top and then add the remaining mixture.
11. Press down and fold over the bacon to totally cover the mixture.
12. Cover in foil and bake in a bain-marie for 1½ hours. Allow to cool slightly and pour off excess fat.

Serve cold with toast and the chutney.

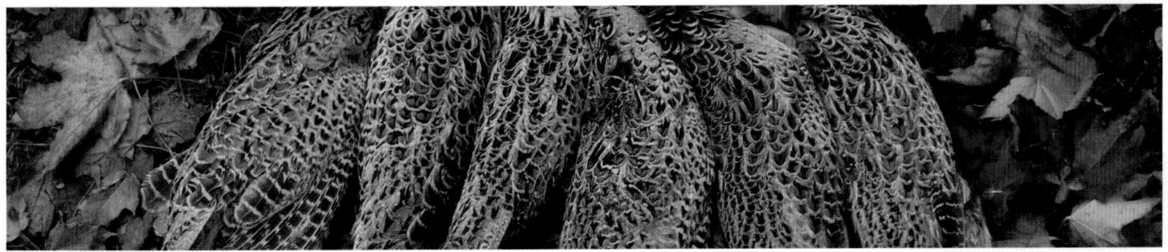

Leek Tart with Roasted Red Pepper Sauce

INGREDIENTS ££

French Pastry
200g (7 oz) plain flour
85ml (3 fl oz) vegetable oil
85ml (3 fl oz) water
Pinch of salt

Red Pepper Sauce
3 red peppers, *de-seeded and roughly chopped*
Olive oil
1/4 tsp Herbes de Provence
2-4 tbsp double cream

6 leeks, *finely sliced*
30g (1 oz) butter
250ml (9 fl oz) double cream
6 eggs
3 egg yolks

METHOD

SERVES 8

Preheat the oven to 180°C / 350°F / gas mark 4

1. Fry the leeks in the butter until soft and allow to cool slightly.
2. **To make the pastry**, put the flour in a bowl, make a well and pour in the oil and water. Mix together adding more water or flour if necessary. *(Don't be alarmed by the consistency of the pastry).*
3. Mix together the cream and eggs, then add the leeks and season generously.
4. Grease, then flour, a loose-bottomed quiche tin and line with the pastry by kneading it into place *(no rolling required, the thinner the pastry the better).*
5. Pour in the mixture and bake for about 30 minutes until the centre is firm and the top golden.
6. **To make the sauce**, put the peppers into a small saucepan, drizzle with olive oil, cover with a lid and cook over a low heat until soft. Purée, add the herbs and cream and season to taste. *

Serve straight from the oven with warm red pepper sauce.

Broccoli Soup

INGREDIENTS £

2 heads of broccoli
570ml (20 fl oz / 1 pt) chicken stock
150ml (5 fl oz / 1/4 pt) cream
30g (1 oz) butter
2 tbsp sesame seeds

METHOD

SERVES 8

1. Peel the main stem of the broccoli with a potato peeler and cut the broccoli into small chunks.
2. Cook the broccoli in the chicken stock until very soft.
3. Blend the soup, then add the cream.
4. Melt the butter in a small saucepan with the sesame seeds and when the butter starts to darken add the mixture to the soup.
5. Season to taste *(lots of black pepper).*

Serve with fresh bread or toast.

Roasted Vegetable Soup

INGREDIENTS ££

1.35kg (3 lbs) of mixed vegetables (eg: 4 carrots 3 courgettes, 1 red pepper, 1 aubergine, 4 tomatoes, 1 onion)
Olive oil
½ tsp **Worcestershire sauce**
1 tbsp **tomato ketchup**
290ml (10 fl oz / ½ pt) **milk**
4 tbsp **cream**
1.1 L (40 fl oz / 2 pts) vegetable **stock**
Pinch of cumin
½ tsp Herbes de Provence
Crème fraîche, *for decoration*

METHOD

SERVES 8

Preheat the oven to 180°C / 350°F / gas mark 4

1. Roughly chop the vegetables into similar sized pieces. Place on a baking tray, sprinkle with olive oil, salt and pepper and roast for about 35 minutes until soft, turning frequently.
2. Put the remaining ingredients *(except for the crème fraîche)* in a large saucepan, add the roasted vegetables and blend until smooth.
3. To serve, bring up to temperature *(do not boil)*, season to taste and garnish with crème fraîche and fresh herbs.

Serve with fresh bread or toast.

Carrot & Coriander Soup

INGREDIENTS £

45g (1½ oz) **butter**
1 onion, *chopped*
450g (1 lb) carrots, *chopped*
1 L (35 fl oz / 1¾ pts) chicken or vegetable **stock**
2 tbsp fresh coriander *(chopped)* or 1 tsp dried coriander
2 tbsp **cream**
Sprigs of corriander

METHOD

Serves 8

1. Melt the butter in a large saucepan and cook the onion over a gentle heat until soft.
2. Add the carrots, season and continue to cook for a further 5 minutes.
3. Add the stock and coriander, cover with a lid and simmer until the carrots are really soft.
4. Blend, using a hand blender, until smooth. *
5. Add the cream, bring up to temperature and serve garnished with a little cream and a sprig of fresh coriander.

Serve with fresh bread or toast.

French Onion Soup

INGREDIENTS £

5 large onions, *peeled and sliced (total weight 900g / 2 lbs approx)*
85g (3 oz) **butter**
3 tbsp plain **flour** *(approx)*
1.7 L (60 fl oz / 3 pts) beef **stock**
175ml (6 fl oz / 0.3 pt) **white wine**
8 slices of French **baguette**
140g (5 oz) **cheese**, *grated*
Parsley, *for garnish*

METHOD

Serves 8

1. Soften and brown the onions in butter with plenty of seasoning.
2. Sprinkle over the flour and mix in well. Add the stock and wine gradually, cover and simmer for 30 minutes. *
3. Lightly toast the slices of baguette in the oven, sprinkle with cheese and brown in the oven.
4. Adjust seasoning if necessary and serve with a slice of the grilled baguette and a sprig of parsley placed on the top.

Courgette & Mint Soup

INGREDIENTS £

45g ($1^1/_2$ oz) **butter**
2 onions, *chopped*
900g (2 lb) courgettes
(approximately 6 courgettes), roughly chopped
1.1 L (40 fl oz / 2 pts) chicken **stock**
40 mint leaves, *approx*

METHOD

SERVES 8

1. Melt the butter in a large saucepan and cook the onions over a gentle heat until soft.
2. Add the courgettes and cook for a further 5 minutes.
3. Add the stock and half the mint leaves, cover with a lid and simmer for 30 minutes. *
4. Add the rest of the mint, blend, season to taste and serve immediately *(adding half the mint at the last minute gives a good mint aroma, flavour and colour, once you have added it serve the soup straight away, otherwise it will spoil).*

Serve with fresh bread or toast.

Thai Sweet Potato & Coconut Soup

INGREDIENTS ££

2 tbsp vegetable oil
1/2 onion, *chopped*
1/2 red pepper, *chopped*
1/2 red chilli, *deseeded and chopped*
1 garlic clove, *crushed*
15g (1/2 oz) fresh ginger, *peeled and chopped*
1 kg (2 lb 4 oz) sweet potato, *peeled and chopped*
1 L (35 fl oz / 1 3/4 pts) water
1 tbsp sugar
2 tbsp fresh coriander
200ml (7 fl oz) **coconut milk** *(stir before use as it separates)*

METHOD

SERVES 8

1. Warm the vegetable oil in a large saucepan and cook the onion, red pepper, chilli, garlic and ginger over a low heat until the onion is soft.
2. Add the sweet potato, water, sugar and plenty of seasoning and cover with a lid, simmer until the sweet potato is very soft.
3. Add the coriander and blend until smooth. *
4. Add the coconut milk, bring up to temperature and season to taste. *

Quail Egg, Bacon & Avocado Salad

INGREDIENTS £££

8-12 quail **eggs**
8 rashers of smoked bacon, *chopped*
2 avocados
20 baby tomatoes, *halved*
Lettuce, *torn into small pieces*
Walnuts, *roughly chopped*

Dressing
1 tsp honey or sugar
85ml (3 fl oz) olive oil
85ml (3 fl oz) **walnut oil**
85ml (3 fl oz) **balsamic vinegar**
2 tsp wholegrain **mustard**

METHOD

SERVES 8

1. Put the eggs into a saucepan of cold water. Bring to the boil, cook for 6 minutes then plunge into cold water.
2. Fry the bacon until crisp.
3. **To make the dressing**, warm the honey in a jar *(without a lid)* in the microwave for a few seconds until runny. Add the rest of the ingredients and shake well *(shake again before use as it separates)*. *
4. Peel the eggs and cut in half lengthways.
5. Cut up the avocado and coat with a little dressing.
6. Arrange the lettuce, quail eggs, tomatoes, avocado, bacon and walnuts on the plate and pour over the dressing.

Baked Camembert with Red Onion Marmalade

INGREDIENTS £££

Marmalade
30g (1 oz) unsalted butter
3 red onions, *finely sliced*
2 tbsp Demerara sugar
1 tbsp balsamic or red wine vinegar
175ml (6 fl oz / 0.3 pt) red wine
2 tbsp redcurrant jelly or Crème de cassis, *(optional)*

Puff pastry
2 Camemberts
Egg for glazing, *beaten*
Lettuce, *torn into pieces*

METHOD

SERVES 8

Preheat the oven to 180°C / 350°F / gas mark 4

1. **To make the marmalade**, melt the butter in a frying pan and soften the onions *(if you are making the marmalade in bulk and storing it in a jar, cook the onions in 1-2 tbsp of olive oil instead of butter).*
2. Add the remaining ingredients and simmer to reduce to a marmalade consistency.
3. Divide the pastry into two, roll out each piece into a square and place the camemberts in the centres.
4. Prick the top of the camemberts with a fork *(be careful not to pierce the base)* and wrap each cheese completely in the pastry, using the beaten egg to stick the pastry together. Decorate with pastry off-cuts.
5. Place on a lined baking tray, glaze with the egg * and bake for about 25-30 minutes until a golden brown.

Serve straight from the oven. Dress the plate with dressed salad and surround each camembert with warm red onion marmalade. Serve it at the table, cut like a cake.

Avocado Fouetté with Tuna / Crab & Tomato Concassé

INGREDIENTS £££

Fish Mix
2 tomatoes
260g (9 oz) fresh crab/tinned tuna (2 tins), *drained*
1 tbsp fresh chives, *chopped*
Olive oil *(if the fish was in brine)*
Tabasco

Sauce
175ml (6 fl oz) tomato passata

Avocado Mousse
2 shallots
3-4 avocados
1 tbsp lemon juice
290ml (10 fl oz / ½ pt) double cream *(optional)*
Tabasco

Garnish
1 tomato
½ tbsp fresh chives, *chopped*
Fresh parsley

METHOD — SERVES 8

1. Quarter all the tomatoes *(3 in total)*, remove the core and seeds and dice very finely.
2. **To make the fish mix**, combine all the ingredients *(save ⅓ of the diced tomatoes for garnishing)*, season and taste. If the fish tastes dry add a little olive oil. *
3. **To make the mousse**, blend the shallots in a food processor. Add the rest of the ingredients except the cream and blend into a smooth paste.
4. Whip the cream until stiff, then fold in the avocado mixture, season to taste. * *(If preparing in advance, press cling film on the mousse so that air can't get to it and refrigerate. It can only be made a maximum of 2 hours in advance).*
5. Place a mousse ring in the centre of each plate and half fill with the avocado mixture.
6. Add a layer of fish and press gently into shape.
7. Spoon the tomato passata around the ring and garnish the plate with the remaining chopped tomato and chives.
8. Carefully remove the ring and garnish with a sprig of parsley.

Stilton, Port & Walnut Pâté

INGREDIENTS £££

340g (12 oz) Stilton cheese
400g (14 oz) cream cheese
110g (4 oz) unsalted butter, *soft*
85g (3 oz) walnuts
1 tsp fresh chives, *chopped, and some for garnish*
175ml (6 fl oz / 0.3 pt) Port
8 baby tomatoes, *for garnish*

METHOD — SERVES 8

1. Blend the Stilton, cream cheese, walnuts *(save some for garnish)* and butter in a food processor.
2. Add the Port and chives, season to taste.
3. Transfer into ramekins, smooth over the top and refrigerate.

Serve with warm freshly baked bread and garnish with quartered baby tomatoes, walnuts and chives.

Cauliflower Soup with Wild Mushrooms

INGREDIENTS £

12g (½ oz) dried wild mushrooms
150ml (5 fl oz / ¼ pt) water
60g (2 oz) butter
6 tbsp olive oil
2 onions, *chopped*
680g (1½ lbs) cauliflower *(2 small), leaves discarded, florets and stalks roughly chopped*
400g (14 oz) potato, *roughly chopped*
1.1 L (40 fl oz / 2 pts) chicken stock
400ml (14 fl oz) milk
200ml (7 fl oz) double cream
2 tbsp chives, *finely chopped*

METHOD

SERVES 8

1. Soak the mushrooms in a little warm water for at least 30 minutes.
2. Warm the butter and 4 tbsp of olive oil in a large saucepan and cook the onions over a gentle heat for about 5 minutes.
3. Add the cauliflower and potato, season, cover with a lid and cook over a gentle heat for about 10 minutes, stirring occasionally.
4. Add the stock and bring to the boil, then add the milk and gently return to the boil *(this way scum should not form from the milk).*
5. Simmer uncovered for 10-15 minutes until the vegetables are soft.
6. Pour in the cream and blend until smooth. Season to taste. *
7. Drain the mushrooms *(adding the mushroom liquid to the soup)* and pat dry with kitchen paper.
8. Warm 2 tbsp of olive oil in a frying pan. When it is really hot fry the mushrooms for a couple of minutes until crisp. *
9. To serve, spoon the mushrooms into the centre of the soup and sprinkle with chives and olive oil.

Cauliflower with Mayonnaise & Chives

INGREDIENTS £

Mayonnaise
3 egg yolks
3 tsp Dijon mustard
6 tbsp olive oil
12 tbsp vegetable oil
3 tsp tarragon or white wine vinegar

1 large cauliflower
2-3 tbsp fresh chives, *chopped*
French bread, *(optional)*
Paprika

METHOD

SERVES 8

1. Whisk together the egg yolks and mustard.
2. Continue to whisk, adding the oil drop by drop. *(As the mixture thickens the oil can be added more quickly).*
3. Mix in the vinegar, seasoning *(a little salt and lots of pepper)* and chives. *
4. Remove the leaves and trim the base of the cauliflower so that the whole cauliflower will sit flat on a plate *(do not remove any florets).*
5. Plunge the cauliflower into salted boiling water and cook for exactly 5 minutes.
6. Drain well, then wrap the cauliflower in a tea towel and gently shake any remaining water out of it. Place on a large warmed plate and pour the mayonnaise mix over, completely covering the cauliflower.
7. Sprinkle with chives, ground pepper and paprika and serve immediately.

Serve with French bread. Encourage guests to help themselves.

Endive (Chicory) & Roquefort Salad with Walnut Dressing

INGREDIENTS ££

3 endives *(chicory)*
Handful of red seedless grapes *(cut in half)*
55g (2 oz) walnuts, *roughly chopped*
170g (6 oz) Roquefort cheese, *cubed*

Walnut Dressing
1 tbsp wholegrain or Dijon mustard
1 tbsp white wine vinegar
1 tsp sugar
2 tbsp water
2 tbsp walnut oil
2 tbsp olive oil

METHOD

SERVES 8

1. **To make the dressing**, put the mustard, white wine, sugar and water in a jam jar and shake to dissolve the sugar. Add the oils and shake well to combine. Season to taste.
2. To prepare the endive, trim the bottom and separate the leaves washing the outer leaves. Trim the bottom of each leaf, if necessary.
3. Combine the salad leaves with the grapes and walnuts and pour over the dressing.
4. Arrange on a plate and scatter over the Roquefort.

Shredded Duck on Rocket in Tortilla Baskets with Hoisin Sauce

INGREDIENTS £££

2 duck legs
Spring onions *(optional), cut into juliennes (thin strips)*
4 **tortillas**
1 **egg**, *beaten*
60g (2 oz) rocket
Cucumber *(optional), cut into juliennes (thin strips)*

Hoisin Sauce *(or use readymade **hoisin sauce**)*
8 tbsp (120ml / 4 fl oz) **soy sauce**
6 tbsp runny honey
4 tbsp smooth **peanut butter**
4 tsp rice vinegar
4 tsp rapeseed oil
1 tsp tabasco
2 garlic cloves, *crushed*
Pinch of cinnamon
Pinch of coriander
Pinch of nutmeg

METHOD

SERVES 8

Preheat the oven to 180°C / 350°F / gas mark 4

1. Season the duck and bake in the oven for 1½ hours *(allow more cooking time if they are large)*, tipping away any fat halfway through. Allow to cool slightly.
2. Shred the duck by pulling it apart with two forks.
3. Soak the spring onions in cold water to make them curl *(leave for at least 15 minutes).*
4. **To make the tortilla baskets**, cut the tortilla like a cake into 16 segments. Brush one side with egg and place egg side down in a muffin tin, so that all the points are either in the bottom of the tin, or all pointing out. Depending on the size of the tortilla, use about 5 pieces for each basket.
5. Bake in the oven for 8 minutes until slightly brown and allow to cool. *
6. **To make the Hoisin sauce**, put all the ingredients into a bowl and whisk vigorously to combine. Season with pepper only.
7. Plate each basket, fill with rocket and top with the shredded duck and hoisin sauce. Garnish with the spring onions and cucumber.

Warm Goats' Cheese Salad with Fig Compôte / Red Currant Jelly

INGREDIENTS ££

8 thick slices of goats' cheese
8 slices of French bread, *lightly toasted*
Olive oil
Herbes de Provence
4 tbsp fig jam or redcurrant jelly
Mixed lettuce leaves, *torn into small pieces*
Black seedless grapes
Walnuts, *roughly chopped*

Dressing
85ml (3 fl oz) olive oil
85ml (3 fl oz) walnut oil
85ml (3 fl oz) balsamic vinegar
2 tsp wholegrain mustard
1 tsp honey or sugar

METHOD

SERVES 8

Preheat the oven to 180°C / 350°F / gas mark 4

1. Place the goats' cheese on the toast, drizzle lightly with olive oil, add a pinch of Herbes de Provence to each piece and bake for about 15 minutes until browned. Spoon the fig jam or redcurrant jelly over.
2. **To make the dressing**, warm the honey in a jar *(without a lid)* in the microwave for a few seconds until runny. Add the rest of ingredients, season and shake well *(shake again before use as it separates).* *
3. Arrange the lettuce, grapes and walnuts on the plate, drizzle over the dressing and place the goats' cheese toasties on top.

Beetroot Salad with Goats' Cheese, Green Beans, Baby Leaf Salad & Romesco Sauce

INGREDIENTS ££

600g (1 lb 6 oz) beetroot
100ml (4 fl oz) white wine vinegar
4 bay leaves
4 garlic cloves, *peeled*
1 tbsp olive oil
300g (10½ oz) fine green beans
200g (7 oz) baby leaf salad
300g (10½ oz) goats' cheese, *crumbled*

Romesco Sauce
40g (1¼ oz) hazelnuts
40g (1¼ oz) flaked almonds
1 red pepper
3 tomatoes, *halved*
2 hot peppadews
2 tbsp red wine vinegar
1 garlic clove
2 tbsp olive oil

METHOD

SERVES 8

Preheat the oven to 180°C / 350°F / gas mark 4

1. Put the beetroot into a saucepan of water, add the vinegar, bay leaves and garlic, bring to the boil and simmer for 1 hour.
2. **To make the sauce**, roast the nuts in the oven for approximately 5 minutes until golden. When cool, rub the hazelnuts together to remove the skins, discard the skins.
3. Peel the beetroot, then roast with the red pepper *(don't cut up the beetroot or the pepper, cook them whole)* and 1 tbsp olive oil for 30 minutes until skin of the pepper has crinkled. After 10 minutes of cooking add the tomatoes.
4. Remove from the oven and immediately put the pepper into a bowl, cover in cling film and leave for 10 minutes *(this helps the skin come off)*, then peel, cut open and remove the seeds.
5. Put all the sauce ingredients in the mini bowl of a food processer and blend until smooth.
6. Dice the beetroot (about 8 mm / ¼ inch cubes).
7. Blanch the green beans in boiling water for 3 minutes, then refresh in cold water.
8. Plate the salad and green beans, arrange the beetroot and goats' cheese on top and top with the sauce.

Globe Artichokes

INGREDIENTS £££

8 globe artichokes
2 lemons, *roughly cut into pieces*
2 tbsp olive oil
French dressing *(see goats' cheese salad for recipe)* or butter

METHOD

SERVES 8

1. Prepare the artichokes by pulling off the stalks *(twist as you pull)* close to the base so they will sit upright without rolling *(if too difficult remove with a knife)*. Remove some of the outer leaves.
2. You will probably need to use two saucepans filled with water to cook them in. Add one lemon, 1 tbsp of oil and some salt to each saucepan and cook for about 45 minutes. *(They are cooked when an inner leaf will pull out easily)*.
3. Drain upside-down and serve immediately. They can be served hot with melted butter, or cold with French vinaigrette.

To eat, pull off the leaves one by one, dip the end into the butter / dressing and eat just the soft, fleshly end, discarding the leaves. The outer leaves will be a bit too tough to eat. The best bit is the centre, the heart of the artichoke and is worth waiting for, but watch out for the choke, which should be cut out before eating the heart!

Cheese Puffs with Cranberry

INGREDIENTS ££

Puff pastry, *chilled*
1 Camembert cheese, Roquefort or strong cheese
2 tbsp cranberry jelly
Egg or milk, *to glaze*
Rocket or lettuce, *finely sliced*

METHOD

SERVES 8

Preheat the oven to 180°C / 350°F / gas mark 4

1. **To make the pastry basket**, roll out the pastry and cut into 8 squares, approximately 10x10 cm (4x4 inch) in size. About 1 cm (½ inch) in from the edge of the squares, cut two large L's, parallel with the outer edges, in two opposite corners of the squares. Fold the two outer L-shaped pieces over to the opposite corner to make a central well for the cheese. *(Use the glaze to hold the pastry in place)*.
2. Stab the central well with a fork *(to prevent it from rising)*, cut the cheese into fat slices and arrange in the well *(if the cheese is positioned on the raised outer edge of the puff pastry it will prevent the pastry from rising)*. *
3. Glaze the pastry and bake for 15 minutes. Top each one with about ¼ tsp of cranberry jelly and bake for a further 10 minutes until the cheese has melted and the pastry is golden. Serve hot on a bed of rocket or lettuce.

Haddock Smokies

INGREDIENTS ££

2 fillets undyed smoked **haddock**, *skinned*
4 ripe tomatoes, *skinned and deseeded*
290ml (10 fl oz / ½ pt) double **cream**
100g (4 oz) fresh **Parmesan**, *grated*
4 slices of brown **bread**, **buttered**

METHOD

SERVES 8

Preheat the oven to 180°C / 350°F / gas mark 4

1. Chop the fish and tomatoes into 1 cm (½ inch) squares and divide them between 8 ramekins.
2. Pour in the cream, top with cheese and black pepper * and bake for 15 minutes.

Allow to cool for a few minutes before serving with fresh brown bread and butter.

Tomato & Lemongrass Consommé

INGREDIENTS ££

6 lemongrass stalks
8 spring onions
3 L (5¼ pts) water
1 chilli
8 thick slices of ginger, *cut into thin sticks*
6 garlic cloves
6 kaffir lime leaves *(if not available, use 2 bay leaves and the zest of ½ a lime)*
2 vegetable **stock** cubes
2 **egg whites**, *beaten*
2 tbsp lime juice
2 tbsp **fish sauce**
50g (2 oz) fresh coriander, *stalks removed*

Garnish

4 mild red chillies, *cut into very thin rounds*
8 mushrooms, *finely sliced*
4 tomatoes, *deseeded and chopped*
2 spring onions, *finely sliced*
24 cooked **prawns**

METHOD

SERVES 8

1. Crush the lemongrass and spring onions and cut into 8 cm *(3 inch)* lengths.
2. Put the lemongrass, water, chilli, ginger, garlic, lime leaves and stock into a large saucepan and bring to the boil and simmer for 45 minutes.
3. Strain the liquid through a sieve into another saucepan *(keep the saucepan to hand)*, pressing down on the cooked ingredients to release all the flavour and juices.
4. Add the lime juice, fish sauce and whisk in the egg whites.
5. Pour the soup through a sieve lined with muslin. *
6. To serve, bring back to the boil then add the coriander and season to taste.
7. Divide the garnish between the bowls and pour over the soup.

Mushroom & Sherry Pâté

INGREDIENTS £

30g (1 oz) **butter**
2 onions, *roughly chopped*
2 garlic cloves, *crushed*
200g (7 oz) mushrooms, *sliced*
3 tbsp **crème fraîche**
250g (9 oz) **cream cheese**
3 tbsp **sherry**
8 slices of **bread**

METHOD

SERVES 8

Preheat the oven to 180°C / 350°F / gas mark 4

1. Melt the butter in a frying pan and cook the onion and garlic until soft.
2. Add the mushrooms, season and cook for a further 5 minutes, then remove from the heat and allow to cool slightly.
3. Put in a food processor and blend with the crème fraîche, cream cheese and sherry until smooth. Season to taste.
4. Pour the mixture into 8 ramekins * and bake for 30 minutes.
5. **To make Melba toast**, lightly toast the bread in a toaster and allow to cool.
6. Remove the crusts and slide the knife through the middle of the piece of toast *(place your hand flat on top of the slice of toast with your fingers on full stretch. Start cutting from a corner and once you have reached the middle, rotate the piece of toast until you have sliced straight through).*
7. Cut in half diagonally and place on a baking tray, toasted side down and bake for 4-5 minutes.
8. Serve the pâté in the ramekins *(a few minutes after they have come out of the oven)* on a starter plate with Melba toast balanced on top.

Spring Rolls / Samosas with Chilli Sauce

INGREDIENTS ££

7½ tbsp vegetable oil
1 red onion, *finely chopped*
2 garlic cloves, *crushed*
15g (½ oz) fresh ginger, *finely sliced*
2 carrots, *peeled and cut into juliennes (fine sticks)*
4 mushrooms, *finely sliced*
½ green pepper, *deseeded and finely sliced lengthways*
½ yellow pepper, *deseeded and finely sliced lengthways*
8 sheets of samosa pastry *(*filo pastry *could be used)*
2 eggs, *beaten*
Lettuce, *torn into pieces*

Chilli Sauce
2 tsp white wine vinegar
2 tbsp soy sauce
2 tsp sugar
2 tbsp olive oil
1 tsp sesame seeds
1 fresh chilli, *finely chopped*
2 tbsp fresh coriander, *finely chopped*
1 tsp fresh ginger, *grated*

METHOD

SERVES 8

1. **To make the sauce**, place the vinegar, soy sauce and sugar in a jam jar and shake to dissolve the sugar. Add the rest of the ingredients and leave for 1 hour so that the flavours can infuse. *
2. Warm 1½ tbsp of vegetable oil in a frying pan, add the onion, garlic and ginger and cook until soft.
3. Add the carrots, mushrooms and green and yellow peppers and cook for about 7 minutes until al dente. Season to taste.
4. **To make a spring roll**: take a square sheet of pastry, place it so that one corner is at the top, resembling a diamond shape, glaze with egg and place ⅛ of the filling on the pastry, in the shape of a sausage, about two thirds down from the middle. Fold up the bottom corner of the pastry, roll it slightly and turn in each side, then roll the parcel away from you creating a spring roll. * Glaze with egg.
5. **To make a samosa**: take a square sheet of pastry and cut it lengthways into three equal sized strips, glaze with egg and place a spoonful of the filling on the top end of one of the strips of pastry. Fold the top left hand corner over the mixture so that the top side of the pastry comes in line with the right hand side of the pastry *(so the folded pastry forms a triangular shape)*, then fold the triangle down towards you. Fold it over to the left *(folding the top right corner over so that the top side of the parcel comes in line with the left side of the pastry)*, continue folding in this way until you come to the end of the strip of pastry. * Glaze with egg.
6. Warm 6 tbsp of vegetable oil in a frying pan and fry the parcels over a medium heat for about 2 minutes until golden brown.
7. Serve on a bed of salad and drizzle over the sauce *(to serve the spring rolls, slice each one in half at an angle and arrange on the salad)*.

Wild Mushroom Risotto with Rocket & Parmesan

INGREDIENTS ££

12g (1/2 oz) dried wild mushrooms *(cep / porcini)*
290ml (10 fl oz / 1/2 pt) warm water
1 tbsp olive oil
30g (1 oz) butter
1 onion, *chopped*
1 garlic clove, *crushed*
200g (7 oz) mushrooms, *sliced*
1/2 lemon, *juiced*
185g (6 1/2 oz) risotto rice *(Arborio rice)*
60ml (2 fl oz) dry white wine
450ml (16 fl oz) vegetable stock *(use 2 cubes)*
1 tbsp fresh parsley, *chopped*
40g (1 1/4 oz) Parmesan cheese, *grated*
Shavings of Parmesan cheese, *for presentation*
Rocket, *for garnish*

METHOD

SERVES 8

1. Place the dried mushrooms in a bowl and pour over the warm water. Leave to soak for at least 40 minutes. *
2. Warm the oil and half of the butter in a large saucepan, add the onion and garlic and cook over a gentle heat until soft. *
3. Meanwhile, melt the remaining butter in a smaller saucepan, add the fresh mushrooms and lemon juice and cook for about 5 minutes. *
4. Add the rice to the saucepan of onion and garlic and stir over the heat for about a minute.
5. Add all of the mushrooms *(both fresh and dried with the liquid they have been soaking in)*, pour in the wine and cook until most of the liquid has been absorbed.
6. Add 3/4 of the stock, stirring occasionally, adding more stock when necessary *(do not let the mixture become dry, if you run out of stock use hot water)*. Simmer for about 20-25 minutes until the rice is tender, but still firm to the bite.
7. Stir in the parsley and Parmesan and season to taste.
8. Place a mousse ring in the centre of each plate and fill with the risotto.
9. Carefully remove the ring and garnish with rocket, Parmesan shavings and black pepper and serve immediately.

Spiced Mackerel on a Watercress Salad

STARTERS

INGREDIENTS ££

8 mackerel fillets, *boned*
Crème fraîche

Marinade
½ tsp cayenne pepper
1 tsp smoked paprika
½ tsp ground ginger
½ tbsp caster sugar
¼ tsp English mustard powder
1 tsp red wine vinegar
¼ tsp chilli powder
1 tbsp rapeseed oil

Watercress Salad
¼ tbsp lemon juice
1 tbsp olive oil
½ tsp Dijon mustard
45g (1½ oz) watercress

Relish
½ tbsp olive oil
½ large onion, *chopped*
1 garlic clove, *chopped*
1½ tomatoes, *deseeded and finely chopped*
½ tbsp tomato purée
½ tbsp fresh ginger, *grated*
½ small green chilli, *finely chopped*
½ tsp cumin
¼ lime, *juiced*
½ tbsp fresh coriander, *chopped*

METHOD

SERVES 8

1. **To make the marinade**, mix together all the ingredients.
2. Slash 3 times diagonally across the skin side of each fillet, coat all over in the marinade and leave to marinate for at least 1 hour. *
3. **To make the relish**, warm the oil in a frying pan and cook the onion and garlic over a gentle heat until soft.
4. Add the fresh tomatoes, tomato purée, ginger, chilli and cumin and simmer for 10 minutes. *
5. Stir in the lime juice and coriander just before serving.
6. **To make the salad**, mix together the lemon juice, olive oil, and mustard and toss the watercress in the dressing just before serving.
7. Place the fillets on a lined baking tray, skin side up and cook under a hot grill for about 4 minutes until the skin is crisp.

Serve the fillets, hot, on a bed of watercress salad with the warm relish, topped with a teaspoon of crème fraîche.

Horseradish potatoes go well if serving as a main course.

Salmon Mousse on French Bread with Dill Oil

INGREDIENTS £££

200g (7 oz) smoked salmon *(to make the roses)*
16 thin slices of French bread, *toasted*
1 lemon, *cut into 8 segments*
Fresh dill, *for garnish*

Salmon Mousse
2 tsp English mustard
1 tbsp lemon juice
4 sprigs of dill
60g (2 oz) smoked salmon, *off cuts*
200g (7 oz) cream cheese
250ml (9 fl oz) crème fraîche

Dill Oil
$^{1}/_{2}$ tsp dried dill
4 tbsp olive oil

METHOD

SERVES 8

1. Blend the mousse ingredients in the food processor *(do not over blend the mixture, use the pulse button just to combine the ingredients)* and refrigerate.
2. Combine the dill oil ingredients to make the dressing. *
3. To prepare the smoked salmon for plating, cut it into strips about 4 cm ($1^{1}/_{2}$ inch) and loosely roll, pinching one end and opening the other to create a rose.
4. Plate the French bread *(two slices per person)* and spoon a generous heap of the salmon mixture on each piece.

Garnish with a salmon rose, a segment of lemon, dill oil, fresh dill and black pepper.

Fennel Salad

INGREDIENTS ££

100g ($3^{1}/_{2}$ oz) pine nuts
2 fennel bulbs
125g ($4^{1}/_{2}$ oz) dried cranberries, *roughly chopped*
Salad

Dressing
3 tbsp olive oil
1 tbsp balsamic vinegar
1 tsp honey
1 garlic clove, *crushed*
$^{1}/_{4}$ tsp English mustard powder

METHOD

SERVES 8

1. Toast the pine nuts in the oven.
2. **To make the dressing**, put all the ingredients in a jar and shake well to combine, season to taste.
3. Remove any hard outside bits from the fennel bulbs then slice very finely.
4. Add the dressing and the cranberries to the fennel and mix well.
5. Just before serving stir in the toasted pine nuts and adjust seasoning if necessary.

Serve in a ramekin surrounded by a few lettuce leaves.

Smoked Salmon & Prawn Méli-mélo

INGREDIENTS £££

300g (10½ oz) cream cheese
1 tsp fresh dill, *chopped*
2 tsp lemon juice
300g (10½ oz) frozen cooked prawns, *defrosted and excess water squeezed out*
4 slices of wholemeal bread
8 x 10 cm strips of smoked salmon
1 lemon, *cut lengthwise into 8 wedges*
Fresh dill, *for garnishing*
½ small cucumber, *sliced*

Dill Oil
½ tsp dried dill
4 tbsp olive oil

METHOD

SERVES 8

1. Mix together the cream cheese, dill, lemon juice and black pepper, then gently stir in the prawns.
2. **To make the dill oil**, combine the dried dill and olive oil.
3. Lightly toast the bread and allow to cool.
4. Remove the crusts and cut each piece into half to make a rectangle.
5. Slide the knife through the middle of each piece of toast *(place your hand flat on top of the toast with your fingers on full stretch, rotate the toast until you have sliced through it).*
6. Place on a baking tray, toasted side down and bake for 4-5 minutes until golden and allow to cool. *
7. Place a piece of the toast off centre on each starter plate, spoon a portion of the prawn mixture over each one.
8. Place a second piece of toast on top so that the edges curl upwards and arrange the strips of smoked salmon, a segment of lemon and a sprig of fresh dill on top of each one.
9. Arrange the cucumber on the plate, drizzle with dill oil and dust with black pepper.

Rocket & Baby Spinach Salad with Sun-Dried Tomatoes, Mozzarella, Avocado & Warm Garlic Mushrooms

INGREDIENTS ££

20g (3/4 oz) butter
2 garlic cloves, *crushed*
340g (12 oz) mushrooms, *finely sliced*
80g (3 oz) bag of pre-washed baby spinach
80g (3 oz) bag of rocket
8 pieces of sun-dried tomatoes, *chopped*
150g (5½ oz) mozzarella, *chopped*
1-2 avocados, *peeled and chopped*

Dressing
6 tbsp balsamic vinegar
2 tsp sugar
6 tbsp olive oil

METHOD

SERVES 8

1. **To make the dressing**, put the vinegar and sugar in a small saucepan, bring up to the boil and simmer for a few minutes to reduce slightly. *(If you have reduced it to a syrup, add a little water to make it the right consistency)*. Allow to cool a little and then add to the oil.
2. Warm the butter in small frying pan and gently fry the garlic for a few minutes. Add the mushrooms, season and cook until soft. *
3. Combine the baby spinach and rocket and arrange the salad on the starter plates.
4. Top with the remaining ingredients.
5. Vigorously stir the dressing and spoon it over the salad.
6. Place the warm mushrooms on top and serve immediately.

Chicken Liver Pâté

INGREDIENTS ££

400g (14 oz) chicken livers
225g (8 oz) **butter**
2 onions, *chopped*
2 garlic cloves, *crushed*
2 tbsp **brandy**

Clarified Butter
110g (4 oz) **butter**
Pinch of nutmeg
12 sprigs of thyme

METHOD

SERVES 8

1. Wash and dry the livers and trim off any fat and membrane.
2. Divide the butter into four quarters, melt one quarter in a frying pan, add the onion and cook on low heat until soft.
3. Add the garlic and cook for a further minute and allow to cool slightly.
4. Pour the mixture into a food processor *(you will be adding more ingredients to it later)*.
5. Melt another quarter of the butter in the frying pan and fry the livers for about 5 minutes *(they should be cooked on the outside and remain slightly pink on the inside)*. Allow to cool slightly and add to the food processor.
6. Add the brandy and the rest of the butter to the food processor and blend the mixture until smooth, season to taste.
7. Divide the mixture evenly between 8 ramekins and refrigerate to set *(they take about 30 minutes to set)*. *
8. Once the pâté has set make the clarified butter; put all the ingredients in a small saucepan and warm gently to melt the butter *(don't let it boil)*.
9. Once the butter has melted swirl the saucepan to mix the ingredients and pour over the pâté. Place ramekins back in the fridge for the butter to set. *

Place the ramekins on a starter plate and serve with toast.

Smoked Haddock Fish Cakes with Tartar Sauce

INGREDIENTS ££

450g (1 lb) potatoes
30g (1 oz) butter
450g (1 lb) smoked haddock
1 lemon, *grated zest*
1 egg, *hard boiled and chopped*
2 tbsp fresh parsley, *chopped*
Lettuce, *torn into pieces*

Tartar Sauce
200g (7 oz) mayonnaise
1 small shallot, *chopped*
2 small gherkins, *chopped*
2 tbsp capers
1 tsp horseradish sauce
1/4 tsp English mustard powder

Coating
2 eggs, *beaten*
110g (4 oz) white breadcrumbs

METHOD

SERVES 8

1. Peel and quarter the potatoes and cook for 25 minutes in salted water until very soft.
2. Drain, add the butter and mash in the saucepan.
3. **To make the tartar sauce**, blend the mayonnaise and shallot in a mini food processor. Add the rest of the ingredients to the food processor to combine. *(Do not blend into a smooth paste).* *
4. Place the fish in a saucepan and add water so that it just covers the fish. Cover with a lid, bring to the boil and simmer for about 5 minutes until the fish is just cooked *(the flesh of the fish will flake cleanly when pulled apart).*
5. Pour off the water and allow the fish to cool a little.
6. Remove the skin and bones, then flake the fish.
7. Add it to the potato, together with the lemon zest, chopped egg and parsley and stir gently to combine. Season to taste.
8. Make the mixture into a round and cut it like a cake into 16 equal portions.
9. Using your hands, make each portion into a ball, then dip into the beaten egg and roll in the breadcrumbs. Flatten slightly into a fish cake shape. *
10. Over a low heat, melt the butter in a frying pan and brown the fish cakes on each side.

Serve the fish cakes on a bed of lettuce with a spoonful of tartar sauce.

Smoked Mackerel Pâté with Cucumber Pappardelle

INGREDIENTS £££

Pâté

3 smoked mackerel fillets, *skinned and pin boned*
1 tsp horseradish sauce
2 tsp Dijon mustard
2 tbsp crème fraîche
Salt and pepper
1 tbsp lemon juice
100g (3½ oz) unsalted butter, *cubed*

Cucumber Pappardelle

½ cucumber
4 tbsp white wine vinegar or cider vinegar
½ lemon, *juiced*
1 tbsp fresh dill, *chopped*
1 tbsp rapeseed oil

Melba Toast

Brown bread, *sliced*
Sesame oil
Sesame seeds
Poppy seeds

Parsley or dill to garnish

METHOD

SERVES 8

1. **To make the pâté**, blend all the ingredients in a food processor until smooth. Season to taste.
2. Line a dish with cling film. Fill the dish with the pâté, smooth over the top and refrigerator to set. *
3. **To make the cucumber pappardelle**, cut cumber in half lengthways and remove the seeds with spoon *(discard the seeds).* Use a potato peeler to shave off strips of cucumber.
4. Mix the cucumber with the other ingredients and chill for about 20 minutes.
5. **To make Melba toast**, lightly toast the bread in a toaster and allow to cool.
6. Remove the crusts and slide the knife through the middle of the piece of toast *(place your hand flat on top of the slice of toast with your fingers on full stretch. Start cutting from a corner and once you have reached the middle, rotate the piece of toast until you have sliced straight through).*
7. Brush with sesame oil and sprinkle with sesame seeds and poppy seeds.
8. Cut the toast into quarters *(cutting through each corner)* and place on a lined baking tray, toasted side down and bake for 4-5 minutes at 180°C / 350°F / gas mark 4 until golden.
9. Serve the pâté with the cucumber pappardelle *(drain the cucumber before serving)* and melba toast and garnish with parsley or dill.

Thai Butternut Squash / Pumpkin Soup

INGREDIENTS ££

800ml (28 fl oz) coconut milk
2 tbsp red *(or yellow)* Thai curry paste
700ml (24 fl oz) fish or vegetable stock *(use 4 cubes)*
6 tbsp Thai fish sauce
6 lemongrass, *(if using fresh; cut into 3 and bruise with the flat of a knife)*
6 lime leaves, *destalked and cut into strips*
1 tsp turmeric powder
1.2 kg (2 lb 11 oz) butternut squash or pumpkin, *peeled and cut into bite sized chunks*
800g (1 lb 12 oz) salmon fillet *(optional), skinned and cut into large bite sized chunks*
800g (1 lb 12 oz) frozen peeled tiger prawns *(optional), thawed*
3 heads pak choi, *sliced (about 1 cm / ½ inch thick slices)*
2 tbsp lime juice
1 bunch coriander, *destalked & roughly chopped*

METHOD

SERVES 8

1. Put the coconut milk, curry paste, stock, fish sauce, lemon grass, lime leaves and turmeric into a large saucepan with the butternut squash or pumpkin and simmer about 15 minutes, until the vegetables are tender. *
2. If adding seafood, add the fish just before the vegetables are tender and cook for about 5 minutes until the fish is cooked *(do not stir too much otherwise you will break up the fish).*
3. Just before serving remove the lemongrass, add the pak choi and stir until wilted.
4. Add the lime juice and season to taste.

Serve and scatter the coriander on top.

Red Onion & Goats' Cheese Tartlets

INGREDIENTS ££

Red Onion Marmalade
30g (1 oz) unsalted butter
4 small red onions, *finely sliced*
2 tbsp Demerara sugar
1 tbsp balsamic or red wine vinegar
170ml (6 fl oz) red wine
2 tbsp redcurrant jelly

55g (2 oz) butter
150g (5½ oz) goats' cheese, *cubed (approx 1 cm)*
Filo pastry
Salad for garnish
2 sprigs of thyme

METHOD

SERVES 8

Preheat the oven to 180°C / 350°F / gas mark 4

1. To make the marmalade, melt the butter in a frying pan and soften the onions.
2. Add the remaining ingredients and simmer to reduce to a marmalade consistency.
3. Melt the butter gently in a saucepan. Using some of the butter, grease, then flour the tartlet tins.
4. Open out the pastry *(but do not separate the layers yet)* and cut into approx 12 cm (4¾ inch) squares *(you will need 24 squares in total)*.
5. Separate the layers and, using a pastry brush, coat 8 pieces on both sides with the melted butter. Place one piece in each tartlet tin.
6. Coat one side of the remaining pieces of pastry with the melted butter and place a second and a third layer into each tin, buttered side up *(place them on top of one another so that the corners do not overlap and a star shape is formed)*.
7. Bake for about 7 minutes until crisp and golden brown.
8. Spread the onion marmalade over the base of the tartlets
9. Top with the goats' cheese and then a sprinkling of thyme. *
10. Bake for 10-15 minutes to warm through and melt the cheese.

Serve on a bed of dressed salad.

STARTERS

Crab Samosas with Harissa & Watercress

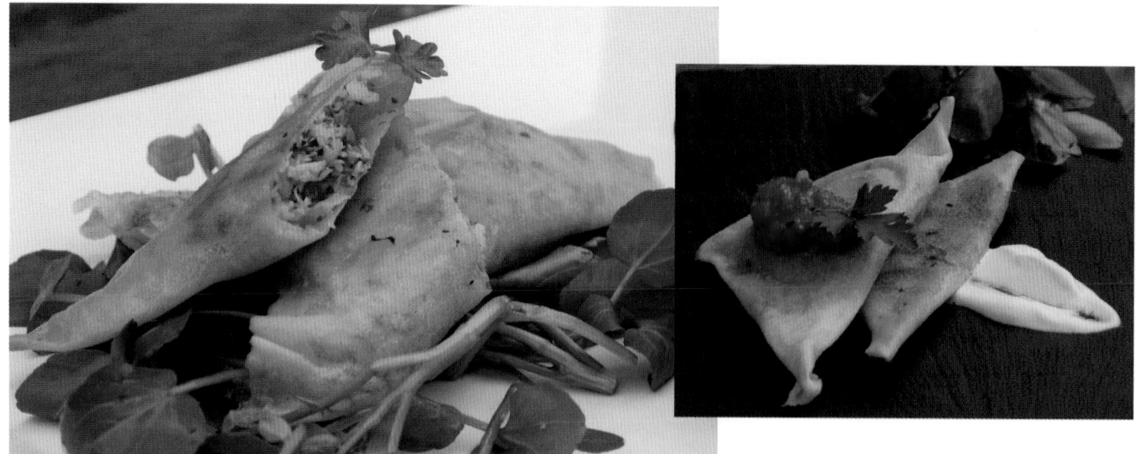

INGREDIENTS ££

3 tbsp fresh mint, *chopped*
3 tbsp fresh parsley, *chopped*
3 tbsp fresh coriander, *chopped*
1 scotch bonnet, *finely chopped*
1 garlic clove, *crushed*
1 tsp cumin seeds, *toasted & ground*
1 tbsp lemon juice
270g (9½ oz) crab meat
8 sheets samosa pastry
1 egg, *beaten*
4 tbsp vegetable oil
Watercress
1 lemon, *cut into wedges*

Harissa Paste
1 tsp cumin seeds
¼ tsp caraway seeds
½ scotch bonnet, *finely chopped*
2 garlic cloves, *crushed*
25g (1 oz) roasted red peppers
1 tsp red wine vinegar
2 tbsp olive oil

METHOD Serves 8

1. **To make the Harissa paste**, dry fry the cumin and caraway seeds for about a minute, then crush in a pestle and mortar.
2. Add the seeds to the mini bowl of a food processor with all the other Harissa paste ingredients and blend to a paste. Season to taste.
3. **To make the samosa filling**, mix together the mint, parsley, coriander, scotch bonnet, garlic, cumin and lemon juice.
4. Pick through the crab meat, remove any shell fragments and stir into the herb mix. Season to taste.
5. **To make a samosa**: take a square sheet of pastry and cut it downwards into three equal sized strips, glaze with egg and place a spoonful of the filling on the top end of one of the strips of pastry. Fold the top left hand corner over the mixture so that the top side of the pastry comes in line with the right hand side *(so the folded pastry forms a triangular shape),* then fold the triangle down towards you. Fold it over to the left *(folding the top right corner over so that the top side of the parcel comes in line with the left side of the pastry)*, continue folding in this way until you come to the end of the strip of pastry.
6. Warm the vegetable oil in a frying pan and fry the samosas over a medium heat until golden brown. Turn and brown the other side then drain on kitchen paper to remove excess oil.
7. Slice in half at an angle and serve warm with dressed watercress, a wedge of lemon and Harissa paste.

Mezzelune (simular to ravioli)

INGREDIENTS ££

Pasta
225g (8 oz) plain flour
1 tbsp olive oil
2 eggs, *beaten*
2 egg yolks
1 tbsp milk
1 egg, *to glaze*

Fillings to choose from:

Spinach Filling
110g (4 oz) frozen spinach, *thawed*
3 tbsp ricotta cheese

Sun-dried Tomato Filling
180g (6½ oz) Cheddar cheese
7 pieces of sun-dried tomatoes

Mushroom Filling
15g (½ oz) butter
120g (4½ oz) mushrooms, *finely chopped*
1 onion, *finely diced*
2 tsp Boursin cheese

Sauces to choose from:

Boursin Sauce
200ml (7 fl oz) cream
60g (2½ oz) Boursin cheese

Tomato Sauce
1 tbsp olive oil
1 onion, chopped
2 garlic cloves, *crushed*
1 x 400g tin of tomatoes
1½ tsp sugar
1 tsp dried basil
1 tsp white wine vinegar

METHOD

SERVES 8

1. **To make the pasta**, put the flour in a bowl, make a well in the centre and add the rest of the ingredients to the well, combine using a spoon and then use your hands *(if too dry add a little more milk but don't make it too sticky)*. Knead into a smooth dough.
2. Wrap in cling film and refrigerate for 30 minutes to cool.
3. **To make the filling** *(you don't need to make them all)*:
   a) Spinach - squeeze the water out of the spinach and blend with the cheese in a food processor. Season to taste.
   b) Sun-dried tomato - blend the cheese and sun-dried tomatoes in a food processor until almost a paste and season.
   c) Mushroom - warm the butter in a frying pan and cook the onions until soft. Add the mushrooms and cook for a further 5 minutes, *(you may need to turn up the heat to reduce excess liquid)* then spread out on a plate and leave to cool. Mix with the Boursin cheese and season to taste.
4. **To make the sauce** *(choose one)*:
   a) Boursin - warm the cream and the cheese until it has melted *(do not boil)*. Season to taste.
   b) Tomato - warm the oil in a small saucepan and cook the onion and garlic over a gentle heat until soft. Add the tomatoes, sugar, basil and white wine vinegar, season and simmer for 10 minutes *(add water if it becomes too dry)*. Use a hand blender to blend until smooth. Season to taste.
5. Roll out the pasta as thinly as you can *(it really does need to be very thin)* and using a crinkly pastry cutter *(approximately 8 cm / 3¼ inch in diameter)* cut out 24 circles.
6. Glaze half of each circle with egg, place a teaspoonful of the filling on the glazed side near the centre and fold over the other half of the pasta, forming a semicircle. Press the edges down all round the outside of the semicircle to seal the filling in. Cover with cling film until cooking. *
7. To cook the pasta, put 1 tsp of salt and 1 tbsp of olive oil in a large saucepan of water and bring it to the boil. Add the mezzelune, turn down the heat and cook for 5-6 minutes until al dente.
8. Arrange 3 mezzelune on a starter plate, drizzle over the sauce and olive oil and garnish with parsley or basil.

STARTERS

Tartlets with Mixed Pepper & Black Olive / Mushroom / Tomato & Mustard / Roquefort & Pear Fillings

INGREDIENTS £

Puff Pastry *(readymade)* or
Shortcrust Pastry
170g (6 oz) plain flour
42g (1½ oz) butter
42g (1½ oz) lard
3 tbsp water
Pinch of salt

Mixed Pepper & Black Olive Filling
2 tbsp vegetable oil
2 onions, *chopped*
1 yellow pepper, *diced*
1 green pepper, *diced*
100g (3½ oz) black olives, *sliced*
1 tsp herbes de Provence
140g (5 oz) Cheddar cheese, *grated*

Tomato & Mustard Filling
4 tsp Dijon mustard
1 tsp English mustard
160g (5½ oz) Cheddar, Parmesan and Emmental cheese, *grated*
3 tomatoes, *finely sliced*
Pinch of herbes de Provence

Mushroom Filling
2 tbsp vegetable oil
2 onions, *chopped*
600g (1 lb 5 oz) mushrooms, *sliced*
6-8 tbsp crème fraîche

Roquefort & Pear Filling
4 pears, *peeled, cored and chopped*
Pinch of dried rosemary
100g (3½ oz) Roquefort cheese, *chopped*

Dressed salad, *for presentation*

METHOD

SERVES 8

Preheat the oven to 180°C / 350°F / gas mark 4

1. Grease and then flour 8 tartlet tins.
2. **To make the shortcrust pastry**, blend all the ingredients in a food processor, tip out on to a floured chopping board and knead into a ball.
3. Roll out the pastry so that it is very thin. Using a pastry cutter, cut out 8 circles and press each one into a tartlet tin
4. Blind bake the pastry for 7-10 minutes (put a layer of greaseproof paper over the pastry and weigh it down with baking beans - *this prevents the pastry base from ballooning*. Remove the baking beans and greaseproof paper and, if the pastry still looks damp, cook for a further 5 minutes. *
5. **To make the mixed pepper & black olive filling**; warm the vegetable oil in a frying pan and cook the onions until soft. Add the peppers, olives and herbes de Provence and cook for a further 5 minutes. Season to taste. * Sprinkle the cheese into the pastry cases and spoon the filling into the tartlets.

   To make the tomato and mustard filling; mix the mustards together and spread over the base of the pastry. Top with the cheese and arrange the slices of tomato over the top. Sprinkle a pinch of herbes de Provence over the top of each tartlet.

   To make the mushroom filling; warm the vegetable oil in a frying pan and cook the onions until soft. Add the mushrooms, season and cook for a further 5 minutes *(if lots of liquid comes out of the mushrooms, turn up the heat to reduce it)*. Stir in the crème fraîche, season to taste * and spoon the filling into the tartlets.

   Pear and Roquefort filling; arrange a pear in each tartlet, sprinkle with rosemary and top with the Roquefort cheese.
6. Bake for 20-25 minutes and serve on a bed of dressed salad.

MAIN COURSES

MAIN COURSES

MAIN COURSES

MAIN COURSES

MAIN COURSES

MAIN COURSES

Stuffed Chicken Breasts with Goats' Cheese, Sun-dried Tomatoes & Rocket served with a Tomato & Basil Sauce

INGREDIENTS £££

4 chicken breasts
15g (½ oz) butter

Tomato & Basil Sauce
1 tbsp olive oil
1 onion, *finely chopped*
2 garlic clove, *crushed*
1 x 400g tin of tomatoes
100ml (4 fl oz) chicken stock
1½ tsp sugar
1 tsp dried basil
1 tsp white wine vinegar
2 tsp fresh basil, *finely chopped*

Stuffing
2 tbsp oil from sun-dried tomato jar
4 shallots, *finely chopped*
10 large pieces of sun-dried tomato, *finely chopped*
1 tsp sugar
1 tsp white wine vinegar
110g (4 oz) rocket, *roughly chopped*
110g (4 oz) goats' cheese, *roughly chopped*

METHOD

SERVES 8

Preheat the oven to 180°C / 350°F / gas mark 4

1. **To make the tomato sauce**; warm the oil in a small saucepan and cook the onion and garlic over a gentle heat until soft. Add the tomatoes, stock, sugar, dried basil and white wine vinegar, season and simmer for 10 minutes. Use hand blender to purée the sauce *(to make it completely smooth, push through a sieve).** Add the fresh basil just before serving and season to taste.
2. **To make the stuffing**; warm the oil in a frying pan and cook the shallots over a gentle heat until soft. Add the sun-dried tomatoes, sugar and vinegar and cook for another minute. Add the rocket and cook for a further minute until the rocket has wilted. Remove from the heat, season to taste and stir in the goats' cheese. *
3. Trim the chicken and prepare it for stuffing – *place the palm of your hand firmly on top of the chicken, fingers on full stretch and slice the meat almost in half, horizontally, creating a pocket.*
4. Stuff each chicken breast and secure using cocktail sticks.
5. Brown the chicken in butter in a hot **stainless steel** frying pan *(the cocktail sticks will damage a non-stick surface).* Transfer to a lined baking tray * and bake for about 25 minutes.
6. To serve, remove the cocktail sticks, slice the chicken and arrange on a plate with the sauce. *(Remember to add the fresh basil to the sauce and adjust seasoning, if necessary, just before serving).*

Pork Fillet Wrapped in Spinach & Parma Ham with Madeira Mushroom Sauce

INGREDIENTS £££

30g (1 oz) butter
300g (10½ oz) baby spinach, *washed*
2 tbsp olive oil
10 slices of Parma ham
2 pork fillets, *trimmed*
1 tbsp vegetable oil

Madeira Mushroom Sauce
30g (1 oz) butter
4 shallots, *finely chopped*
200g (7 oz) mushrooms, *sliced*
2 garlic cloves, *crushed*
2 tbsp plain flour
850ml (30 fl oz / 1½ pts) chicken stock
4 tbsp Madeira
4 tbsp cream

METHOD

SERVES 8

Preheat the oven to 180°C / 350°F / gas mark 4

1. Melt the butter in a saucepan and cook the spinach for a few minutes until just cooked. Drain, squeeze out any excess liquid and allow to cool.
2. Lay a large piece of cling film on a chopping board and brush with olive oil. Lay out 5 slices of Pama ham across the width of the board, so it overlaps slightly.
3. Spread half of the spinach over the ham.
4. Heat the vegetable oil in a frying pan. When it is very hot seal the fillets.
5. Place one fillet on top of the spinach and remove the other from the pan *(keep the frying pan with its juices to make the sauce)*.
6. Season and then using the cling film, roll the ham around the fillet and secure tightly with the cling film. Prepare the second fillet in the same way and chill for 1 hour. *
7. **To make the sauce**, melt the butter in the frying pan and cook the shallots over a gentle heat until soft.
8. Add the mushrooms and garlic and cook for a further 5 minutes.
9. Sprinkle over the flour, stir and slowly stir in the stock.
10. Add the Madeira and simmer to reduce by half.
11. Add the cream and season to taste. *
12. Remove the cling film from the pork fillets and place on a lined baking tray. * Bake for 25 minutes.
13. Allow to rest for 5 minutes before slicing into thick slices.

Arrange the slices on a plate and spoon the sauce around.

Cod with Bacon, Rosemary & Lemon Beurre Noisette

INGREDIENTS ££

2 tbsp fresh rosemary, *finely chopped*
½ lemon, *grated zest*
8 fillets **cod**
16 slices streaky bacon
Knob of **butter**

Beurre noisette
120g (4½ oz) **butter**
1 tbsp lemon juice

METHOD

SERVES 8

Preheat the oven to 200°C / 400°F / gas mark 6

1. Mix together the rosemary and lemon zest.
2. To prepare the fish, cut the fillet in half *(across the fish rather than down the length of the fillet)* and roll in the rosemary and lemon mixture.
3. Cut a length of baking paper twice as long as the baking tray and put one end of the paper on the baking tray. Arrange the bacon on the baking paper *(so that it does not overlap)*. Fold over the other end of the paper to cover the bacon and tuck the end under to secure in place. Bake in the oven for 1 hour.
4. Heat a knob of butter in a frying pan and cook the fish in the hot pan, skin side down first and cook until the skin lifts off the base of the pan *(4-5 minutes)*, turn and seal the other side for just a few seconds.
5. Place on a lined baking tray * *(keep the frying pan for making the sauce)* and bake for 3-6 minutes, depending on the size of the fish.
6. **To make the beurre noisette**, melt the butter in the frying pan. Continue to cook until it becomes golden brown. Remove from the heat and add the lemon juice *(be careful as it will spit)*.

Serve immediately, plate the fish, lean the bacon against it and spoon the sauce around the plate.

Pan Fried Sea Bass with Ginger Mash & Pickled Fennel

INGREDIENTS ££

1 fennel
290ml (10 fl oz / ½ pt) **white wine vinegar**
55g (2 oz) caster sugar
1kg (2 lb 4 oz) potatoes, *peeled*
100g (3½ oz) **butter**
60ml (2 fl oz) double **cream**
90g (3 oz) root ginger, *finely grated*
8 **sea bass** fillets, *pin boned*
1 tbsp olive oil
30g (1 oz) **butter**

METHOD

Serves 8

Preheat the oven to 180°C / 350°F / gas mark 4

1. To prepare the fennel, remove the top stalks and cut in half lengthways. Cut out the core in a wedge shape and discard. Finely slice the fennel and put in a bowl.
2. Put the white wine vinegar, sugar and a good pinch of salt into a pan, bring to the boil and simmer until the sugar has dissolved.
3. Remove from the heat and pour over the sliced fennel. Cover with cling film and leave to marinate for 3-4 hours or overnight. *
4. Put the potatoes in a saucepan of salted water, bring to the boil and simmer for about 25 minutes until very soft.
5. Drain the potatoes well, add the butter and cream and mash until smooth. Season to taste.
6. Put the potato in a dish, cover in foil * and reheat in the oven for about 20 minutes. Mash in the ginger just before serving.
7. Carefully score the skin of the fish 4-5 times *(take care not to cut all the way through the fish)* and season.
8. Heat the oil and butter in a frying pan. When the pan is really hot cook the fish, skin side down, for 1½ - 2 minutes, pressing gently on the fish to stop it from curling up *(the fish will stick initially, but as it cooks it releases itself. Don't move it around the pan as the skin will break up)*.
9. Carefully turn the fish and cook for a few seconds on the other side.
10. Put the fillets on a lined baking tray, skin side up, * and cook in the oven for 5 minutes.

To serve, arrange the fennel in the centre of the plate, top with a large quenelle of potato and place the fish on top. Drizzle the plate with olive oil.

Coronation Chicken

INGREDIENTS ££

2 medium chickens
1 Homepride curry sauce, *390g tin*
600g (1 lb 5 oz) mayonnaise
Small bunch of grapes, *washed*
2 tbsp mango chutney
55g (2 oz) flaked almonds, *toasted*

METHOD

SERVES 12

Preheat the oven to 180°C / 350°F / gas mark 4

1. Place the chickens upside-down in a roasting pot, pour in some water *(1 cm / ½ inch deep)* cover and bake for 2 hours.
2. Strip the chicken while warm and chop into bite size pieces *(no gristle or skin!).*
3. Empty the curry into a bowl and use the curry tin to measure the amount of mayonnaise. Use a tin full plus 2 heaped tbsp.
4. Stir in the chutney, season and taste.
5. Stir in the grapes and the chicken, taking care not to break up the chicken pieces. Transfer to a serving dish and decorate with toasted almonds. *

Serve chilled.

Roast Leg of Lamb with Garlic & Rosemary

INGREDIENTS £££

Leg of lamb, *on the bone*
6-8 cloves of garlic, *peeled and halved*
Fresh rosemary
Olive oil

Gravy
2 tbsp plain **flour**
570ml (20 fl oz / 1 pt) **stock**
2-3 tbsp red currant jelly *(optional)*

METHOD

SERVES 8

Preheat the oven to 220°C / 425°F / gas mark 7

1. Calculate the cooking time; allow 20 minutes per 450g (1 lb), plus an extra 20 minutes.
2. Stab the meat with a knife and push the garlic and rosemary into the holes.
3. Coat in oil, sprinkle with salt * and roast, turning the oven down to 180°C / 350°F / gas mark 4 after 20 minutes.
4. Use the juices from the roast meat to make the gravy. Pour the juices from the roasting tin into a jug, allow to settle for a few minutes and then spoon off most of the fat that will have risen to the surface. There will be juices from the meat stuck to the baking tray, so use a scraper and a little of the stock to help dissolve it.
5. Put the flour in a saucepan, add enough of the juice to make a roux.
6. Add the rest of the juice and the stock, season and whisk, using a coiled whisk. Bring to the boil and simmer for a few minutes, stirring occasionally. Add the red currant jelly and taste before serving.

Let the meat rest out of the oven for 15 minutes before carving *(cover in foil and a tea towel to keep warm)*.

Serve with mint sauce and red currant jelly.

Cod with Tomato, Basil, Parmesan & Pesto Mash

INGREDIENTS ££

675g (1½ lbs) potatoes, *peeled*
4-6 tbsp pesto *(to taste)*
8 x 175g (6 oz) fillets of cod, *skinned & boned*
6-8 tomatoes, *skinned, de-seeded & sliced*
A few sprigs of fresh basil, *chopped*
110g (4 oz) Parmesan, *coarsely grated*
Paprika
Parsley, *to garnish*

Pesto Sauce
1 tbsp pesto *(readymade or see recipe on following page)*
150ml (5 fl oz / ¼ pt) cream
Seasoning

METHOD

SERVES 8

Preheat the oven to 180°C / 350°F / gas mark 4

1. Quarter the potatoes and cook for 25 minutes in salted water until very soft.
2. Drain the potatoes, then mash. If using ready made pesto add and season to taste * *(If using fresh pesto, combine with the mashed potato just before cooking the cod).*
3. Season the cod fillets on both sides, place on a lined, greased baking tray and spread the potato over each one.
4. Arrange the sliced tomatoes on top of the potato, sprinkle with basil and Parmesan and dust lightly with paprika.
5. Season and bake for about 20-30 minutes until the fish is cooked *(the flesh of the fish will flake cleanly when it is cooked).*
6. To make the sauce, put the ingredients in a small saucepan and warm.

Place the fish in the centre of the plate, spoon the sauce around it, garnish with parsley and serve immediately.

Pesto

INGREDIENTS £££

55g (2 oz) fresh basil leaves
1 large garlic clove, *crushed*
1 tbsp **pine nuts**
10 tbsp olive oil
30g (1 oz) **Parmesan cheese**
Pinch of salt

METHOD

SERVES 8

1. To make the pesto, blend the basil, garlic, pine nuts, olive oil and some salt in a food processor. With the food processor running add the Parmesan to the mixture through the feeding tube.

Chicken & Tomato Casserole

INGREDIENTS £

8 large chicken thighs
4 tbsp plain **flour**
55g (2 oz) **butter**
2 onions, *finely sliced*
2 garlic cloves, *crushed*
1 green pepper, *sliced*,
1 yellow pepper, *sliced*
2 x 400g tins of chopped tomatoes
570ml (20 fl oz / 1 pt) chicken **stock**
2 tsp dried mixed herbs
½ tsp **white wine vinegar**
4 tsp capers

METHOD

SERVES 8

Preheat the oven to 180°C / 350°F / gas mark 4

1. Wash and dry the chicken thighs and trim off any excess fat.
2. Put the flour in a bowl, season, add the chicken and toss to lightly coat in flour.
3. Melt the butter in a large frying pan, add the chicken and cook on a medium heat for 8-10 minutes until golden brown.
4. Transfer the chicken to a casserole dish, leaving the juices in the frying pan
5. Add the onion and garlic to the frying pan and cook over a gentle heat until soft.
6. Add the green and yellow peppers and cook for a further 5 minutes.
7. Add the tomatoes, stock, mixed herbs, white wine vinegar and seasoning, stir and then pour over the chicken.
8. Cover with the lid * and cook in the oven for 1 hour.
9. About 5 minutes before serving stir in the capers *(if there is lots of fat on the top spoon it off, or use kitchen paper to soak up excess fat before adding the capers).*

Roast Loin of Pork with Sage & Onion Stuffing

INGREDIENTS ££

Loin of Pork *(140-200g / 5-7 oz per person)*

Stuffing
½ onion, *finely chopped*
55g (2 oz) **breadcrumbs**
1 tbsp fresh sage or 1 tsp dried sage, *chopped*
1 pear, *peeled and finely chopped*
Water

Gravy
1 tbsp plain **flour**
570ml (20 fl oz / 1 pt) **stock**

METHOD

Preheat the oven to 220°C / 425°F / gas mark 7

1. Calculate the cooking time; allow 25 minutes per 450g (1 lb), plus an extra 25 minutes.
2. **To make the stuffing**, combine all the ingredients, add a few drops of water so that the mixture forms a ball.
3. Cut open the joint lengthways to make a cavity and fill with the stuffing. Tie up with string, oil the skin and rub in some salt. *
4. Roast, turning the oven down to 180°C / 350°F / gas mark 4 after the first 20 minutes of cooking.
5. Use the juices from the roast meat to make the gravy. Pour the juices from the roasting tin into a jug, allow to settle for a few minutes and then spoon off most of the fat that will have risen to the surface. There will be juices from the meat stuck to the baking tray, so use a scraper and a little of the stock to help dissolve it.
6. Put the flour in to a saucepan, pour in enough of the juices to make a roux.
7. Add the rest of the juices and the stock, season and whisk, using a coil whisk. Bring to the boil and simmer for a few minutes, stirring occasionally.

Let the meat rest out of the oven for 15 minutes before carving. Cover in foil to keep warm.

Pork Medallions with Calvados Sauce

INGREDIENTS £££

2 sprigs of fresh rosemary *(or 2 tsp of dried)*
3 egg yolks
8 pork medallions
30g (1 oz) butter
30g (1 oz) plain flour
70g (2½ oz) hazelnuts, *finely chopped*

Calvados Sauce
175ml (6 fl oz) Calvados
500ml (17½ fl oz) cider *(medium)*
1 tsp soy sauce
2 tbsp honey
2 shallots, *finely chopped*
1½ tbsp cornflour
2 tbsp cream

METHOD

SERVES 8

Preheat the oven to 180°C / 350°F / gas mark 4

1. Add the rosemary to the egg yolks, mix well and leave to marinade for 2 hours.
2. Bash the meat with a rolling pin to tenderize. Melt the butter in a frying pan and fry the medallions for about 5 minutes on each side until golden brown *(keep the remaining juices for the sauce).*
3. **To make the sauce**, put the cider in a saucepan, add the shallots and simmer to reduce to half its volume.
4. Flame the Calvados and add to the cider and shallots. *(To flame the Calvados, start by turning off the extractor fan. Heat the Calvados over a high heat. Have a saucepan lid to hand. When it begins to shudder turn off the heat, stand well back and put a match to it. Allow it to burn for a few seconds and then cover with the lid to extinguish the flames).*
5. Mix the cornflour in a glass with a little water and add to the cider and shallots, together with the soy sauce and the honey. Simmer, with a lid on, over a medium heat for 5 minutes. *
6. Roll the edges of the pork in seasoned flour, then in the egg marinade and then in the nuts. Place on a lined baking tray, cover with foil * and bake for 20 minutes.
7. Heat the sauce and add the cream before serving.

Apple Sauce

INGREDIENTS £

2 apples, *peeled, cored and chopped*
½ lemon, *juiced*
2 tbsp water
10g (¼ oz) butter
Sugar *(optional)*

METHOD

SERVES 4-6

1. Put the apples, lemon juice and water into a saucepan, cover and cook over a low heat until very soft.
2. Remove from the heat and mash in the butter.
3. Taste and add sugar if it is too tart *(tartness varies depending on the type of apples used).* Allow to cool.

Cod Fillets Topped with Prawns & Filo Twists

INGREDIENTS £££

8 portions of cod fillets, *washed, skinned and boned*
½ lemon
Bunch of dill, *leaves only, chopped*
200g (7 oz) cream cheese
400g (14 oz) frozen prawns, *defrosted, washed and dried*
4 sheets of filo pastry
4 tsp vegetable oil
2 tbsp Parmesan, *grated*
Parsley, *for garnishing*

Pea Purée
150ml (5 fl oz) chicken stock *(dissolve 1 stock cube in the water)*
250ml (9 fl oz) dry white wine
500g (1 lb 2 oz) frozen peas
150ml (5 fl oz) cream

METHOD

Serves 8

Preheat the oven to 180°C / 350°F / gas mark 4

1. **To make the pea purée**, put the stock and wine in a saucepan and bring to the boil.
2. Add the peas and simmer for about 3-4 minutes.
3. Drain the peas over a bowl to reserve the liquid *(as you may need some of it).*
4. Blend the peas with the cream until smooth, adding some of the reserve liquid to get the right consistency. Season to taste.
5. To prepare the fish, place on a lined baking tray, squeeze over the lemon juice and season with salt and pepper.
6. Mix the dill with the cream cheese and carefully stir in the prawns. Season with black pepper and spread evenly over the fish.
7. Brush both sides of the filo pastry with vegetable oil, then cut into strips about 5 x 15 cm (2 x 6 inch) in size, scrunch up the pastry and place on top of the fish.
8. Sprinkle with Parmesan and bake for 15-20 minutes until the fish is cooked *(the flesh of the fish will flake cleanly when it is cooked).*
9. Serve on a bed of pea purée and garnish with parsley.

Lemon & Sage Crusted Fillet of Pork with Pepper & Olive Tapenade

INGREDIENTS £££

Crust
2 slices of bread
8 fresh sage leaves
3-4 tbsp fresh parsley
1 garlic clove
½ lemon, *grated zest*
1 tsp olive oil

Knob of butter
600g (1 lb 5½ oz) pork fillet, *cut into two*
30g (1 oz) plain flour
1 egg, *beaten*
Parsley, *to garnish*

Sauce
½ tbsp olive oil
½ red onion, *finely diced*
1 garlic clove, *crushed*
½ red pepper, *finely diced*
½ yellow pepper, *finely diced*
½ green pepper, *finely diced*
45g (1½ oz) black olives, *sliced*
150ml (5 fl oz / ¼ pt) chicken stock
200ml (7 fl oz) white wine
1 tsp cornflour

METHOD

SERVES 8

Preheat the oven to 180°C / 350°F / gas mark 4

1. To make the lemon crust, place the bread, sage, parsley, garlic, lemon zest, and olive oil in food processor and blend into a breadcrumb consistency. Empty the breadcrumbs on to a large plate.
2. To prepare the meat, melt a knob of butter in a frying pan over a high heat *(be careful not to burn it)* and seal the meat until golden in colour.
3. Roll the pork in the flour, then in the egg and finally in the breadcrumbs. Place on a lined baking tray * and bake for 30 minutes *(if you want to serve it slightly pink)* or 40 minutes.
4. **To make the sauce**, warm the olive oil in a saucepan and cook the onions and garlic for 5 minutes.
5. Add the peppers and cook until soft.
6. Add the olives, stock and white wine, bring to the boil and reduce slightly.
7. To thicken the sauce, mix the cornflour in a glass with a little water and add to the sauce. Bring to the boil and season to taste.
8. Slice the pork fillet thickly, allowing three slices per person. Arrange on a plate, spoon over the tapenade and season with parsley.

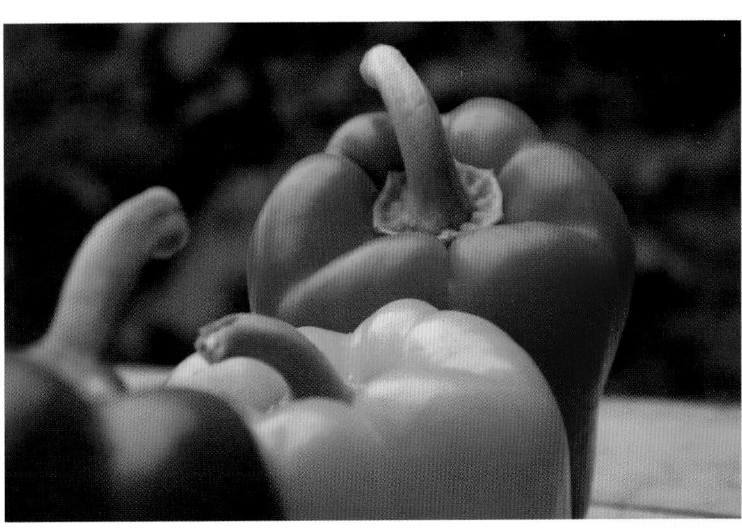

Peppered Crusted Pork Medallions with Brandy Sauce

INGREDIENTS £££

2 tbsp coloured peppercorns
8 pork medallions
30g (1 oz) butter
3 slices of bread, *made into breadcrumbs*
1 tbsp fresh parsley, *chopped*
30g (1 oz) plain flour
2 eggs, *beaten*

Brandy Sauce
290ml (10 fl oz / ½ pt) brandy
1 tbsp cornflour, *diluted in a little water*
290ml (10 fl oz / ½ pt) beef stock
2-3 tbsp red currant jelly, *to taste*
4 tbsp cream

METHOD

SERVES 8

Preheat the oven to 180°C / 350°F / gas mark 4

1. Coarsely grind the peppercorns in a pestle and mortar and spread out on a plate.
2. Bash the meat with a rolling pin to tenderize and press the medallions on the pepper, one side at a time, to evenly coat them.
3. Melt the butter in a frying pan and fry the medallions for about 5 minutes on each side until golden brown *(keep the remaining juices for the sauce).*
4. Combine the breadcrumbs and parsley. Roll the edges of the pork in flour, then in the egg and lastly in the breadcrumb mixture. Place on a lined baking tray, * and bake for 20 minutes.
5. **To make the sauce**, add the brandy to the pan and flame to remove the alcohol *(to flame, start by turning the extractor fan off and have a saucepan lid to hand. Heat the brandy over a high heat. When it begins to shudder, turn off the heat, stand well back and put a match to it. Allow it to burn for a few seconds and then cover with the lid to extinguish the flames).*
6. Add the diluted cornflour *(to thicken the sauce)*, stock and red currant jelly and simmer gently until the sauce thickens. Add the cream just before serving and bring up to temperature, season to taste.

Cheese Fondue

INGREDIENTS ££

Approximately 150-200g (6-7 oz) cheese per person *(other cheeses such as Beaufort & Comté can be used).*
350g (12¼ oz) Emmental cheese, *grated*
250g (8¾ oz) Gruyère cheese, *grated*
55g (2 oz) Parmesan cheese, *grated*
290ml (10 fl oz / ½ pt) dry white wine
3 tsp cornflour
2 tbsp brandy
1 clove of garlic, *peeled*
Pinch of mustard powder
Pinch of ground nutmeg
Pinch of cayenne pepper

Fresh bread, *cut into chunks.*
A selection of dried meats, cured ham, salami etc, *arranged on a plate.*

METHOD

SERVES 8

1. Rub the sides and base of a thick based saucepan with a clove of garlic.
2. Put the cheese into the saucepan, cover with wine *(the Swiss use a dry white called Fendant)* and stir over a low heat until the cheese has melted.
3. Mix together the cornflour and the brandy and add to the melted cheese. Stir rigorously, bring to the boil and cook for a few minutes.
4. Season with the mustard, cayenne pepper and nutmeg and carry to the table.

White wine, not water, should be drunk with a cheese fondue to aid the digestion of the cheese.

Stuffed Chicken Breasts with Prune, Feta & Rosemary served with a Sun-Dried Tomato Sauce

INGREDIENTS ££

8 chicken breasts
15g (½ oz) butter
Fresh parsley, *for garnishing*

Sauce
2 tbsp olive oil
1 onion, *chopped*
8 pieces of sun-dried tomatoes
6 tbsp white wine
570ml (20 fl oz / 1 pt) chicken stock
2 tbsp tomato purée
4 tsp cornflour *(if needed)*

Stuffing
2 tbsp olive oil
2 onions, *chopped*
16 prunes, *roughly chopped*
130g (4½ oz) feta cheese, *roughly chopped*
1 tsp dried rosemary

METHOD

SERVES 8

Preheat the oven to 180°C / 350°F / gas mark 4

1. **To make the sauce**, warm the oil in a saucepan and cook the onion over a gentle heat until soft.
2. Blend the sun-dried tomatoes in a food processor until fairly smooth, then add them to the onion.
3. Add the white wine, stock and tomato purée, season and simmer for 5 minutes, *(to thicken the sauce, add a little water to the cornflour in a glass. Add to the sauce, a little at a time to adjust the consistency. Cook for a few minutes to allow it to thicken).* Check for seasoning before serving. *
4. **To make the stuffing**, warm the olive oil in a saucepan and cook the onion until soft. Remove from the heat, stir in the prunes, feta cheese and rosemary and season.
5. Trim the chicken and prepare it for stuffing - *place the palm of your hand firmly on top of the chicken, fingers on full stretch and slice the meat almost in half, horizontally, creating a pocket.*
6. Stuff each chicken breast and secure using cocktail sticks.
7. Brown the chicken in butter in a hot **stainless steel** frying pan *(the cocktail sticks will damage a non-stick surface).* Transfer to a lined baking tray * and bake for about 25 minutes.
8. To serve, remove the cocktail sticks, slice the chicken and arrange on a plate with the sauce.

Serve on a bed of bulgur wheat and garnish with parsley.

Lasagne

MAIN COURSES

INGREDIENTS ££

Mince
1 tbsp vegetable oil
2 onions, *peeled and chopped*
2 garlic cloves, *crushed (optional)*
500g (1 lb 2 oz) beef steak mince
2 x 400g tin of chopped tomatoes
2 beef stock cubes, *crushed*
1 tbsp tomato ketchup
1 tsp dried basil
1 tsp dried oregano
Dash of Worcestershire sauce

White Sauce
60g (2 oz) plain flour
60g (2 oz) butter
800ml (28 fl oz) milk
1 tsp Dijon mustard

125g (4½ oz) lasagne sheets, *(approx)*
170g (6 oz) strong cheese, *grated*

METHOD

SERVES 8

Preheat the oven to 180°C / 350°F / gas mark 4

1. **To make the mince,** warm the oil in a saucepan and then cook the onion and garlic until soft.
2. Stir in the mince, as it cooks the meat will stick together so keep breaking it up.
3. Add the rest of the mince ingredients and season. Bring to the boil, cover with a lid and simmer for about 30 minutes, stirring occasionally *(if the mince is too liquid remove the lid for the last 10 minute of cooking).* Pour off any excess fat. *
4. **To make the white sauce**, melt the butter in a saucepan over a medium heat, remove from the heat and stir in the flour to make a roux.
5. Return to the heat and gradually add the milk, stirring until all the liquid has been incorporated and the sauce is smooth and glossy.
6. Add the mustard, season and allow to cool slightly.
7. Spread a layer of mince over the bottom of an ovenproof dish and allow to cool slightly *(otherwise the lasagne will curl up).*
8. Cover with a layer of lasagne, followed by a layer of white sauce and sprinkle with cheese. Continue layering in this way, starting with the mince and finishing with a layer of white sauce sprinkled with cheese. *
9. Bake for about 45-55 minutes until the pasta is cooked.

Serve with garlic bread and dressed salad.

Honey Roast Ham with Cumberland Sauce / Mustard & Parsley Sauce / Watercress Sauce

INGREDIENTS ££

1.5 kg (3 lbs 5 oz) Gammon joint
Cloves
2 tbsp brown sugar
Fresh parsley, *to garnish*

Cumberland Sauce
1 orange
1 lemon
9 tbsp redcurrant jelly
250ml (9 fl oz) **red wine**
*(**Port** can be used)*
1½ tsp wholegrain **mustard**
1½ tsp ground ginger

Mustard & Parsley Sauce
400ml (14 fl oz) **white wine**
570ml (20 fl oz / 1 pt) chicken **stock**
2 tsp English **mustard**
2 tsp sugar
2 tbsp cornflour
3 tbsp fresh parsley, *chopped*

METHOD

SERVES 8

1. Boil the ham in a large saucepan allowing 30 minutes of cooking time per kilo (2¼ lbs), plus an extra 30 minutes. *(To reduce the saltiness of the meat, soak it over night in a large saucepan of water. Otherwise, when cooking the meat, bring to the boil and change the water, replacing it with fresh boiling water from the kettle).*
2. **To make the Cumberland sauce**, remove the zest of the orange and lemon so that you have long strands of zest. Cook the redcurrant jelly, red wine, orange and lemon zest in a saucepan for about 5 minutes to reduce slightly. Add the mustard and ginger and stir well. *
3. **To make the mustard and parsley sauce**, bring the wine and chicken stock to the boil and simmer to reduce it to half its volume. Add the mustard and sugar and season to taste. Mix the cornflour in a glass with a little water and add to the sauce, cook for a minute to allow the sauce to thicken. * Add the parsley just before serving.
4. **To make the watercress sauce**, melt the butter in a saucepan, add the shallots and cook over a gentle heat until soft. Add the wine, stock and bay leaf, bring to the boil and simmer for 2-3 minutes. * Remove the bay leaf, add the cream and watercress and bring up to temperature. Season (add a pinch of sugar if bitter) and serve immediately.

Watercress Sauce
15g (½ oz) salted butter
2 small shallots, *chopped*
100ml (3½ fl oz) white wine
55ml (2 fl oz) vegetable stock *(use 1 cube)*
1 bay leaf
100ml (3½ fl oz) double cream
85g (3 oz) watercress, *remove big stalks & chop finely*

Glazed Oranges *(for garnish)*
1-2 oranges
3 tbsp soft brown sugar

5. **To make the glazed oranges**, slice the oranges finely, dab dry with kitchen paper, place on a lined baking tray, sprinkle with sugar and bake for 30 minutes. Allow to cool on the baking tray.
6. Transfer the meat to a lined baking tray and cut away the skin and some of the fat. Score the fat through to the meat, making a criss-cross pattern.
7. Stick a clove in the centre of each square and sprinkle with brown sugar.
8. Preheat the oven to 180°C / 350°F / gas mark 4 and bake for 30 minutes to caramelise and bring back to temperature. *(Keep a close eye on it as the top burns very easily. If you are warming from cold, cover with foil for the first 15 minutes and heat for a little longer).*

Slice the meat finely, pour the sauce over some of the meat and garnish with parsley.

Spaghetti Bolognese

INGREDIENTS ££

675g (1½ lbs) spaghetti
(85g / 3 oz per person)
Knob of butter
Parmesan or strong
cheese, *grated*

Bolognese Sauce
1 tbsp vegetable oil
2 onions, *peeled and sliced*
2 garlic cloves, *crushed (optional)*
500g (1 lb 2 oz) beef steak mince
3 x 400g tin of chopped tomatoes
110g (4 oz) mushrooms, *sliced (optional)*
1 beef stock cube
1 tbsp tomato ketchup
1 heaped tsp dried basil
1 heaped tsp dried oregano
Dash of Worcestershire sauce
Dash of red wine *(optional)*

METHOD

SERVES 8

1. **To make the Bolognese Sauce**, warm the oil in a frying pan and cook the onion and garlic until soft.
2. Stir in the mince. As it cooks the meat will stick together, so keep breaking it up.
3. Add the rest of the ingredients, season, cover with a lid and simmer for 1 hour, stirring occasionally (if the sauce becomes too thick, add a little water).
4. Pour off any access fat and check the seasoning.
5. **To cook the spaghetti,** refer to the instructions on the packet to give you an idea of the cooking time. Add salt and a few drops of oil to the boiling water *(to stop the spaghetti sticking together).* When the spaghetti is cooked drain it in a colander and pour boiling water over it. Put a knob of butter in the hot saucepan and return the spaghetti to the pan stirring to coat it with the butter *(to prevent the spaghetti clogging together on the plate).*

Serve the Bolognese on a bed of spaghetti. The grated cheese should be served separately in a bowl and sprinkled over the Bolognese.

French Bread Pizza

INGREDIENTS £

2 tbsp olive oil
½ onion, *finely chopped*
1 garlic clove, *crushed*
4 tbsp tomato purée
4 tbsp water
¼ tsp sugar
¼ tsp dried oregano
1 baguette
2 slices of ham, salami or cooked bacon, *chopped*
55g (2 oz) Cheddar cheese or mozzarella, *grated or finely sliced*

METHOD

SERVES 1

Preheat the oven to 180°C / 350°F / gas mark 4

1. Warm the oil in a frying pan and cook the onion and garlic over a gentle heat until soft.
2. Add the tomato purée, water, sugar and oregano, season and blend in the mini bowl of a food processor until almost smooth.
3. Cut the bread in half lengthways, and spread the tomato mixture over the bread, then add the meat and top with cheese.
5. Grill or bake until the cheese has melted.

Additional toppings: sweetcorn, peppers, pineapple, anchovies, olives, tuna fish, mushrooms, artichokes, red onion.

Marmalade Chicken Casserole

INGREDIENTS £

3 tbsp plain flour
8 large chicken legs or 16 small legs
55g (3 oz) butter
2 onions, *sliced (optional)*
4 tbsp marmalade
1 tsp ground cinnamon
1 tsp ground coriander
1.1 L (40 fl oz / 2 pts) chicken stock
2 tsp lemon juice

METHOD

SERVES 8

Preheat the oven to 180°C / 350°F / gas mark 4

1. Put the flour in a bowl, add lots of seasoning and toss the chicken lightly to coat in flour.
2. Melt the butter in a large frying pan, add the chicken and cook for about 10 minutes turning occasionally until golden brown.
3. Transfer the chicken to a casserole dish and gently fry the onion in the remaining juices until soft.
4. Add the marmalade, cinnamon, coriander and stock to the onion, bring to the boil and simmer for 5 minutes.
5. Pour over the chicken, cover with the lid * and cook in the oven for 1 hour.
6. Just before serving stir in the lemon juice and season to taste.

Serve with mashed or baked potatoes and a green vegetable.

MAIN COURSES

Cottage / Shepherd's Pie

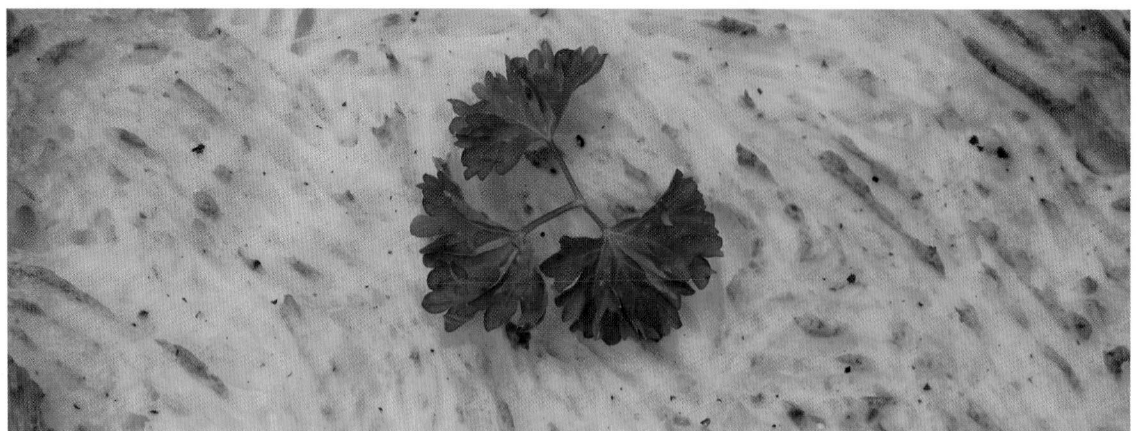

INGREDIENTS £

1 tbsp vegetable oil
2 onions, *sliced*
2 carrots, *sliced*
2 garlic cloves, *crushed (optional)*
450g (1 lb) beef steak mince or minced lamb
55g (2 oz) mushrooms, *sliced*
1 tbsp tomato purée
1 tbsp plain **flour**
150ml (5 fl oz / ¼ pt) beef **stock**
1 tin of baked beans

Mashed Potato
340g (12 oz) potatoes
30g (1 oz) **butter**
2-3 tbsp **milk**

METHOD

SERVES 6

Preheat the oven to 180°C / 350°F / gas mark 4

1. Warm the oil in a frying pan and cook the onion, carrots and garlic until soft.
2. Meanwhile, peel and quarter the potatoes and cook for 25 minutes in salted water until very soft.
3. Stir the mince into the frying pan. As it cooks the meat will stick together so keep breaking it up. Season and simmer for 10 minutes, pouring off any excess fat.
4. Add the mushrooms and tomato purée to the mince, stir well and then gradually stir in the flour a little at a time.
5. Add the stock, cover and simmer for 20 minutes, stirring occasionally.
6. When the potatoes are soft drain, then mash them in the saucepan with the butter, milk and plenty of seasoning.
7. To finish off the mince, add the baked beans, taste and adjust the seasoning if necessary. Spoon into a 1.7 litre (3 pts) ovenproof dish and cover with mashed potato, use a fork to make a pattern on the top. *
8. Bake in the oven for 40 minutes.

Serve with peas.

Toad in the Hole

INGREDIENTS £

450g (1 lb) sausages
215ml (7½ fl oz) milk
30g (1 oz) butter
Pinch of salt
70g (2½ oz) self raising flour
2 eggs
55g (2 oz) cheese, *grated (optional)*

METHOD

SERVES 6

Preheat the oven to 200°C / 400°F / gas mark 6

1. Cook the sausages in the oven for about 20 minutes so that they are slightly brown and then remove them from the oven. Pour off any fat.
2. To make the batter, gently heat the milk, butter and salt in a saucepan.
3. When the butter melts bring to the boil, then remove the pan from the heat, add the flour and beat the mixture until smooth.
4. Add one egg, continue to beat, add the second egg and beat until the mixture is smooth.
5. Lightly grease a baking dish with butter and spread half of the batter over the base.
6. Arrange the cooked sausages in the batter and spread the rest of the mixture over the sausages.
7. Sprinkle with cheese and bake in the oven for about 20-25 minutes, until golden brown.

Goes nicely with onion gravy *(see page 121)*

MAIN COURSES

Cheese & Potato Pie

INGREDIENTS £

1.125kg (2½ lbs) potatoes
45g (1½ oz) **butter**
1 tbsp vegetable oil
4 large onions, *sliced*
340g (12 oz) strong **Cheddar cheese**, *grated*
2 tomatoes, *sliced*

METHOD

SERVES 6

Preheat the oven to 180°C / 350°F / gas mark 4

1. Peel and quarter the potatoes and cook for 25 minutes in salted water until very soft.
2. Drain, then mash in the saucepan with the butter, and plenty of seasoning.
3. Warm the oil in a frying pan and cook the onions until soft.
4. Season, then spread half of the onions over the base of an ovenproof dish.
5. Cover the onions by spooning half of the mashed potato over the top.
6. Sprinkle evenly with half of the cheese, top with the remaining onions, followed by the mashed potato and finally a layer of cheese.
7. Decorate with the tomatoes and bake in the oven for 40 minutes until the top is golden and bubbly.

Kedgeree

INGREDIENTS ££

2 **eggs**
175g (6 oz) long grain rice
Salt
450g (1 lb) smoked **haddock** fillets
55g (2 oz) **butter**
Cayenne pepper
3 tbsp fresh parsley, *chopped*

METHOD

SERVES 4

1. Put the eggs into a saucepan of cold water, bring to the boil then cook for 10 minutes. Then plunge into cold water.
2. Pour boiling water into a large saucepan, add the rice and a good pinch of salt and bring to the boil. Cover with a lid and simmer gently for about 12-15 minutes then test the rice to see if it is cooked *(check the rice packet for guidelines on cooking time).*
3. Drain *(you will use this pan again),* pour over boiling water, drain thoroughly and spread out over a tray to dry.
4. Put the haddock in a frying pan with just enough water to cover it, bring to the boil and simmer for 10-15 minutes until cooked through.
5. Drain, skin and flake the fish, removing any bones.
6. Peel the eggs, slice one *(for garnish)* and chop the other.
7. Melt the butter in the large saucepan, add a pinch of cayenne pepper, the rice, fish, ½ the parsley and one chopped egg. Stir gently over a medium heat to bring it up to temperature.
8. Garnish with the sliced egg and remaining parsley.

Beef Stroganoff

INGREDIENTS £££

4 tbsp plain flour
3 tsp mustard powder
800g (1 lb 12 oz) beef skirt, *cut into 5 cm / 2 inch strips*
30g (1 oz) butter
2 onions, *sliced*
2 garlic cloves, *crushed*
620g (1lb 6 oz) mushrooms, *sliced*
570ml (20 fl oz / 1 pt) beef stock *(use 2 stock cubes)*
¼ tsp paprika
4 tsp lemon juice
290ml (10 fl oz / ½ pt) soured cream
2 tbsp parsley, *chopped*

METHOD

SERVES 8

Preheat the oven to 160°C / 320°F / gas mark 2-3

1. Mix together the flour, mustard powder and seasoning in a casserole dish, add the beef and toss to coat in the flour mixture.
2. Melt the butter in a frying pan, add the onion and garlic and cook until soft.
3. Add the mushrooms to the frying pan and cook for a further 5 minutes or until the mushrooms are soft.
4. Pour the mushroom mixture into the casserole dish and stir well.
5. Add the beef stock, paprika and lemon juice, cover with the lid * and bake for 1½ hours.
6. About 5 minutes before the end, stir in the soured cream and season to taste.
7. Sprinkle with chopped parsley and serve immediately.

Serve with boiled rice and a salad.

Panéed Turkey with Coconut, Ginger & Coriander Sauce

INGREDIENTS £

3 slices **bread**
2 tbsp fresh parsley, *finely chopped (optional)*
1 lime, *grated zest*
50g (1¾ oz) plain **flour**
8 turkey escalopes
2 **eggs**, *beaten*
30g (1 oz) **butter**

Sauce
400ml tin of **coconut milk**
200ml (7 fl oz) **milk**
30g (1 oz) fresh root ginger, *peeled & grated*
2 bay leaves
30g (1 oz) **butter**
1 tbsp plain **flour**
1 lime, *grated zest and juice*
4 tbsp fresh coriander, *chopped*
2 tsp sugar

METHOD

SERVES 8

Preheat the oven to 180°C / 350°F / gas mark 4

1. Blend the bread, parsley and lime zest in a food processor until you have a fine breadcrumb consistency. Empty the breadcrumbs on to one end of a clean, dry chopping board.
2. Sprinkle the flour on the other end of the chopping board and season with salt and pepper.
3. To prepare the meat, bash each fillet into shape with a rolling pin to tenderise.
4. Roll one escalopes in the seasoned flour until it is completely covered, dip it in the beaten egg and then roll it in the breadcrumbs. Prepare the remaining escalopes in the same way.
5. Warm half the butter in a large frying pan and cook four of the escapoles on both sides until golden, then transfer on to a lined baking tray. Melt the remaining butter and cook the other four escalopes until golden, * then bake for 20 minutes.
6. **To make the sauce**, put the coconut milk, milk, ginger and bay leaves in a saucepan and warm over a gentle heat until it is nearly boiling.
7. Remove from the heat and leave to infuse for 20 minutes. * Then pour the milk through a seive into a jug, squeezing the milk out of the ginger.
8. Melt the butter in a saucepan, add the flour and stir over a gentle heat for about 30 seconds to make a roux.
9. Remove from the heat and pour the milk mixture into the saucepan, a little at a time, stirring until the sauce is smooth.
10. Return to the heat and bring the sauce up to the boil, stirring occasionally. *
11. Add the juice and zest of the lime, coriander and sugar and bring up to temperature . Season to taste. *

Serve on a bed of three grain rice.

Cajun Spiced Chicken on Creamed Corn

INGREDIENTS ££

8 chicken breasts *(with the skin on)*

Spice marinade
1 tsp chilli powder
1 tsp cayenne pepper
4 tsp paprika
1 tsp crushed black pepper
2 tsp dried oregano
2 tsp thyme
2 tsp salt
2 tsp vegetable oil

Creamed Corn
500g (1 lb 2 oz) frozen sweetcorn, *thawed*
1 tbsp vegetable oil
1 onion, *chopped*
2 garlic cloves, *crushed*
Pinch of ground nutmeg
3 tbsp double **cream**
2 tbsp **Parmesan**, *grated*

METHOD

SERVES 8

Preheat the oven to 200°C / 400°F / gas mark 6

1. Combine the marinade ingredients in a large bowl.
2. Rub the marinade over the chicken leave for at least one hour *(even better overnight)* to marinate. *
3. **To make the creamed sweetcorn**, cook the sweetcorn in boiling water for about 5 minutes, then drain.
4. Warm the oil in a saucepan and cook the onions and garlic until soft.
5. Add the sweetcorn and the rest of ingredients, season and blend until smooth *(add a splash of milk if it seems too dry).* Season to taste. *
6. Warm a large frying pan and cook the chicken, skin side down for approximately 8 minutes until crispy, then turn and cook the other side for about 2 minutes.
7. Transfer onto a lined baking tray * and bake for 15 minutes.
8. Remove from the oven, cover with foil and allow to rest for 5 minutes.
9. Slice the chicken at an angle and serve on the creamed sweetcorn.

Bangers & Mash with Onion Gravy

INGREDIENTS £

Sausages *(quantity depends on size of sausages)*

Onion Gravy
45g (1½ oz) butter
225g (8 oz) onions, *sliced*
½ tsp ground cumin
1 tbsp sugar
570ml (20 fl oz / 1 pt) beef stock
1 tbsp plain flour
150ml (5 fl oz / ¼ pt) red wine

Mashed Potato
675g (1½ lbs) peeled potatoes
30g (1 oz) butter
2 tbsp cream or milk *(optional)*

METHOD

SERVES 6

Preheat the oven to 180°C / 350°F / gas mark 4

1. Prick each sausage several times with a fork and bake in the oven for about 40 minutes, or until nicely browned, turning once during cooking. *(Sausages can be cooked under the grill).* Place the sausages on kitchen paper before serving.
2. **To make the gravy,** melt the butter in a small saucepan and cook the onions until soft and slightly golden in colour.
3. Add the cumin and sugar and cook for another 5 minutes to slightly caramelise the onions.
4. Add a little stock to the flour and mix together to make a smooth paste, then add the rest of the stock and slowly pour it on to the onion mixture. Bring to the boil, stirring occasionally.
5. Add the wine, season and simmer for 30 minutes. Stir occasionally to ensure that it does not stick to the bottom of the pan.
6. **To make the mashed potato,** peel and quarter the potatoes and boil for 25 minutes in salted water until very soft.
7. Drain, then mash in the saucepan with the butter and cream / milk and plenty of seasoning.
8. Use a mousse ring to mould the potato, cut the sausages in half at an angle and arrange on the mashed potato.

Serve with peas and tomato ketchup.

Orange Crusted Salmon with Hollandaise Sauce

INGREDIENTS £££

8 salmon fillets, *skinned and boned*
Fresh parsley

Topping
125g (4½ oz) bread
4 tbsp olive oil *(extra for greasing)*
1 large orange, *grated zest*
8 tbsp fresh parsley, *chopped and a few sprigs, to garnish*

Hollandaise Sauce
6 egg yolks
1½ tsp sugar
Pinch of salt
1 tbsp + 1 tsp (20ml) tarragon vinegar
4 tbsp (60ml) lemon juice
285g (10 oz) unsalted butter, *good quality*

METHOD

SERVES 8

Preheat the oven to 180°C / 350°F / gas mark 4

1. Place the salmon fillets on a lined baking tray.
2. Blend the topping ingredients in the food processor, season and press some mixture firmly on each piece of fish so that it stays in place.
3. Bake in the oven for about 15-20 minutes until the fish is cooked through and the topping is golden brown.
4. Prepare the sauce ingredients and only start making the sauce 5 minutes before the fish will be ready.
5. **To make the sauce**, blend the egg yolks, sugar and salt in the small bowl of the food processor. Leave the food processor running until the sauce is served.
6. Warm the vinegar and lemon juice in a small saucepan until it starts to boil *(do not reduce the mixture by continuing to boil).*
7. Melt the butter in a second saucepan.
8. Very slowly, pour the vinegar and lemon mixture through the feeding tube of the food processor.
9. In the same way pour in the butter, check for seasoning and serve immediately. Garnish with parsley.

Stuffed Chicken Breasts with Spinach, Parmesan Cheese & Pine Nuts

INGREDIENTS ££

Stuffing
Vegetable oil
2 onions, *finely chopped*
175ml (6 fl oz) white wine
175ml (6 fl oz) chicken stock
(dissolve 1 stock cube in boiling water)
400g (14 oz) frozen spinach, *thawed and well drained*
1 tbsp dried Parmesan cheese
Pinch of ground cinnamon
Pinch of ground nutmeg
45g (1½ oz) pine nuts
100g (3½ oz) cream cheese

8 chicken breasts
30g (1 oz) butter

Mushroom Sauce
15g (½ oz) butter
1 onion, *finely chopped*
3 cloves of garlic, *crushed*
10 mushrooms, *sliced*
175ml (6 fl oz) white wine
175ml (6 fl oz) stock
(dissolve ½ a stock cube in boiling water)
175ml (6 fl oz) cream

METHOD

SERVES 8

Preheat the oven to 180°C / 350°F / gas mark 4

1. **To make the stuffing**, warm the vegetable oil in a saucepan and cook the onions until soft. Add the white wine, chicken stock, spinach, Parmesan, cinnamon, nutmeg and seasoning and cook for a few minutes.
2. Stir in the pine nuts and cream cheese and remove from the heat.
3. **To make the mushroom sauce**, melt the butter in a small saucepan and cook the onion and garlic until soft. Add the mushrooms, cook for a further 2 minutes, then add the wine, stock, and cream and season to taste. *(To thicken the sauce, add a little water to 1 tbsp of cornflour in a glass, add to the sauce, a little at a time, to adjust the consistency and cook for a couple of minutes to allow it to thicken).*
4. Trim the chicken and prepare it for stuffing; place the palm of your hand firmly on top of the chicken and slice the meat almost in half horizontally, creating a pocket.
5. Stuff each chicken breast and secure using cocktail sticks.
6. Brown the chicken in butter in a hot stainless steel frying pan *(the cocktail sticks will damage a non-stick surface).* Transfer to a lined baking tray * and bake for about 25 minutes.

To serve, remove the cocktail sticks, slice the chicken and arrange on a plate with the sauce.

Beef Bourguignon

INGREDIENTS ££

1 kg (2 lb 4 oz) beef, *diced*
850ml (½ pt / 30 fl oz) **red wine**
6 tbsp plain **flour**, *seasoned*
4 tbsp vegetable oil
1 onion, *diced*
2 garlic cloves, *crushed*
400g (14 fl oz) button mushrooms, *halved if large*
250g (9 oz) streaky bacon, *sliced*
1.1 L (2 pt / 40 fl oz) beef **stock**
1 bay leaf

METHOD

SERVES 8

Preheat the oven to 180°C / 350°F / gas mark 4

1. Soak the beef in the red wine for 30 minutes.
2. Remove the beef and roll it in the seasoned flour *(retain the red wine as you will use it later).*
3. Warm the oil in a frying pan, shake the excess flour off the beef and fry for about 5 minutes until golden brown. Put in a casserole dish *(if you don't have a casserole dish you can use a large saucepan).*
4. Add a little more oil to the frying pan and fry the onions and garlic until soft.
5. Add the mushrooms and cook for a further 5 minutes, then add them to the casserole dish.
6. Cut the bacon into 1cm (3/8 inch) slices and fry until golden, then add to the casserole dish.
7. Pour in the red wine and stock, add the bay leaf, season, cover with the lid and cook in the oven *(if using a saucepan gently simmer on the hob)* for approximately 2 hours *(until sauce thickens and meat is tender).* Check seasoning before serving.

Serve with mashed potato and French beans or a green salad.

Chicken Breasts Baked in a Cherry Tomato, Black Olive & Baby Spinach Sauce

INGREDIENTS £££

8 chicken breasts
90g (3¼ oz) **butter**
2 onions, *finely chopped*
2 garlic cloves, *crushed*
2 x 400g tins of chopped tomatoes
24 black olives, *sliced*
340g (12 oz) cherry tomatoes
500g (18 oz) fresh spinach, *stalks removed*
8 tbsp **mascarpone**

METHOD

SERVES 8

Preheat the oven to 180°C / 350°F / gas mark 4

1. Trim the chicken breasts and season.
2. Melt a third of the butter in a large frying pan and cook 4 chicken breasts on both sides until golden *(about 5 minutes on each side)*. Use half of the remaining butter to cook the other 4 chicken breasts in the same way.
3. Transfer to an ovenproof dish and then fry the onion and the garlic in the same pan until soft *(add a little more butter if necessary)*.
4. Add the tinned tomatoes and simmer for 2-3 minutes.
5. Then stir in the olives, season and pour over the chicken. *
6. Bake for 25-30 minutes until the chicken is cooked.
7. Cut the tomatoes in half across the core and place them on a greased baking tray. Sprinkle with salt and bake for about 10 minutes.
8. Five minutes before serving melt the remaining butter in a large saucepan, add the spinach, pushing it down into the pan. Cover with a lid and cook for about 3 minutes until the spinach has wilted down, then drain really well.
9. Remove the chicken breasts from the sauce and slice thickly ready for plating.
10. Stir the spinach into the tomato sauce and spoon some sauce on to each plate. Top with the slices of chicken and a tablespoon of mascarpone. Arrange the baby tomatoes around the plate.

Thai Green Chicken Curry

INGREDIENTS ££

½ tbsp olive oil
1 onion, *finely diced*
1 garlic clove, *crushed*
10g (¾ oz) ginger, *grated*
1 lime, *juice and grated zest*
4 tbsp fresh coriander, *chopped*
1 tsp Thai green **curry paste**
2 tbsp sweet chilli sauce
1 x 400ml tin **coconut milk**
200ml (7 fl oz) water
800g (1 lb 12 oz) chicken breasts, *cut into bite sized chunks* or turkey breast escalopes, *cut into strips*
100g (3½ oz) green beans, *cut in half*
1 courgette, *sliced*

METHOD

SERVES 6

1. Warm the oil in a pan, add the onion and cook over a gentle heat until soft.
2. Add the garlic, ginger, lime zest, half the coriander, Thai green curry paste, sweet chilli sauce, coconut milk and water and simmer for 5 minutes.
3. Carefully stir the chicken into the hot sauce, bring it back to the boil and continue to simmer for a further 20 minutes. *
4. Add the green beans and courgette and simmer for approximately 10-12 minutes until the vegetables are cooked.
5. Add the lime juice and the rest of the coriander and season to taste.

Serving suggestions; rice, **poppadoms**, **naan bread**, mango chutney.

Fish Pie

INGREDIENTS £££

1.35 kg (3 lb) potatoes, *peeled and cut into even sizes*
4 eggs
900g (2 lb) fish, mixture of cod, salmon and smoked haddock
1 onion, *finely chopped*
1 bay leaf
1 tsp ground pepper
1.1 L (40 fl oz / 2 pts) milk
85g (3 oz) butter
4 tbsp plain flour
225g (8 oz) peas, *frozen*
225g (8 oz) prawns *(optional)*
225g (8 oz) frozen spinach, *thawed and drained*

METHOD

SERVES 8

Preheat oven 180°C / 350°F / gas mark 4

1. Put the potatoes into a saucepan of salted water and simmer for 25 minutes until really soft.
2. Put the eggs into a saucepan of cold water, bring to the boil and simmer for 10 minutes. Then plunge into cold water.
3. Put the fish, onion, bay leaf, pepper and milk into a large saucepan, bring to the boil and simmer for 2 minutes. Then remove the fish and pour the milk through a sieve into a jug, discarding the bay leaf.
4. Allow the fish to cool slightly, then flake into large chunks. Carefully look for and remove any fish bones or skin.
5. When the potatoes are cooked, drain and return them to the saucepan. Add 15g (½ oz) of the butter, 4 tbsp of the sieved milk and mash until smooth. Season to taste.
6. **To make the white sauce**, melt the remaining butter over medium heat, remove from the heat and stir in the flour to make a roux. Return to the heat and gradually add the sieved milk, stirring until the liquid has been incorporated and the sauce is smooth and glossy. Cook for a few minutes until it thickens, season and allow to cool slightly.
7. Add the fish mixture, onions, peas and prawns to the sauce and stir carefully making sure you don't break up the fish too much.
8. Peel and quarter the eggs.
9. Spread the spinach over the base of a casserole dish, arrange the eggs on top, pour over the sauce mixture and spoon over the mashed potato. Use a fork to make a pattern on top. *
10. Bake for 45 minutes until golden brown on top *(be careful not to overcook the pie as the fish will become tough).*

MAIN COURSES

Navarin of Lamb

INGREDIENTS

3 tbsp vegetable oil
1 onion, *sliced*
2 garlic cloves, *crushed*
1 kg (12 lb 4 oz) lamb, *trimmed and diced*
100g (3½ oz) **celery**, *sliced*
350g (12 oz) carrot, *diced*
4 tbsp plain **flour**
4 beef **stock** cubes, *crushed*
4 tbsp tomato purée
570 ml (1 pt / 20 fl oz) **white wine**
1.1 L (2 pts / 40 fl oz) water
1 bay leaf
4 sprigs of thyme

METHOD

SERVES 8

Preheat the oven to 180°C / 355°F / gas mark 4

1. Heat the vegetable oil in a large saucepan and cook the onion and garlic until soft.
2. Add the lamb and cook until golden.
3. Add the celery and carrot and cook for a further 2 minutes.
4. Sprinkle the flour and stock cubes over, add the tomato purée and stir to make a thick paste.
5. Add the wine and bring to the boil.
6. Transfer to a casserole dish *(if you don't have a casserole dish you can cook it on the hob on a low heat so it simmers gently).* Add the water, bay leaf, thyme and seasoning.
7. Cover with a lid and cook in the oven for 2 hours until meat is tender. Season to taste *(remove the bay leaf and sprigs of thyme before serving).*

Quiche Lorraine

INGREDIENTS £

15g (½ oz) butter
1 onion, *chopped*
3 rashers bacon, *chopped*
2 eggs
150ml (5 fl oz / ¼ pt) whole milk
55–110g (2-4 oz) Cheddar cheese, *grated*

French Pastry
100g (3½ oz) plain flour
45ml (1½ fl oz) vegetable oil
45ml (1½ fl oz) water
Pinch of salt

METHOD

SERVES 4

Preheat the oven to 180°C / 350°F / gas mark 4

1. Melt the butter in a frying pan and cook the onions and bacon until the onions are soft. Allow to cool slightly.
2. **To make the pastry**, put the flour in a bowl, make a well and pour in the oil and water. Mix together, adding more water or flour if necessary. *(Don't be alarmed by the consistency of the pastry - it should be smooth and stretchy).*
3. Mix together the milk and eggs, then add the onion and bacon mixture and season generously.
4. Grease, then flour a 20 cm (8 inch) quiche tin *(preferably a loose-bottomed tin)* and line with the pastry by kneading it into place *(no rolling required).* The thinner the pastry the better.
5. Pour in the mixture, sprinkle with cheese and bake for about 30 minutes until the centre is firm and the top is golden.

Serve hot or cold.

Dumplings

INGREDIENTS £

100g (3½ oz) self raising flour
50g (2 oz) beef suet
1 tbsp chopped fresh herbs *(eg. thyme, rosemary, parsley)*
5 tbsp cold water, *approx.*
Pinch of salt

METHOD

SERVES 8

1. Mix all the ingredients together in a bowl and add the water, a little at a time, until it forms a ball.
2. Divide into 8 balls, then place into the stew or casserole, cover with a lid and cook for 20 minutes.

MAIN COURSES

Chilli Beef

INGREDIENTS £

2 tbsp vegetable oil
2 large onions, thinly sliced
2 garlic cloves, *crushed*
500g (1 lb 6 oz) lean mince beef
1 fresh chilli, *deseeded and finely sliced*
3 tsp dried oregano
Pinch ground cinnamon
1 tsp ground cumin
3 beef stock cubes, *crushed*
3 x 440g tins chopped tomatoes
2 x 400g tins red kidney beans, *drained and washed*
2 tsp chilli powder
50g (1 oz) high cocoa plain chocolate

METHOD

SERVES 8

1. Warm the oil in a frying pan and cook the onion and garlic until soft.
2. Stir in the mince *(as it cooks the meat will stick together so keep breaking it up).* Pour off any excess fat.
3. Stir in the fresh chilli, oregano, cinnamon, cumin, stock cubes, tomatoes and kidney beans, season and cook over a low heat for 2–3 hours, stirring occasionally, or bake in oven in a covered dish for 2 hours at 160°C / 320°F / gas mark 2-3.
4. Half an hour before serving check the seasoning and add the chilli powder to taste.
5. Add the chocolate, allow to melt and serve with rice.

Chicken Curry

INGREDIENTS ££

85g (3 oz) butter
1 tbsp vegetable oil
2 onions, *chopped*
2 garlic cloves, *crushed*
1 kg (2 lb) chicken, *chopped*
2 bay leaves
1 x 400g (14 oz) tin chopped tomatoes
150ml (5 fl oz / ¼ pt) chicken stock
55g (2¾ oz) baby leaf spinach
Crème fraîche
25g (¾ oz) flaked almonds, *toasted (optional)*

Spices *(Instead of using the following spices you may substitute them with 1½ -2 tbsp curry powder, depending on the type you are using).*
1 tsp chilli powder
6 cloves, *ground with a pestle and mortar*
4 cardamom pods, *remove and discard shells*
¼ tsp ground cinnamon
1 tsp ground garam masala
¼ tsp ground ginger

Long grain rice (70g /2½ oz per person for a small portion)

METHOD

SERVES 8

1. Warm the butter and oil in a large saucepan and cook the onions and garlic for about 5 minutes.
2. Add the meat, bay leaves and all the spices *(or curry powder if using)*, stir well and continue to cook for a further 5 minutes.
3. Add the tomatoes, chicken stock and seasoning and bring to the boil.
4. Simmer uncovered for approximately 1 hour to reduce to the right consistency.
5. Cook the rice in salted water *(following the cooking directions on the back of the packet, but beware, they are not always correct!)*. When the rice is cooked drain, then pour over boiling water. Serve immediately.
6. Remove the bay leaves from the curry, check the seasoning and stir in the spinach about 3 minutes before serving.

Serve the curry with the rice, spoon a teaspoon of crème fraiche on top of the curry and sprinkle with almonds.

Suggestions for side dishes:

Chutney, Sultanas, Sliced Tomatoes, Yoghurt and Cucumber, Peanuts or Cashew Nuts, Desiccated Coconut, Sliced hard boiled Eggs

Panéed Turkey with Piquante Sauce

INGREDIENTS ££

Piquante Sauce
1 tbsp olive oil
1 onion, *finely chopped*
1 garlic clove, *crushed*
120g (4½ oz) Demerara sugar
240ml (8½ fl oz) malt vinegar
½ tsp smoked paprika
2 tbsp Worcestershire sauce
2 tbsp tomato ketchup
2 x 400g tins chopped tomatoes

3 slices of bread
2 tbsp fresh parsley, *finely chopped (optional)*
8 turkey escalopes
55g (2 oz) plain flour
1 egg, *beaten*
30g (1 oz) butter

METHOD

SERVES 8

Preheat the oven to 180°C / 350°F / gas mark 4

1. **To make the sauce**, warm the oil in a frying pan and cook the onion and garlic over a gentle heat until soft.
2. Put the malt vinegar and Demerara sugar into a separate saucepan, bring to the boil and simmer to reduce to a third of its volume.
3. When the onion and garlic is soft, add the vinegar solution and the rest of the ingredients.
4. Bring to the boil and simmer for 10 minutes. * Season to taste.
5. Blend the bread and parsley in a food processor until you have a fine breadcrumb consistency. Empty the breadcrumbs on to half of a clean, dry chopping board.
6. Sprinkle the flour on the other half of the chopping board and season with salt and pepper.
7. **To prepare the meat**, bash each escalope into shape with a rolling pin to tenderise.
8. Roll one escalope in the seasoned flour until it is completely covered, dip it in the beaten egg and then roll it in the breadcrumbs. Prepare the remaining escalopes in the same way.
9. Warm half the butter in a large frying pan and cook four of the escalopes on both sides until golden, then transfer to a lined baking tray. Melt the remaining butter and cook the other four escalopes until golden. * Bake for 20 minutes.

Roast Leg or Shoulder of Lamb with Apricot & Thyme

INGREDIENTS ££

Leg or shoulder of lamb,
on the bone
6 **dried apricots**, *sliced into thirds*
Sprigs of fresh thyme
Olive oil
1 tbsp apricot jam

Gravy
2 tbsp plain **flour**
570ml (20 fl oz / 1 pt) **stock**
1 tbsp **white wine**
½ tsp **soy sauce**
Pinch of dried thyme
2 tbsp apricot jam

METHOD

SERVES 8

Preheat the oven to 220°C / 425°F / gas mark 7

1. Calculate the cooking time; allow 20 minutes per 450g (1 lb), plus an extra 20 minutes *(a shoulder usually needs at least 2 hours).*
2. Stab the meat with a small knife and push the apricot pieces and thyme into the holes.
3. Coat in oil, sprinkle with salt * and roast. Turn the oven down to 180°C / 350°F / gas mark 4 after 20 minutes.
4. 30 minutes before the end of cooking time coat the lamb in 1 tbsp of apricot jam.
5. Use the juices from the roast meat to make the gravy. Pour the juices from the roasting tin into a jug, allow to settle for a few minutes and then spoon off most of the fat which will have risen to the surface. There will be juices from the meat stuck to the baking tray, so use a scraper and a little of the stock to help dissolve it.
6. Add the flour to a saucepan, pour in enough of the juice to make a roux.
7. Add the rest of the juice and the stock, season and whisk using a coil whisk.
8. Add the white wine, soy sauce and thyme, bring to the boil and simmer for a few minutes, stirring occasionally. Add the apricot jam and taste before serving.

Let the meat rest out of the oven for 15 minutes before carving *(cover in foil and a tea towel to keep warm).* To serve the shoulder, remove the scapular bone by twisting and pulling *(it should come out relatively easily if the meat is cooked).* It is then easier to carve.

Serve with mint sauce and red currant jelly.

Roast Chicken / Turkey

INGREDIENTS ££

1 whole chicken or turkey
Vegetable oil
Bacon *(4 slices for chicken or 5 slices for turkey) (optional)*
1 potato

Gravy
Juices from the meat
2 tbsp plain **flour**
570ml (20 fl oz / 1 pt) chicken **stock**

Approximate quantities and cooking times.

6 people	2.7 kg (6 lb)	2½ + hrs
8 people	3.6 kg (8 lb)	2¾ + hrs
10 people	4.5 kg (10 lb)	3 hrs
12 people	5.4 kg (12 lb)	3¼ hrs
14 people	6.4 kg (14 lb)	3¾ hrs
16 people	7.2 kg (16 lb)	4¼ hrs

METHOD

SERVES 8

Preheat the oven at 200°C / 400°F / gas mark 6

1. Weigh the bird *(or look at the weight on the packaging)* and calculate the cooking time:
   a. **For a chicken**, allow 20 minutes per 450g / lb plus 20 minutes (eg a 1.8 kg / 4 lb bird would take about 1 hr 40 mins to cook).
   b. **For a turkey**, see chart below. *(Plan for the turkey to be cooked 15-30 minutes before you want to serve it, just in case it is not cooked in time. You can sit the turkey on the side in its roasting tin, covered in tin foil and several warmed tea towels to keep it warm if it is cooked before you need it).*
2. Rinse the bird inside and out, drain then dry with kitchen paper and place in a large roasting tin with the neck and giblets. *(The giblets and neck are cooked to flavour the juices that will be used to make the gravy. Discard them when the chicken/turkey is cooked).*
3. Coat the skin with vegetable oil and cover the breasts *(and thighs if cooking a turkey)* with bacon to stop the meat from drying out. Also to help prevent the meat from drying out, place a peeled raw potato in the cavity of the bird.
4. Place a few knobs of butter on the meat and loosely cover the whole bird in greased tin foil, tucking the edges into the tin.
5. Put in the oven for 30 minutes and then reduce the temperature to 180°C / 350°F / gas mark 4.
6. Half an hour before the bird is cooked, remove the foil and pour off the juices and sauce to make the gravy.
7. Allow the juices to settle for a few minutes and then spoon off most of the fat that will have risen to the surface. There will be juices from the meat stuck to the baking tray, so use a scraper and a little stock to help dissolve it.
8. Put the flour in a small saucepan and pour in enough of the juices to make a roux.
9. Add the rest of the juices and the stock, season and whisk using a coil whisk. Bring to the boil and simmer for a few minutes, stirring occasionally.
10. To test to see if the bird is cooked, push a skewer into the thick parts of the meat. If the juices runs clear it is cooked, if it is pink it requires further cooking.

Serve with sausages, stuffing and bread sauce.

Almond & Apricot Stuffing

INGREDIENTS £

1 onion, *finely chopped*
225g (8 oz) breadcrumbs
2 heaped tbsp chopped parsley *(1 heaped tbsp dried)*
30g (1 oz) dried apricots, *chopped (optional)*
30g (1 oz) almonds, *chopped (optional)*
180-200ml (6-7 fl oz) water *(depending on the dryness of breadcrumbs)*
30g (1 oz) butter

METHOD

SERVES 8

1. To make the stuffing, mix all the ingredients *(except the butter)* together with enough water to make the mixture into a soft ball.
2. Melt half the butter in a frying pan and add the stuffing, pressing it firmly into the pan. *(We recommend that you cook the stuffing separately, rather than inside the chicken).*
3. Cook for about 10 minutes until lightly browned and then turn to brown the other side, adding the other half of the butter to the pan.

It can be served straight from the pan, or kept warm in the oven. It can be made in bulk and frozen in batches, uncooked.

Bread Sauce

INGREDIENTS £

Try Colmans bread sauce **mix!** *(One packet requires 290ml / 10 fl oz / ½ pt) of* milk *and will serve four people. You can add extra* milk *and white* breadcrumbs *to make it go further).*

If you prefer to make your own here is a simple recipe:
30g (1 oz) butter
1 onion, *blended*
570ml (20 fl oz /1 pt) milk
110g (4 oz) white bread, *crust removed, made into breadcrumbs*

METHOD

SERVES 8

1. Melt the butter in a small saucepan and cook the onions over a gentle heat until soft.
2. Add all the other ingredients, season and slowly bring to the boil, stirring all the time. Simmer gently for 10 minutes continuing to stir to prevent burning.
3. Leave for a couple of hours to allow the flavours to infuse.
4. Reheat to serve, check seasoning and adjust consistency with milk, if necessary.

Can be made in bulk and frozen in small batches. If using from frozen, check the seasoning before serving, you will probably need to add more salt.

MAIN COURSES

Beef Wellington

INGREDIENTS £££

½ onion, *peeled & quartered*
30g (1 oz) butter
Fillet of beef
75g (2¾ oz) mushrooms
100ml (3½ fl oz) beef stock
50ml (2 fl oz) red wine
1 tsp cornflour, *if needed*
Puff pastry, *chilled*
1 egg, *beaten (for glazing)*
2 tbsp cream

METHOD

SERVES 8

Preheat the oven to 220ºC / 425ºF / gas mark 7

1. **To make the pâté**, blend the onions in a food processor. Melt the butter in a medium sized saucepan, add the onions and gently cook them until the mixture no longer tastes bitter.
2. Seal the meat in a very hot frying pan then transfer to a lined baking tray.
3. Blend the mushrooms in the food processor, add to the onions, season and cook for about 10 minutes until very soft, stirring occasionally.
4. Transfer just under half the pâté to a plate and spread it out so that it cools quickly.
5. Add stock and red wine to the saucepan of pâté, stir well, season and simmer for about 10 minutes. *(To thicken the sauce, add a little water to 1 tsp of cornflour in a glass. Add to the sauce a little at a time to adjust the consistency. Cook for a couple of minutes to allow it to thicken).* *
6. Cover the top of the meat with the pâté, pressing into place with your hands.
7. Cover the meat with a single layer of pastry, tucking the pastry under the meat and removing any overlapping layers *(keep the leftovers, don't use up all the pastry as you need some to decorate)*. Mould using your hands and seal any joins with beaten egg.
8. With the left over pastry cut leaf shapes, or use a patterned pastry cutter to decorate *(use the beaten egg to stick in place)*.
9. Glaze the pastry with beaten egg * and bake until cooked to your liking, 25-35 minutes *(If the pastry browns too quickly cover with tin foil)*.
10. Add the cream to the sauce and bring up to temperature.

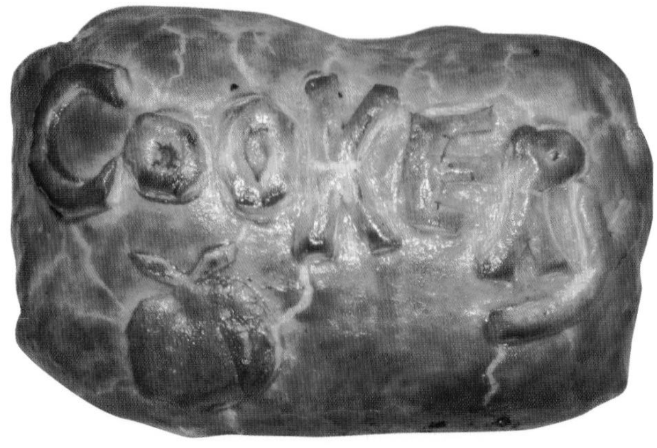

Herb Crusted Rack of Lamb with a Mint Hollandaise

INGREDIENTS £££

Crust
3 slices of white **bread**
1 lemon, *grated zest and juice*
6 sage leaves
2 tbsp rosemary leaves, *chopped*
1 tsp olive oil

30g (1 oz) **butter**
1 tbsp olive oil
3 lamb racks, *trimmed*
1 tsp Dijon **mustard**
2 tbsp red currant jelly

Mint Hollandaise Sauce
4 **egg yolks**
1 tsp lemon juice
Pinch of cayenne pepper
½ tsp salt
2 tbsp **sherry vinegar**
1 shallot, *finely chopped*
220g (8 oz) unsalted **butter**, *good quality*
1 tbsp fresh mint, *chopped*

METHOD

SERVES 8

Preheat the oven to 200°C / 400°F / gas mark 6

1. **To make the crust**, blend the bread, lemon zest, sage leaves and rosemary in the food processor. Stir in the lemon juice and oil *(a little at a time until you get the right consistency, it does not want to be too wet)* and season.
2. Melt the butter and oil in a frying pan and seal all sides of the meat. Transfer to a lined baking tray and allow to cool for a few minutes.
3. Spread the mustard and the red currant jelly over the large side of the racks of lamb then press the crust on top so that it sticks. *
4. Roast the lamb in the oven for 20 plus minutes *(depending on how rare you want the meat)* then allow the meat to rest out of the oven for at least 15 minutes before carving (*cover in foil and a tea towel to keep warm).*
5. **To make the hollandaise sauce**, blend the egg yolks, lemon juice, cayenne pepper and salt in the small bowl of the food processor *(leave the food processor running until the sauce is served).*
6. Warm the sherry vinegar and shallot in a small saucepan until it starts to boil *(do not reduce the mixture by continuing to boil it).*
7. Melt the butter in a second saucepan.
8. Very slowly, pour the vinegar and shallot mixture through the feeding tube of the food processor.
9. In the same way, pour in the butter.
10. Stir in the mint, check the seasoning and serve immediately.

Serve 2-3 cutlets per person.

Jubilee Chicken

INGREDIENTS ££

1 whole chicken
½ lime
1 garlic clove, *peeled*
5 cm (2 inch) piece of ginger

Sauce
200ml (7 oz) crème fraîche
200ml (7 oz) mayonnaise
3 tsp ginger, *grated*
1½ lime, *grated zest and juice*
2 Granny Smith apples, *cored and chopped*
30g (1 oz) pine nuts, *toasted*
2 tbsp fresh flat leaf parsley, *chopped*
Flat leaf parsley sprigs, *to garnish*

METHOD

SERVES 6

Preheat the oven to 180°C / 350°F / gas mark 4

1. Wash chicken inside and out and put the lime, garlic and ginger in the cavity.
2. Place the chicken upside-down in a pot roast, pour in some water so that there are 2½ cm (1 inch) of water in the bottom. Cover and bake for 2 hours.
3. Remove from the oven, allow to cool a little and then strip the chicken *(which is easier if the chicken is still warm)* discarding the skin, bones and gristle.
4. Chop the chicken into bite size pieces.
5. **To make the sauce**, combine the crème fraîche, mayonnaise, ginger, lime juice and zest. Season to taste.
6. Add the apples, chicken, half of the nuts and parsley and gently mix together.
7. Transfer to a serving dish and sprinkle the rest of the nuts and parsley over the top to garnish.

MAIN COURSES

Lamb Tagine

INGREDIENTS ££

900g (2 lb) left over *(cooked)* lamb, *diced*
2 tbsp plain **flour**
2 tbsp fresh rosemary, *chopped*
3 tbsp olive oil
2 red onions, *chopped*
1 aubergine, *cubed*
2 medium carrots, *cubed*
1 tbsp tomato purée
720ml (25 fl oz / 1¼ pts) **stock**
100g (3½ oz) fresh spinach

METHOD

SERVES 8

Preheat the oven to 160°C / 320°F / gas mark 2-3

1. Put the lamb into a casserole dish, sprinkle over the flour and rosemary and toss to cover the meat in flour.
2. Warm 2 tbsp of the oil in a frying pan, add the meat and fry gently until slightly brown, then return the meat to the casserole dish.
3. Add another tbsp of oil to the pan, fry the onions, aubergine and carrots over a gentle heat for about 10 minutes, until they are golden. Then transfer them to the casserole dish.
4. Add the tomato purée, stock and seasoning to the dish. Stir carefully so you don't break up the lamb and cook in the oven for 2 hours. *
5. Check the seasoning and stir in the spinach just before serving.

Spicy Sausage Casserole

INGREDIENTS £

1 tbsp vegetable oil
900g (2 lbs) **sausages**, *pierce skin with a fork*
8 rashers streaky bacon, *chopped*
2 onions, *sliced*
4 garlic cloves, *crushed*
1 tsp red chilli, *deseeded and finely chopped*
2 tsp sugar
2 tbsp wholegrain **mustard**
2 x 400g tins red kidney beans, *drained and rinsed*
2 x 400g tins butter beans, *drained and rinsed*
4 x 400g tins chopped tomatoes
290ml (10 fl oz / ½ pt) beef **stock**
½ tsp hot chilli powder, *if needed*

METHOD

SERVES 8

1. Warm the oil in a large saucepan, add the sausages and bacon and cook over a gentle heat until browned *(stir occasionally so that the meat does not catch on the bottom of the pan).*
2. Remove the sausages and bacon from the pan, pour off the excess fat, retaining about 1 tablespoonful to fry the onions in.
3. Add the onions and garlic to the pan and cook until soft.
4. Add the chilli and cook for a further 2 minutes. Then add the sugar, wholegrain mustard, tinned tomatoes and beans.
5. Cut the sausages into bite size pieces and return them to the pan.
6. Add the stock, season * and simmer *(with the lid off)* for about 20 minutes.
7. Adjust the seasoning before serving. If it is not spicy enough, add a little chilli powder.

Serve with crusty white bread.

MAIN COURSES

Chicken Breasts Stuffed with Wild Mushrooms, Pine Nuts & Apricots with a Brandy Sauce

INGREDIENTS £££

8 chicken breasts
30g (1 oz) butter, *for frying chicken breasts*

Stuffing
55g (2 oz) dried wild mushrooms
30g (1 oz) butter
2 onions, *finely chopped*
8 shallots, *finely chopped*
8 dried apricots, *finely chopped*
4 tbsp brandy
4 tbsp balsamic vinegar
4 tbsp pine nuts, *toasted*

Sauce
290ml (10 fl oz / ½ pt) chicken stock
290ml (10 fl oz / ½ pt) cream
½ of the stuffing mixture

METHOD

SERVES 8

Preheat the oven to 180°C / 350°F / gas mark 4

1. **To make the stuffing**, soak the mushrooms in a little warm water for at least 15 minutes *(use just enough water to cover them).*
2. Melt the butter in a saucepan and cook the onion and shallots over a gentle heat for 5 minutes.
3. Drain the mushrooms *(retaining the water to add to the sauce)* roughly chop any large pieces and add them to the saucepan.
4. Add the rest of the ingredients for the stuffing and continue to cook until the onions are soft. Season to taste. *
5. Remove ½ the mixture, leave other half in the saucepan for the sauce.
6. Trim the chicken and prepare it for stuffing by cutting it open – *place the palm of your hand firmly on top of the chicken, fingers on full stretch and slice the meat almost in half, horizontally, creating a pocket.*
7. Stuff each chicken breast and secure using cocktail sticks.
8. Brown the chicken in butter in a hot stainless steel frying pan *(the cocktail sticks will damage a non-stick surface)*. Transfer to a lined baking tray * and bake for about 25 minutes.
9. **To make the sauce**, put the chicken stock, mushroom water and cream in the saucepan containing half of the stuffing and simmer to reduce by half. Season to taste. *

To serve, remove the cocktail sticks, slice the chicken and arrange on a plate with the sauce.

Roast Duck Legs with Morello Cherry Sauce

INGREDIENTS ££

2 tsp fennel seeds
2 tsp coriander seeds
1 whole star anise
8 duck legs, *trimmed & scored*
Spring onions

Morello Cherry Sauce
350g (12 oz) morello cherry jam
300ml (10 fl oz / ½ pt) **red wine**

METHOD

SERVES 8

Preheat the oven to 180°C / 350°F / gas mark 4

1. Put fennel seeds, coriander seeds and star anise into a pestle and mortar, season and coarsely crush.
2. Rub it over the duck legs * and bake in the oven for 1½ hours, tipping away any fat halfway through.
3. To prepare the garnish, finely slice the spring onions lengthways, cover with water and refrigerate for at least 20 minutes *(this makes them curl).*
4. **To make the sauce**, heat the jam and red wine and simmer to reduce for 10 minutes.

Sesame Seed Crusted Sea Bass with Asian Noodle Broth

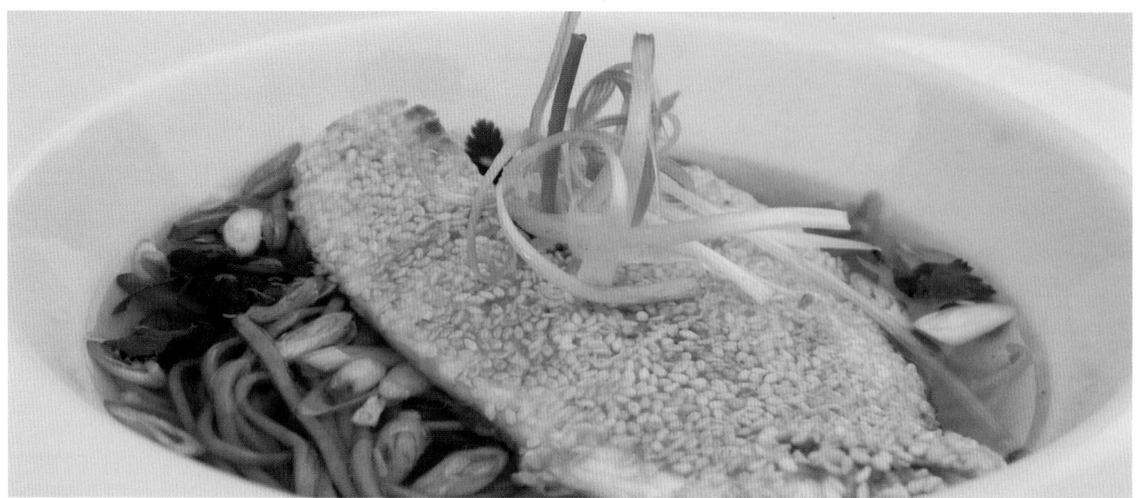

INGREDIENTS ££

Broth

2.2 L (80 fl oz / 4 pts) fish stock *(use 4 cubes)*
20g (¾ oz) piece of ginger, *whole*
1 red chilli *(cut in half lengthways)*
2 sticks lemon grass, *bashed with a rolling pin*
2 tsp sesame oil
2 tsp fish sauce
2 tsp clear honey
2 tsp soy sauce

8 sea bass fillets, *skinned*
8 tsp sesame seeds
340g (12 oz) Soba noodles (Chinese medium egg noodles)
8 spring onions, *finely sliced at an angle*
1-2 red chillies, *finely sliced at an angle*
25g (1 oz) fresh coriander, *slightly chopped*
¼ tsp vegetable oil

METHOD

SERVES 8

1. **To make the broth**, put fish stock, ginger, chilli, lemon grass, sesame oil, fish sauce, honey and soy sauce in a saucepan. Bring to the boil and simmer for 10 minutes. Then strain and discard the bits.
2. To prepare the fish sprinkle 1 tsp of sesame seeds onto one side of each fillet and press them on to the fish.
3. Cook noodles in a saucepan full of boiling, salted water for 5 minutes or until cooked, then drain and rinse in cold water to stop them from cooking any further.
4. Divide the noodles, spring onions, chilli and coriander leaves between 8 warm bowls.
5. Warm ¼ tsp vegetable oil in a frying pan and cook the fish, seed side down for 1 minute. Then turn and cook the other side for 2 minutes.
6. Bring the broth to the boil and carefully pour over the noodles.

Place the fish on top and serve immediately.

Coq au Vin

INGREDIENTS ££

8 chicken breasts
2-3 tbsp vegetable oil
250g (9 oz) streaky bacon, *diced*
100g (2½ oz) **celery**, *sliced*
2 garlic cloves, *crushed*
1 onion, *sliced*
4 tbsp **flour** *(plus extra to coat chicken)*
570ml (20 fl oz / 1 pt) **red wine**
570ml (20 fl oz / 1 pt) chicken **stock**

METHOD

SERVES 8

Preheat the oven to 180°C / 350°F / gas mark 4

1. Roll the chicken breasts in seasoned flour.
2. Warm the vegetable oil in a frying pan and seal the chicken by cooking it for a few minutes on each side, until golden in colour. Then transfer to a casserole dish.
3. Fry the bacon until just golden, then add the celery, garlic and onion, season and cook over a low heat until soft.
4. Sprinkle over the flour and stir to make a roux.
5. Add the red wine a little at a time to make a thick sauce, then pour the mixture over the chicken.
6. Add the chicken stock, cover and bake for 2 hours *(add a little more water during cooking if necessary).*

Duck with Ruby Sauce

MAIN COURSES

INGREDIENTS £££

6-8 duck breasts
Sprigs coriander to garnish

Sauce
290 ml (10 fl oz / ½ pt) **red wine**
2 tsp **balsamic vinegar**
6 tbsp red currant jelly
2 tsp **soy sauce**
Dash of Tabasco
1 tsp sugar
1 orange, *zest & juice*

Spices
1 tsp ground coriander
1 tsp ground cinnamon
Pinch of ground nutmeg
1 tsp salt
½ tsp ground black pepper

METHOD

SERVES 8

Preheat the oven to 220°C / 425°F / gas mark 7

1. Trim the fat from the breasts and score the skin through to the flesh, making a criss-cross pattern.
2. Combine spices and rub over the scored skin.
3. Seal the meat in a very hot frying pan. Start skin side down and fry for about 3 minutes to brown and crisp the skin. Fry the other side in the pan only for a few seconds. Pour out the fat as you go.
4. **To make the sauce**, add all the ingredients to a pan and simmer to reduce to half its volume. *
5. Bake the duck for 6-8 minutes, depending on size. *(To see if cooked, stick a sharp knife into the middle of a duck breast, hold for five seconds, remove and place the tip of the blade to your lip. If it feels warm the duck is cooked to perfection, but not everyone likes duck this rare. Cut one open just to double check. It carries on cooking once removed from the oven).*

To serve, slice the duck, arrange on the plate and pour over the sauce. Garnish with coriander sprigs.

Tarragon & White Wine Chicken Fricassée

INGREDIENTS ££

30g (1 oz) **butter**
8 chicken breasts
2 onions, *chopped*
2 garlic cloves, *crushed*
8 rashers of bacon, *chopped*
300g (10½ oz) mushrooms, *sliced*
2 tsp English **mustard**
350ml (12 fl oz) **white wine**
2 tsp dried tarragon
290ml (10 fl oz / ½ pt) **cream**
Chives, *for garnishing*

METHOD

SERVES 8

Preheat the oven to 180°C / 350°F / gas mark 4

1. Melt the butter in a frying pan and cook the chicken breasts for about 10 minutes until golden in colour. Transfer to an ovenproof dish.
2. Fry the onion, garlic and bacon in the juices from the chicken until soft.
3. Add the mushrooms and cook for a further 5 minutes.
4. Add the mustard, wine, tarragon, cream and seasoning to the pan, pour over the chicken * and bake for 30 minutes.

To serve, slice the chicken, arrange on the plate, spoon the sauce over and garnish with chives.

Chicken Dijonaise

INGREDIENTS ££

30g (1 oz) **butter**
8 chicken breasts
2 onions, *chopped*
8 rashers of bacon, *chopped*
2 tbsp Dijon **mustard**
350ml (12 fl oz / 0.6 pt) **white wine**
1 tsp dried thyme
290ml (10 fl oz / ½ pt) double **cream**
Fresh chives, *for garnish*

METHOD

SERVES 8

Preheat the oven to 180°C / 350°F / gas mark 4

1. Melt the butter in a frying pan, cook the chicken breasts for about 10 minutes until golden in colour. Transfer to an ovenproof dish.
2. Fry the onion and the bacon in the same pan *(in the juices from the chicken)* until soft.
3. Add the mustard, wine, thyme, cream and seasoning to the pan, pour over the chicken * and bake for 30 minutes.

To serve, either leave in the dish and serve at the table, or to plate up, slice the chicken, arrange on the plate and spoon over the sauce. Garnish with chives.

Citrus Marinated Salmon served on Oriental Soba Noodle Salad

INGREDIENTS ££

8 salmon fillets, *boned and skinned*
1-2 tbsp vegetable oil

Fish Marinade
1 tbsp coriander seeds, *toasted and crushed*
2 oranges, *grated zest and juice*
6 spring onions, *chopped*
30g (1 oz) fresh coriander, *chopped including stalks*
2 chillis, *chopped*
6 tbsp white wine
6 tbsp white wine vinegar

Dressing
2 tbsp rapeseed oil
1 tbsp soy sauce
1 tbsp rice wine vinegar
½ garlic clove, *crushed*
½ tbsp fish sauce
½ tbsp sesame seeds, *toasted*
½ tsp sesame seed oil

Soba Noodle Salad
85g (3 oz) Soba noodles
1 large carrots, *grated*
½ large courgette, *deseeded and grated*
¼ large cucumber, *deseeded and grated*
½ chilli, *deseeded and very thinly sliced into long strips*
15g (½ oz) fresh coriander, *including stalks, finely chopped*
7g (¼ oz) fresh ginger, *thinly sliced*
½ tbsp peanut butter or roasted peanuts, *finely chopped (optional)*

METHOD

SERVES 8

1. **To make the marinade**, combine all the ingredients in a large shallow dish. *
2. Warm the oil in a frying pan. When the oil is hot cook the fish for 1 minute on each side.
3. Pour the marinade over the fish and refrigerate overnight. *
4. **To make the dressing**, put all the ingredients in a jar, season and shake to combine. Leave to infuse for an hour. *
5. Plunge the noodles into a pan of boiling water and cook for about 7 minutes. Drain, then refresh in cold water to stop them from cooking any further.
6. In a large bowl mix together the carrot, courgette, cucumber, chilli, coriander, ginger and peanut butter / roasted peanuts.*
7. Add the dressing, stir in the noodles and serve immediately with the salmon placed on top.

Serve cold or at room temperature.

Duck with Wild Berry Sauce

INGREDIENTS £££

6-8 duck breasts
Sprigs of coriander, *to garnish*

Spices
1 tsp ground coriander
1 tsp ground cinnamon
Pinch of ground nutmeg
1 tsp salt
½ tsp ground black pepper

Sauce
200ml (7 fl oz) **red wine**
100ml (3½ fl oz) beef **stock**
2 tbsp red currant jelly
2 tbsp black currant jam
2 tsp cornflour
120g (4½ oz) mixed frozen berries

METHOD

SERVES 8

Preheat the oven to 220ºC / 425ºF / gas mark 7

1. Trim the duck fat from the breasts and score the skin through to the flesh, making a criss-cross pattern.
2. Combine spices and rub over the scored skin.
3. Seal the meat in a very hot frying pan, start skin side down and fry for about 3 minutes to brown and crisp the skin. Fry the other side in the pan for only a few seconds. Pour out the fat as you go.
4. **To make the sauce**, put the red wine, beef stock, red currant jelly and black currant jam in a pan, bring to the boil and simmer for 12-15 minutes to reduce.
5. Mix the cornflour in a glass with a little water, add to the sauce and bring to the boil. *
6. Add the frozen berries, bring back to the boil and simmer for about 3 minutes *(be careful not to squash the berries)*.
7. Bake the duck for 6-8 minutes, depending on size. *(To see if it is cooked, stick a sharp knife into the middle of a duck breast, hold for five seconds, remove and place the tip of the blade to your lip. If it feels hot the duck is cooked to perfection, but not everyone likes duck this rare. Cut one open just to double check. It carries on cooking once removed from the oven).*

To serve, slice the duck, arrange on plates and pour the sauce over. Garnish with coriander sprigs.

Fajitas

INGREDIENTS £££

Flour Tortillas
450g (1 lb) plain flour
½ tsp baking powder
1 tsp salt
110g (3¾ oz) lard
250ml (8½ fl oz) warm water

Relish
6 tomatoes *deseeded & finely chopped*
10 radishes, *coarsely chopped*
5 spring onions, *thinly sliced*
3 tbsp fresh basil, *torn*
1 lemon, *juiced (save a bit for the avocado)*

Filling for the Tortillas
560g (1¼ lbs) turkey, chicken or pork, *chopped into small pieces*
Oil for frying
1 lemon, *juice and zest*
2 tbsp sherry
3 garlic cloves, *crushed*
2 tbsp dried coriander leaves
1 tbsp paprika
1 tsp ground cumin
4 tbsp cream

Soured cream
Guacamole
(see Mexican Nachos page 14)
or crushed avocado, lemon juice & seasoning

METHOD

SERVES 4

1. **To make the tortillas,** blend all the ingredients in a food processor. When the mixture comes together remove it from the food processor and knead it into a ball.
2. Place the ball in a bowl, glaze with oil, cover with cling film and leave to stand for about 20 minutes.
3. Divide the mixture into 10 balls. On a floured surface, roll out each piece into a circular shape approx 20 cm (8 inch) in diameter using a rolling pin *(or clean wine bottle).*
4. Warm a frying pan and cook each circular piece *(without adding oil to the pan)* for a few minutes on each side. *(They can change colour slightly but don't cook them for too long because they will become crispy).*
5. Wrap them in foil, separating each one with a layer of foil and reheat together when required.
6. **To make the relish,** simply combine all the ingredients and place in a small serving dish.
7. **To make the filling**, fry the meat in a little oil until almost cooked.
8. Add the rest of the ingredients, except the cream, season and continue to cook over a gentle heat for about 10 minutes *(do not allow it to dry out, add a little water if necessary).* *
9. Add the cream, bring up to temperature and serve.

Serve with soured cream and guaccamole.

MAIN COURSES

Pork with Vermouth Sauce

INGREDIENTS ££

6 pork chops or loin steaks
30g (1 oz) **butter**
4 slices streaky bacon, *chopped*
2 shallots *(or 1 onion)*
finely chopped
1 tbsp plain **flour**
290ml (10 fl oz / ½ pt)
chicken **stock**
90ml (3 fl oz) **Vermouth**
110g (4 oz) mushrooms, *sliced*
2 tbsp Dijon **mustard**

METHOD

SERVES 6

Preheat the oven to 180°C / 350°F / gas mark 4

1. Melt half the butter in a frying pan and brown the meat on each side to seal.
2. Transfer the meat to a lined baking tray and bake for 30 minutes. *(Reserve the juices in the pan to make the sauce).*
3. Melt the remaining butter in the pan with the juices and cook the bacon and shallots until the shallots are soft.
4. Season and stir in the flour a little at a time.
5. Gradually add the stock and Vermouth and bring to the boil.
6. Add the mushrooms and mustard and simmer for 15 minutes.

To serve, spoon a little sauce over each piece of meat and garnish with parsley.

Turkey / Chicken served in a Sherry & Lemon Sauce

INGREDIENTS ££

110g (4 oz) **butter**
6-8 chicken breasts *(or turkey escalopes), cut into chunks*
6 tbsp **sherry**
6 tbsp lemon juice
6 tsp grated lemon zest
570ml (20 fl oz / 1 pt) single **cream**
255g (9 oz) **Cheddar cheese**, *grated*
55g (2 oz) flaked **almonds**

METHOD

SERVES 8

Preheat the oven to 180°C / 350°F / gas mark 4

1. Fry the meat in the butter for about 10 minutes until cooked and golden brown. Transfer the meat to an ovenproof dish.
2. Add the sherry, lemon juice and zest to the frying pan and cook for a couple of minutes. Add the cream and continue to stir. *(Do not allow it to boil).*
3. Pour the sauce over the meat and sprinkle with cheese and a few almonds. *
4. Bake for 15 minutes. *(If heating from cold bake for 30 minutes until warmed through).*

MAIN COURSES

Egg Sauce

INGREDIENTS

Serve with **Fish**

2 **eggs**
15g (½ oz) **butter**
1 tbsp plain **flour**
150ml (¼ pt / 5 fl oz) **milk**

METHOD

SERVES 6-8

Serves 8 to accompany a starter or 6 for main course

1. Put the eggs into a saucepan of cold water, bring to the boil and simmer for 10 minutes.
2. Allow to cool, peel and roughly mash the egg with a fork.
3. Melt the butter in a saucepan then remove from the heat, stir in the flour to make a roux.
4. Return the saucepan to the heat and gradually add the milk *(use a coil whisk to remove any lumps)*. Cook until the sauce looks smooth and glossy.
5. Stir in the eggs, season and cook for a further minute to bring the sauce up to temperature.

Serve hot with fish.

Béchamel Sauce (Basic White Sauce)

INGREDIENTS

30g (1 oz) **butter**
30g (1 oz) plain **flour**
300ml (10 fl oz / ½ pt) **milk**

METHOD

1. Melt the butter in a saucepan over a medium heat.
2. Remove from the heat and stir in the flour to make a roux.
3. Return to the heat and stir in the milk, a little at a time. Use a coil whisk and stir vigorously until the milk is all incorporated and the sauce is smooth and glossy.
4. Reduce the heat and cook the sauce for about 5 minutes. Season to taste.

VEGETARIAN

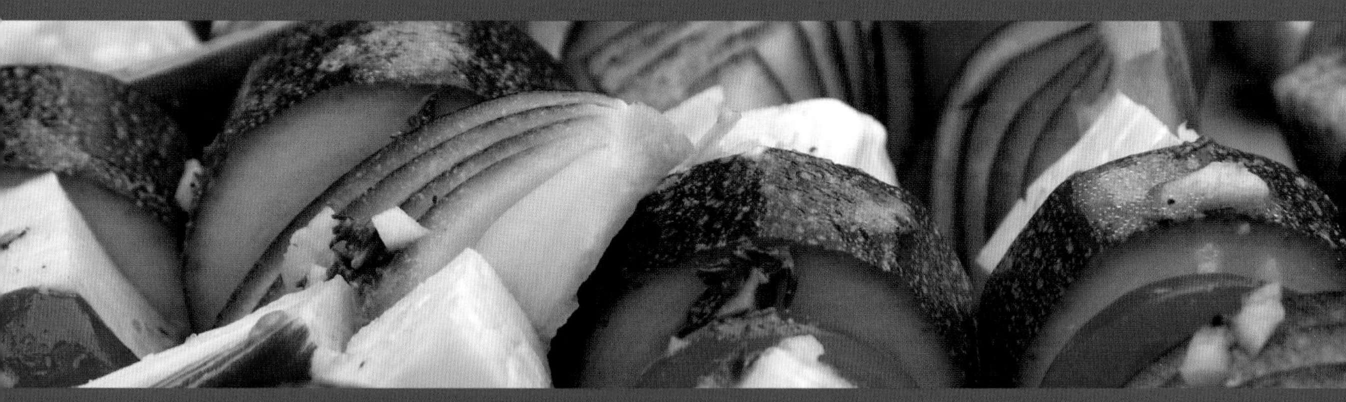

VEGETARIAN

VEGETARIAN

VEGETARIAN

Other Vegetarian Options

Some of the starters in this book can also be served as a vegetarian main course:

Pea & Coriander Falafel with Tzatziki Sauce

VEGETARIAN

INGREDIENTS £

250g (9 oz) frozen peas
1 tbsp olive oil
2 shallots, *finely chopped*
1 tsp ground cumin
1 tsp **sesame seeds**
1 red chilli, *deseeded and finely chopped*
20g (¾ oz) fresh coriander, *chopped*
1 **egg**
1½ - 2 slices of **bread**, *made into breadcrumbs*
Vegetable oil

Tzatziki Sauce
⅛ cucumber, *deseeded and finely diced*
1 tsp lemon juice
½ garlic clove, *crushed*
75ml (2½ fl oz) **yoghurt** or **crème fraîche**

METHOD

MAKES 24 SMALL FALAFELS

1. **To make the sauce**, combine all the ingredients.
2. Cook the peas in boiling water for few minutes and then drain.
3. Heat the olive oil in a small frying pan and cook the shallots for 2-3 minutes to soften slightly.
4. Stir in the ground cumin, sesame seeds and chilli and cook for a further 2-3 minutes.
5. Place the onion mixture and the peas in a food processor, pulse to break up the peas.
6. Add the coriander and the egg and pulse again to combine *(the mixture should resemble a thick, course paste).*
7. Stir in the breadcrumbs and season.
8. Take teaspoons of the mixture and with floured hands shape into 24 small balls. Flatten each one slightly. *
9. Heat some vegetable oil in a frying pan *(enough oil so that it is about 2 cm / ¾ inch deep).* When the oil is hot *(test by dropping in a little of the mixture and seeing if it sizzles)* fry the falafels in batches for about 1 minute on either side until golden and crispy *(they can be cooked in advance and reheated in the oven for about 5 minutes).*

Serve hot with the tzatziki sauce.

Vegetable Lasagne

INGREDIENTS ££

Vegetable Base Ingredients
2 carrots, *peeled*
2 onions, *peeled*
2 red peppers, *deseeded*
½ aubergine
1 small head of broccoli
2 courgettes
2 garlic cloves, *crushed*
250g (9 oz) cherry tomatoes
85g (3 oz) sun-dried tomatoes, *finely chopped (optional)*
55g (2 oz) black pitted olives, *sliced*
4 tbsp olive oil
1 tsp dried basil

Béchamel Sauce
60g (2 oz) butter
60g (2 oz) plain flour
800ml (28 fl oz) milk or stock
1 tsp Dijon mustard *(optional)*

170g (6 oz) cheese, *grated*
125g (4½ oz) lasagne sheets, *approx.*

METHOD

SERVES 8

Preheat the oven to 180°C / 350°F / gas mark 4

1. **To make the vegetable base**, roughly chop the vegetables into walnut sized pieces. Place on a baking tray *(except for the olives and sun-dried tomatoes),* sprinkle with basil, olive oil, salt and pepper and roast for about 35 minutes until soft and browned at the edges.
2. Remove from the oven and add the olives and sun-dried tomatoes.
3. **To make the béchamel sauce**, melt the butter over a medium heat, remove from the heat and stir in the flour.
4. Return to the heat and gradually add the milk, stirring until all the liquid has been incorporated and the sauce is smooth and glossy.
5. Add the mustard, season and allow to cool slightly.
6. Start layering according to the depth of your dish. Start with a layer of the vegetable mixture followed by a layer of lasagne, then a layer of béchamel sauce and a layer of cheese. Continue layering in this way, finishing with a layer of cheese. *
7. Bake for about 45-50 minutes until the pasta is cooked.

Mushroom & Onion Pasty

VEGETARIAN

INGREDIENTS £

1 tbsp olive oil
½ onion, *chopped*
55g (2 oz) mushrooms, *sliced*
55g (2 oz) **Cheddar**, **Emmental** or **Gruyere cheese**, *grated*
Puff pastry
Milk or **egg**, *for glazing*

METHOD

SERVES 1

Preheat the oven to 180°C / 350°F / gas mark 4

1. Warm the oil in a frying pan and soften the onion.
2. Add the mushrooms, season, cook for a few minutes and leave to cool completely *(leftover vegetables can be added)*. Stir in half the cheese.
3. Roll out the puff pastry into a circle and spoon the mixture into the centre.
4. Brush the outside edges of the pastry with milk or egg and bring the edges together to make a Cornish pasty shape.
5. Glaze the pastry and sprinkle over the remaining cheese. * Bake for about 20-25 minutes until golden.

VEGETARIAN

Roasted Butternut Squash & Polenta Croquettes

INGREDIENTS £

340g (12 oz) butternut squash, *peeled and chopped roughly into 2 cm (¾ inch) cubes*
1 tbsp olive oil
285g (10 oz) peeled potatoes
2 spring onions, *finely chopped*
2 garlic cloves, *crushed*
1 **egg yolk**
50g (2 oz) plain **flour**
2 **eggs**, *beaten*
100g (3½ oz) instant polenta
3 tbsp vegetable oil

Sauce
8 tbsp natural **yoghurt**
½ red chilli, *deseeded and finely chopped*
4 tbsp fresh coriander, *chopped*

METHOD

SERVES 4

Preheat the oven to 180°C / 350°F / gas mark 4

1. **To make the sauce**, mix the yoghurt, chilli and coriander together, season and leave for at least an hour for the flavours to infuse.
2. Place the butternut squash on a lined baking tray, drizzle with olive oil, season, toss, cover with tin foil and roast for 40 minutes.
3. Peel and quarter potatoes and cook in salted water for 25 minutes until very soft. Drain and mash in the saucepan with lots of seasoning.
4. When the butternut squash is cooked roughly mash it into the potato.
5. Add the spring onions, garlic, egg yolk and seasoning and mix together. Chill in the fridge for an hour *(the mixture is easier to work with when cold).* *
6. Divide the mixture into 16 and mould into sausage shapes. Roll each one in the flour, then in egg and finally in polenta.
7. Warm the vegetable oil in a large frying pan and fry the croquettes for 3-4 minutes on each side until crisp and golden. Transfer on to kitchen paper. *
8. Serve hot with the sauce and a dressed salad.

Mushroom Pasta Bake

INGREDIENTS £

225g (8 oz) **pasta**
1 onion, *chopped*
1 garlic clove, *crushed*
45g (1½ oz) **butter**
675g (1½ lbs) mushrooms, *sliced*
20g (¾ oz) plain **flour**
150ml (5 fl oz / ¼ pt) vegetable **stock**
Pinch of ground nutmeg
4 tbsp **cream**
170g (6 oz) **cheese**, *grated*

METHOD

SERVES 4

Preheat the oven to 180°C / 350°F / gas mark 4

1. Cook the pasta in salted water until *al dente.*
2. Drain, plunge into cold water to cool and drain once again.
3. Fry the onions and the garlic in half the butter for 5 minutes.
4. Add the mushrooms and cook until soft.
5. Melt the other half of the butter in a saucepan, stir in the flour and gradually add the stock, stirring continuously until combined into a smooth sauce.
6. Add the sauce to the mushrooms, season with salt, pepper and nutmeg, cover with a lid and simmer for a few minutes. Add the cream and stir in half of the cheese.
7. Stir in the pasta, check the seasoning and transfer to an ovenproof dish.
8. Sprinkle with the remaining cheese * and bake in the oven for about 15 minutes.

VEGETARIAN

Sun-Dried Tomato & Mozzarella Tartlet

INGREDIENTS ££

Puff pastry, *chilled*
Pesto
Mozzarella, *finely sliced*
Sun-dried tomatoes, *each cut into four*
Black olives, *finely sliced*
Olive oil
Egg or **milk**, *to glaze*
Rocket or lettuce

METHOD

Preheat the oven to 180°C / 350°F / gas mark 4

1. To make the pastry baskets, roll out the pastry and cut into approximately 10 cm (4 inch) squares. About 1 cm (½ inch) in from the edge of the squares in two opposite corners, cut two large L's, parallel with the outer edges. Fold the two outer L-shaped pieces over to the opposite corner to make a central well for the cheese. *(Use the glaze to hold the pastry in place).*
2. Stab the central well with a fork *(to prevent it from rising),* spoon in a little pesto, add a chunk of cheese, chopped tomatoes and the sliced olives *(avoid placing ingredients on the raised outer edge as this will prevent the pastry from rising).* *
3. Drizzle with olive oil, glaze the pastry, season and bake for 20-25 minutes until the pastry is golden.

Serve hot on a bed of rocket or lettuce.

Roasted Mediterranean Vegetable Couscous

INGREDIENTS ££

To be Roasted

½ aubergine
1 courgette
½ onion, *peeled*
½ red pepper, *deseeded*
½ small bulb of fennel
225g (8 oz) cherry tomatoes, *skinned*
1 garlic clove, *crushed*
2 tbsp olive oil

Couscous

140g (5 oz) couscous
250ml (9 fl oz) vegetable stock

55g (2 oz) feta cheese, *cut into 1 cm cubes*
30g (1 oz) pitted black olives, *chopped*
1 tbsp fresh basil, *roughly chopped*
1 tsp capers

METHOD

SERVES 4

Preheat the oven to 180°C / 350°F / gas mark 4

1. Cut the aubergine and courgette into 2½ cm (1 inch) pieces. Place in a colander and sprinkle generously with salt. Put a small plate on top, weight it down and leave for 1 hour. *(The salt draws out liquid, removing bitterness).* Rinse off the salt and dab dry.
2. Cut the onion, red pepper and fennel into 2½ cm (1 inch) pieces.
3. Put all the ingredients to be roasted in a large baking tray, season and bake for about 35 minutes until browned.
4. **To make the couscous**, pour boiling stock over the couscous, season, stir with a fork and leave for about 5 minutes until all the liquid has been absorbed. Leave to cool.
5. When the roasted vegetables and couscous are cool, combine with the feta cheese, black olives, basil and capers and season to taste. *

Can be served hot or cold.

Petit Pois Risotto with Prawns

INGREDIENTS ££

15g (½ oz) butter
1 onion, *finely chopped*
1 garlic clove, *crushed*
1 leek, *sliced and washed*
170g (6 oz) risotto rice *(Arborio)*
200ml (7 fl oz) white wine
570ml (20 fl oz / 1 pt) vegetable stock *(use 2 stock cubes)*
250g (9 oz) frozen petit pois peas
200g (7 oz) frozen prawns *(optional), thawed and water squeezed out (optional - for fish eaters)*
55g (2 oz) Parmesan, *grated*
5 fresh mint leaves, *finely chopped*
Parmesan shavings, *for garnishing*
2 tsp fresh parsley, *chopped, for garnishing*

METHOD

SERVES 2

1. Melt the butter in a large saucepan and cook the onion and garlic for 5 minutes.
2. Add the leek, cover and cook over a low heat until the onions are soft. *
3. Add the rice and fry for a further 1½ minutes, pour over the wine, season and cook until the rice has almost absorbed the liquid.
4. Pour in half of the stock and simmer over a low heat *(stir frequently as it can stick to the bottom),* gradually add more stock until the rice is cooked. Add the peas about 10 minutes before the rice is cooked and the prawns a few minutes later.
5. Stir in the Parmesan cheese and mint, season to taste and serve immediately, garnish with chopped parsley and Parmesan shavings.

VEGETARIAN

Roasted Butternut Squash with Goats' Cheese & Thyme

INGREDIENTS £

70g (2½ oz) goats' cheese, *crumbled*
50g (2 oz) Parmesan, *grated*
50g (2 oz) white breadcrumbs *(approx 1 slice)*
2 tbsp natural yoghurt
½ -1 tsp fresh thyme
1 butternut squash
Olive oil
1 tsp pesto

METHOD

SERVES 2

Preheat the oven to 180°C / 350°F / gas mark 4

1. Mix the goats' cheese, Parmesan, breadcrumbs, yoghurt and thyme together.
2. Cut off and peel the top seedless section of the butternut squash *(retain the bulbous part for another use – roast vegetable soup perhaps).*
3. Cut into 6 slices, approximately 1 cm (3/8 inch) thick and cook in a saucepan of boiling salted water for 5 minutes until tender. Drain and allow to cool.
4. Place two of the slices on a lined baking tray and spread half the cheese mixture over them, top with another slice of butternut squash, followed by the remaining cheese mixture and place the last slice on top.
5. Secure each stack with two cocktail sticks, drizzle with olive oil * and bake for 30 minutes.
6. Plate up carefully removing the cocktail sticks. Mix the pesto with 1 tbsp of olive oil and drizzle around the plate.

Aubergine & Mozzarella Stack

INGREDIENTS £

½ small aubergine
15g (½ oz) **butter**
1 garlic clove, *crushed*
1 tbsp tomato purée
60g (2 oz) **mozzarella**, *sliced*
3 large fresh basil leaves, *chopped*

METHOD

SERVES 1

Preheat the oven to 180°C / 350°F / gas mark 4

1. Cut the aubergine into 3-4 discs *(crossways so that the stalk can be used as the top)* approximately 1¼ cm (½ inch) thick.
2. Melt the butter in a frying pan, add the aubergine slices to the butter and immediately turn so that both sides are coated in the butter. Cook both sides until golden, remove from the frying pan and allow to cool.
3. In the same frying pan cook the garlic for a few minutes, then stir in the tomato purée and season.
4. Place one slice of aubergine on a lined baking tray, spread with a layer of the tomato mixture, top with a layer of mozzarella and basil. Place the second slice of aubergine on top and repeat the layering, finishing with a slice of aubergine. *
5. Secure the stack with two cocktail sticks and bake for 15-20 minutes *(until the mozzarella has melted).*

Plate up carefully, removing the cocktails sticks.

Red Onion, Black Olive & Feta Cheese Tart

VEGETARIAN

INGREDIENTS ££

15g (½ oz) butter
1 red onion, *finely sliced*
½ tsp dried rosemary
4 tbsp black pitted olives, *sliced*
170g (6 oz) feta cheese, *crumbled*
4 eggs, *beaten*
290ml (10 fl oz / ½ pt) milk
Pinch of dried rosemary

French Pastry
200g (7 oz) plain flour
85 ml (3 fl oz) vegetable oil
85 ml (3 fl oz) water
Pinch of salt

METHOD

SERVES 4

Preheat the oven to 180°C / 350°F / gas mark 4

1. Melt the butter in a small frying pan and cook the onion over a gentle heat until soft. Add the rosemary and allow to cool.
2. **To make the pastry**, put the flour and a pinch of salt in a bowl, make a well and pour in the oil and water, mix together, adding more water or flour if necessary.
3. Grease and flour a loose-bottomed quiche tin and line with the pastry by kneading into place *(no rolling required).* The thinner the pastry the better, so discard any excess.
4. Scatter the olives over the pastry base, followed by the onion and feta cheese.
5. Combine the eggs and the milk, season well and gently pour into the pastry case.
6. Sprinkle over a pinch of rosemary and bake for about 30-35 minutes until the centre is firm and the top golden. *

Serve with dressed salad.

"Healthy" Pastry

INGREDIENTS £

175g (6 oz) plain flour
100ml (3½ fl oz) natural yoghurt
75ml (2½ fl oz) olive oil

METHOD

This quantity will line a 25 cm (10 inch) quiche tin

Preheat the oven to 180°C / 350°F / gas mark 4

1. Combine all the ingredients in a bowl.
2. Place on a floured chopping board and knead for 15-20 seconds until smooth.
3. Roll out thinly and use as required. If using the pastry to make a quiche, grease and flour the tin, line it with the pastry and blind bake the pastry for 15 minutes *(put a layer of greaseproof paper over the pastry and weight it down with baking beans. This prevents the pastry base from ballooning).* Remove the baking beans and greaseproof paper and cook for a further 5 minutes.

Stuffed Red Peppers

VEGETARIAN

INGREDIENTS ££

2 red peppers
½ onion, *peeled and finely chopped*
1 small garlic clove, *crushed*
30g (1 oz) **butter**
55g (2 oz) long grain rice
200ml (7 fl oz) vegetable **stock**
½ tbsp tomato purée
55g (2 oz) mushrooms, *sliced*
45g (1½ oz) **pine nuts** or flaked **almonds**, *toasted*
1 tsp **soy sauce**

METHOD

SERVES 2

Preheat the oven to 180°C / 350°F / gas mark 4

1. Cut the peppers in half lengthways, cutting through the centre of the stalk.
2. Core, deseed and blanch the peppers in boiling water for about 2 minutes.
3. Fry the onion and garlic in butter until soft.
4. Stir in the rice, cook for a couple of minutes, then add the stock, tomato purée and mushrooms.
5. Bring to the boil and simmer for about 15-20 minutes until the rice is tender and all the stock has been absorbed.
6. Stir in the nuts and soy sauce and season to taste.
7. Fill the peppers, place them on a baking tray, cover with foil * and bake for 30 minutes until tender.

VEGETARIAN

Vegetable Falafels with Tzatziki Sauce

INGREDIENTS £

1½ tbsp vegetable oil
½ onion, *finely chopped*
½ garlic clove, *crushed*
½ x 400g tin of chickpeas, *drained, washed & dried*
½ tsp ground cumin
½ tsp ground coriander
2 tbsp fresh parsley, *chopped*
2 **dried figs**, *chopped*
3 **walnuts**, *chopped*
1 tbsp fig jam
½ **egg**, *beaten*
Salad for serving

Tzatziki Sauce
⅛ cucumber, *deseeded and finely diced*
1 tsp lemon juice
½ garlic clove, *crushed*
75ml (2½ fl oz) natural **yoghurt** or **crème fraîche**

METHOD

SERVES 2-3 MAINS (OR 4 STARTERS)

1. **To make the sauce**, combine all the ingredients.
2. Warm ½ tbsp of oil in a large frying pan, add the onion and garlic and cook over a low heat until soft. Use kitchen paper to remove excess oil.
3. Transfer to the small bowl of a food processor *(put the frying pan to one side as you will use it again)*, add the chickpeas, cumin and coriander and pulse until combined, but not quite smooth.
4. Empty into a bowl and stir in the parsley, figs, walnuts and fig jam and season to taste.
5. Stir in most of the egg then check the consistency (if the mixture is too dry to make into balls add more egg).
6. Divide the mixture into about 6 balls and flatten each one slightly.
7. Warm 1 tbsp of oil in the frying pan and fry the falafels over a gentle heat until golden brown. Turn and brown the other side.
8. Serve the falafels with the sauce and **couscous** or salad.

Stuffed Courgette

INGREDIENTS £

½ onion, *chopped*
20g (¾ oz) **butter**
Pinch of thyme
Any left over vegetables, *chopped*
20g (¾ oz) **pine nuts**
1 large courgette
30g (1 oz) **cheese**, *grated*

METHOD

SERVES 1

Preheat the oven to 180°C / 350°F / gas mark 4

1. Soften the onion in the butter with a pinch of thyme and remove from the heat.
2. Stir in the left over vegetables and pine nuts and season to taste. *
3. Cut the courgette in half, leaving the ends on. Cut each half in half again lengthways and spoon out the flesh so you are left with a boat like shell about ½ cm (¼ inch) thick.
4. Fill the courgettes with the vegetables, top with cheese and bake for about 15-20 minutes until the courgette is cooked.

Spanish Omelette

INGREDIENTS £

3 tbsp olive oil
1 onion, *sliced (optional)*
220g (8 oz) chorizo, *chopped (optional - leave out for vegetarian)*
500g (1 lb 2 oz) peeled potatoes
5 **eggs**

METHOD

SERVES 2-3

1. Warm the oil in a medium sized frying pan, add the onion and chorizo and cook over a medium heat for 3-4 minutes.
2. Dice the potatoes *(approx 1½ cm / ⅝ inch cubed)* then rinse and dry really well.
3. Add the potatoes to the pan, season, cover, and continue cooking over a low heat until the potatoes and onions are soft *(for about 15-20 minutes)*, stirring occasionally.
4. Beat the eggs in a bowl, season well and pour into the pan. Stir well and cook gently *(for about 5 minutes)* until half the mixture is firm but the top is still runny.
5. Turn the omelette *(away from the heat, place a large plate over the frying pan and turn the pan holding the plate firmly to it, protecting your hand with an oven cloth, then slide the omelette back into the pan)* and continue cooking *(for about 5 minutes)* until the eggs feel firm to touch and the surface is lightly browned.
6. Carefully turn it out onto a serving dish and serve immediately. The omelette can also be eaten cold, so is excellent for picnics.

Serve with salad and crusty bread.

Courgette & Feta Curry Cakes with a Dill Sauce

INGREDIENTS £

Sauce
100g (3½ fl oz) Greek yoghurt
½ tsp fresh dill, *chopped*

250g (9 oz) courgettes
3 spring onions, *finely chopped*
200g (7 oz) breadcrumbs, *(approx 5 slices)*
½ tbsp fresh mint, *chopped*
½ tbsp curry powder
⅛ tsp ground nutmeg
50g (2 oz) feta cheese, *crumbled*
2 eggs, *beaten*
30g (1 oz) butter
Salad, *to serve*

METHOD

SERVES 4

1. **To make the sauce,** mix the yoghurt and dill together, season and leave to infuse.
2. Coarsely grate the courgettes and squeeze out any excess water.
3. Mix together the courgettes, spring onions, 80g (3 oz) of breadcrumbs, mint, curry powder, nutmeg, feta and ¼ of the egg and add lots of seasoning.
4. Divide the mixture into 8 equal portions and, using your hands, make each portion into a ball.
5. Dip each one into the beaten egg and then roll in the remaining breadcrumbs. Flatten slightly into a fish cake shape. *
6. Melt the butter in a frying pan over a low heat and brown the cakes on each side. *

Serve hot on a bed of salad.

Spinach & Goats' Cheese Quiche

INGREDIENTS £

225g (8 oz) frozen spinach, *drained*
15g (½ oz) butter
3 eggs, *beaten*
85ml (3 fl oz) milk or single cream
110g (4 oz) goats' cheese, *thinly sliced*
Pinch of ground nutmeg
3 tomatoes, *finely sliced*

French Pastry
100g (3½ oz) plain flour
45ml (1½ fl oz) vegetable oil
45ml (1½ fl oz) water
Pinch of salt

METHOD

SERVES 4

Preheat the oven to 180°C / 350°F / gas mark 4

1. Squeeze the spinach to remove the excess liquid, finely chop and fry in the butter for about 5 minutes.
2. Mix together the eggs, milk, spinach, half the goats' cheese, nutmeg and lots of salt and pepper.
3. **To make the pastry**, put the flour in a bowl, make a well and pour in the oil and water. Combine, adding more water or flour if necessary.
4. Grease and flour a loose-bottomed quiche tin and line with the pastry by kneading into place *(no rolling required).* The thinner the pastry the better, so discard any excess.
5. Pour the spinach mixture into the lined tin and arrange the tomato and remaining goats' cheese slices over the top.
6. Bake for about 25 minutes until the centre is firm and the cheese has browned slightly. *

VEGETARIAN

Broccoli & Stilton Quiche

INGREDIENTS ££

2 medium heads of broccoli, *cut into florets*
170g (6 oz) Stilton, *roughly chopped*
4 eggs, *beaten*
290ml (10 fl oz / ½ pt) milk

French Pastry
200g (7 oz) plain flour
85ml (3 fl oz) vegetable oil
85ml (3 fl oz) water
Pinch of salt

METHOD

SERVES 8

Preheat the oven to 180°C / 350°F / gas mark 4

1. Plunge the broccoli florets into salted boiling water and simmer for about 4 minutes until just cooked.
2. **To make the pastry**, put the flour in a bowl, make a well and pour in the oil and water. Mix to combine adding more water or flour, if necessary.
3. Grease and flour a loose-bottomed quiche tin and line with the pastry by kneading into place *(no rolling required).* The thinner the pastry the better, so discard any excess.
4. Arrange the broccoli in the pastry case and scatter the Stilton over.
5. Mix together the eggs and milk, season and pour over the broccoli and Stilton.
6. Bake for about 35 minutes, until the centre is firm and the top golden. *

Smoked Haddock, Asparagus & Gruyere Cheese Quiche

VEGETARIAN

INGREDIENTS £££

Pastry
200g (7 oz) plain **flour**
60g (2¼ oz) lard
60g (2¼ oz) **butter**
Pinch of salt
3 tbsp cold water

½ **egg yolk**, *beaten*

Filling
3 asparagus
1 fillet *(130g / 4¾ oz approx)* smoked **haddock**
Milk, *for cooking the fish in*
180ml (6 fl oz) double **cream**
3 **eggs**, *beaten*
70g (2½ oz) **Gruyere**, *grated*

METHOD

SERVES 6

Preheat the oven to 180°C / 350°F / gas mark 4

1. **To make the pastry**, mix the flour, lard, butter and salt in food processor until it resembles bread crumbs.
2. Empty the mixture into a bowl, add the water *(a small amount at a time)* and kneed into a soft dough *(add more water if needed)*. Rest in the fridge for 30 minutes.
3. Roll out the pastry on a lightly floured surface.
4. Grease, then flour a small loose bottomed tin and line it with the pastry. Trim the edges using the back of a knife.
5. Blind bake the pastry for 25 minutes (put a layer of greaseproof paper over the pastry and weigh it down with rice or baking beans. This prevents the pastry base from ballooning). Remove the rice or baking beans and greaseproof paper and brush the pastry with the beaten egg yolk. Put back into the oven for a further 3-5 minutes until golden.
6. Trim the stalks of the asparagus to remove the woody part and cook in boiling water for approximately 4-5 minutes until tender. Drain, then cool in cold water and chop into bite size pieces.
7. Place the haddock in a frying pan, cover with milk and water *(50% of each)* and poach for 5-7 minutes until haddock is cooked. Allow to cool before draining well and breaking up into pieces to check for bones.
8. Arrange the fish and asparagus on the base of the pastry case.
9. Mix together the cream and eggs, season well and carefully pour into the pastry case.
10. Sprinkle over the cheese and bake for approximately 30-40 minutes until set.

Leek & Blue Cheese Quiche

INGREDIENTS ££

½ egg yolk, *beaten*
10g (½ oz) butter
110g (4 oz) leeks, *finely sliced*
3 eggs
180ml (6 fl oz) double cream
70g (2½ oz) blue cheese

Pastry
200g (7 oz) plain flour
60g (2¼ oz) lard
60g (2¼ oz) butter
Pinch of salt
3 tbsp cold water

METHOD

SERVES 6

Preheat the oven to 160°C/ 325°F/ Gas mark 3

1. **To make the pastry**, mix the flour, lard, butter and salt in food processor until it resembles a bread crumb consistancy.
2. Empty the mixture into a bowl, add the water *(a small amount at a time)* and knead into a soft dough *(add more water if needed)*. Rest in the fridge for 30 minutes.
3. Roll out the pastry on a lightly floured surface.
4. Grease, then flour a small loose bottomed tin and line it with the pastry. Trim the edges using the back of a knife.
5. Blind bake the pastry for 25 minutes *(put a layer of greaseproof paper over the pastry and weigh it down with rice or baking beans. This prevents the pastry base from ballooning)*. Remove the rice or baking beans and greaseproof paper and brush the pastry with the beaten egg yolk. Put the pastry back into the oven for a further 3-5 minutes until golden.
6. Melt the butter in a frying pan and cook the leeks over a gentle heat until soft. Allow to cool slightly.
7. Mix the eggs and cream together and season well.
8. Spread the leeks over the base of the pastry case, pour over the egg mixture and crumble over the cheese.
9. Bake in the oven for 30-40 minutes until set.

Stuffed Portobello Mushrooms with White Bean & Rosemary Purée

VEGETARIAN

INGREDIENTS ££

4 Portobello mushrooms
½ tbsp olive oil

Vegetable Topping
½ tbsp. olive oil
½ red onion, *chopped*
2 tbsp balsamic vinegar
¼ aubergine, *cut into 1 cm (3/8 inch) chunks*
½ small courgette, *cut into 1 cm (3/8 inch) chunks*
4 pieces sun-dried tomatoes, *chopped*
100g (3¾ oz) goats' cheese, *crumbled*

Breadcrumb Topping
½ slice of bread
1 small garlic clove
1 tbsp fresh parsley
15g (½ oz) butter
1 tsp pesto, *for decoration*

White Bean & Rosemary Purée *(optional)*
1 tbsp olive oil
¾ onion, *chopped*
1 garlic clove, *crushed*
1 sprig rosemary, *stalk removed & finely chopped*
1 x 400g tin white beans *(flageolet, cannellini, butter or haricot)*
50ml (2 fl oz) vegetable stock

METHOD

SERVES 4

Preheat the oven to 180°C / 350°F / Gas mark 4

1. Wipe the mushrooms with damp kitchen paper to remove any dirt. Break off the stalks *(you will use them later)* and place the mushrooms *(gill side up)* on a lined baking tray, drizzle with the olive oil, and cook in the oven for 10 minutes.
2. **To make the vegetable topping**, warm the oil in a frying pan and cook the onion over a gentle heat until soft.
3. Add the balsamic vinegar and simmer until all the vinegar has been absorbed, then transfer the onions to a bowl.
4. Add the aubergine and courgettes to the frying pan and cook for about 5 minutes.
5. Dice the mushroom stalks and add them to the pan. Cook until golden in colour then add the vegetables to the bowl of onions.
6. Allow to cool slightly, then gently stir in the tomatoes, goats' cheese and season.
7. **To make the breadcrumb topping**, blend the bread, garlic and parsley in a food processer.
8. To prepare the mushrooms for the topping, drain off the liquid from the baking tray and the mushrooms *(this juice can be kept to flavour a soup)* and spoon over the vegetable mixture.
9. Sprinkle over the breadcrumbs, dot with the butter * and bake in the oven for 10 minutes.
10. **To make the purée**, warm the oil in a small frying pan and cook the onion, garlic and rosemary over a low heat until the onions are soft.
11. Drain the beans and rinse them in cold water.
12. Put all the purée ingredients in a food processor and blend until smooth.
13. Warm, season to taste and serve with the baked mushrooms.

Portobello Mushroom topped with Peas, Cheese & Pine Nuts

INGREDIENTS ££

4 Portobello mushrooms
Rapeseed oil
15g (½ oz) butter
1 small onion, *peeled and finely chopped*
1 garlic clove, *crushed*
150g (5¼ oz) frozen peas
1 tbsp water
175g (6 oz) cream cheese
2 tbsp fresh herbs (parsley, basil and mint), *chopped*
1 tbsp fresh basil, *chopped*
15g (½ oz) pine nuts, *toasted*
½ slice of brown bread, *made into breadcrumbs*
Fresh basil sprig, *to garnish*

METHOD

SERVES 4

Preheat the oven to 180°C / 350°F / Gas Mark 4

1. Wipe the mushrooms with damp kitchen paper to remove any dirt.
2. Remove the stalks *(you will use them later)* and place the mushrooms *(gill side up)* on a baking tray.
3. Season, drizzle with oil and bake in the oven for 15 minutes. Allow to cool slightly.*
4. Melt the butter in a frying pan and start to cook the onions over a gentle heat.
5. Roughly chop the mushroom stalks and add them to the pan, together with the garlic.
6. After 5 minutes add the peas and water, then cook for a further minute. Allow to cool.
7. Mix together the cheese, fresh herbs and pine nuts. Add the mushroom mixture and season.
8. To prepare the mushrooms for the topping, drain off any liquid from the baking tray and from the mushrooms and spoon the mixture onto each mushroom.
9. Sprinkle over the breadcrumbs, drizzle with a little oil * and cook in the oven for 10 minutes, or until the tops are golden.

Nut Roast with Oyster Mushroom Sauce

INGREDIENTS £££

125g (4½ oz) mixed **nuts** (**walnuts**, **almonds**, **hazelnuts**)
50g (2 oz) frozen spinach, *thawed*
¼ onion, *finely chopped*
½ carrot, *grated*
¼ x 400g tinned tomatoes
25g (1 oz) sun-dried tomatoes, *roughly chopped*
½ **egg**, *beaten*
50g (2 oz) **Gruyere cheese**, *grated*
½ tsp fresh sage, *chopped*
¼ tsp fresh mint, *chopped*
¾ tbsp fresh parsley, *chopped*
½ garlic clove, *crushed*
½ vegetable **stock** cube, *crumbled*

Oyster Mushroom Gravy
15g (½ oz) **butter**
125g (4½ oz) oyster mushrooms, *halved*
½ large shallot, *finely chopped*
½ garlic clove, *crushed*
150ml (5 fl oz / ¼ pt) vegetable **stock** *(use one cube)*
1 tbsp **soy sauce**
½ tbsp plain **flour**

For presentation
Creme fraîche
Flat leaf parsley

VEGETARIAN

METHOD

SERVES 5

Preheat the oven to 180°C / 350°F / gas mark 4

1. Put the nuts in the food processor and pulse until finely chopped *(be careful not to over blend and turn them into a powder).*
2. Transfer to a large bowl, season and stir in all the other ingredients.
3. Spoon the mixture into 5 lined mousse rings and bake for 30 minutes *(if making in a loaf tin, grease the tin and bake for one hour).*
4. **To make the gravy**, melt half the butter in a frying pan, add the mushrooms and cook over a gentle heat for approximately 10 minutes, until golden brown. Then remove from the pan and set aside for later.
5. Melt the rest of the butter in the same frying pan, add the shallots and garlic and cook over a gentle heat until soft.
6. Chop three of the cooked mushrooms and mix them with the stock and soy sauce.
7. Sprinkle the flour into the frying pan and stir to make a roux.
8. Stir in the stock and soy mixture, a little at a time until it is all incorporated.
9. Bring to the boil and simmer until it has thickened. Season to taste *

To serve, plate the nut roast, top with the mushrooms, pour the sauce over and top with creme fraîche and parsley.

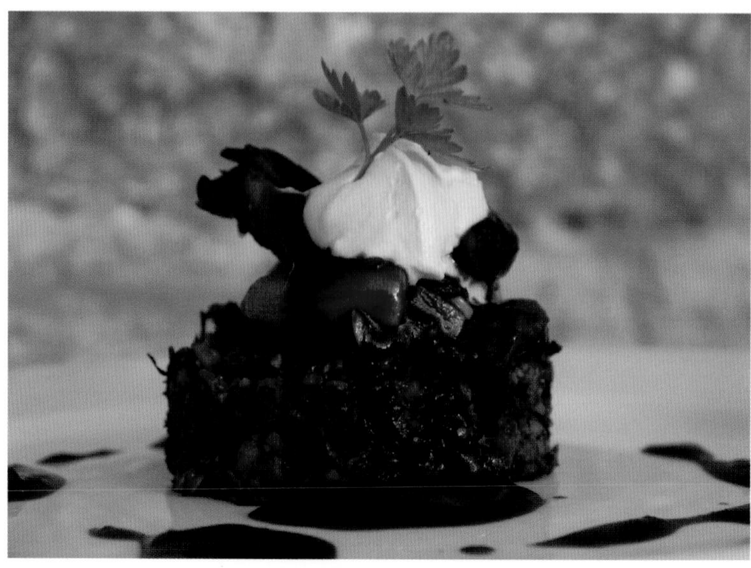

Greek style Halloumi Skewers

VEGETARIAN

INGREDIENTS ££

Marinade
1 tbsp olive oil
2 tbsp lemon juice
1 tsp fresh thyme, *chopped*
1 tsp Dijon **mustard**
1 garlic clove, *crushed*
Pepper, *ground*

250g (9 oz) **halloumi**
2-3 courgettes, *cut into 1-1½ cm (½ inch) chunks*
2 red onions, *peeled and cut into eighths*
16 cherry tomatoes, *halved*

Greek **yoghurt**, *to serve*

METHOD

MAKES 8 SKEWERS

1. Put all the marinade ingredients into a jam jar and shake to combine.
2. Cut the halloumi into cubes about 1-1½ cm (½ inch) in size *(ideally you want 24 squares so that you have 3 per skewer).*
3. Place in a bowl and pour over the marinade. Allow to marinade for at least 1 hour *(stir occasionally to coat the cheese in the marinade).* *
4. Remove the cheese from the marinade *(keep the marinade).*
5. Push the courgette, red onion *(separate out the layers slightly so that they cook),* halloumi and cherry tomatoes onto the skewers and brush with the remaining marinade.
6. Cook on a griddle pan or in the oven:
   a) griddle pan; warm the pan, drizzle with olive oil and cook for approximately 25 minutes, turning the skewers every few minutes and basting with the marinade.
   b) oven; cook for approximately 20 minutes at 180°C / 350°F / gas mark 4. Baste with the marinade half way through cooking.

Serve warm with a dollop of Greek yoghurt.

Baked Onions with Nut Stuffing

INGREDIENTS £

4 large onions

Stuffing
140g (5 oz) long grain rice
1 medium onion, *chopped*
15g (½ oz) **butter**
55g (2 oz) mushrooms, *sliced*
55g (2 oz) **hazelnuts**, *browned in the oven, skinned and roughly chopped*
55g (2 oz) salted **peanuts**, *browned in the oven and roughly chopped*
225g (8 oz) tomatoes, *skinned and roughly chopped*
110g (4 oz) **Cheddar cheese**, *grated*
½ tsp dried basil
¼ tsp dried oregano
1-2 tsp turmeric

METHOD

SERVES 4

Preheat the oven to 180°C / 350°F / gas mark 4

1. Boil the 4 onions in their skins for 45-50 minutes until very tender, then drain and leave to cool.
2. **To make the stuffing**, cook the rice in salted water. When it is cooked, drain and rinse in cold water.
3. Fry the chopped onion in butter until soft, add the mushrooms and cook for a further few minutes.
4. In a bowl, mix together the rice, onion and mushrooms, add all the other ingredients and season to taste.
5. To prepare the onions for stuffing, remove the root of each onion, leaving on the coloured outer skin. Hold each onion on its side and cut through to the centre from tip to root and ease them open for stuffing.
6. Divide the stuffing between the onions, open out the onions and press the stuffing well into the centre. From above, the rice should look like a quarter segment of the onion.
7. Wrap with foil * and bake for about 40 minutes.

Vegetable Profiteroles

INGREDIENTS ££

Choux Pastry
50g (2 oz) butter or margarine
150ml (5 fl oz / ¼ pt) water
70g (2½ oz) plain flour
2 eggs

Filling
1 tbsp vegetable oil
½ onion, *finely diced*
1 garlic clove, *crushed*
80g (2¾ oz) butternut squash, *finely diced*
80g (2¾ oz) courgette, *finely diced*
85g (3 oz) aubergine, *finely diced*
50g (1¾ oz) oyster mushrooms, *chopped*
1 vegetable stock cube
5 tbsp white wine
Fresh basil, *to garnish*

Tomato Sauce
½ tbsp olive oil
½ onion, *chopped*
1 garlic clove, *crushed*
½ a 400g tin of tomatoes
¾ tsp sugar
½ tsp dried basil
½ tsp white wine vinegar

Pesto Dressing
1 tsp pesto
3 tbsp olive oil

METHOD

SERVES 4

Preheat the oven to 200°C / 400°F / gas mark 6

1. **To make the choux pastry** - melt the butter in a saucepan, add the water and bring to the boil.
2. Remove from the heat, add flour and beat with a wooden spoon until the mixture leaves the side of the pan clean *(a little more heat may be needed).*
3. Cool for a minute or two and add the eggs, one at a time beating well.
4. Spoon the mixture onto a greased baking tray *(the mixture should make 4)* and bake for 20-25 minutes until golden.
5. Immediately transfer the profiteroles to a cooling rack and pierce the side of each to allow the steam to escape. *
6. **To make the filling** - heat oil in a sauce pan, add onions, garlic and squash and cook on a low heat until soft.
7. Add the courgettes, aubergine and mushrooms and cook until tender.
8. Crumble in the vegetable stock cube and add the white wine. Cook until reduced and season to taste. *
9. **To make the tomato sauce** - warm the oil in a small saucepan and cook the onion and garlic over a gentle heat until soft.
10. Add the tomatoes, sugar, basil and white wine vinegar, season and simmer for 10 minutes *(add water if it becomes too dry).*
11. Use hand blender to get the sauce to the right consistency *(do not make completely smooth).* Season to taste. *
12. To make the pesto dressing mix the ingredients together.
13. Cut the profiteroles in half and remove the soggy, uncooked batter from the centre. *
14. To serve, warm the sauce and filling. Spoon some tomato sauce on to the plate, place the bottom half of a profiterole on top and fill it with the vegetable mixture, top with the other half and garnish with basil. Drizzle pesto around the plate.

Stuffed Curried Eggs

VEGETARIAN

INGREDIENTS £

8 eggs
4-6 tbsp mayonnaise
½-1 tsp mild Korma curry powder
Chives, *chopped*
Lettuce, *finely sliced*
6 slices of brown bread, *toasted*

METHOD

SERVES 4

1. Put the eggs in a pan of cold water and bring to the boil. Simmer for about 10 minutes.
2. Plunge into cold water * and peel when cool enough to handle.
3. Cut the eggs in half, lengthways. Remove a sliver of egg from the base of each half so that the halves stand up when placed on a plate.
4. Remove the yolks and mash them with the mayonnaise and curry powder. Season to taste and fill each egg with the mixture using a piping bag.

To serve, arrange the lettuce around the outside of the plate. Remove the crust from the toast and cut into small triangles. Use the toast to make a nest in the centre of the plate and place the egg halves in the middle. Decorate with chives.

Spinach Crêpes with Mushrooms

INGREDIENTS ££

Crêpes
1 egg
85g (3 oz) plain flour
150ml (5 fl oz / ¼ pt) milk
30g (1 oz) frozen spinach, *thawed*

Filling
15g (½ oz) butter
285g (10 oz) mushrooms, *thinly sliced*
1 garlic clove, *crushed*
1½ tbsp plain flour
2 tbsp milk
1 tbsp sherry

Topping
55g (2 oz) cheese, *grated*

Vegetable oil

METHOD

SERVES 2

Preheat the oven to 180°C / 350°F / gas mark 4

1. Blend all crêpe ingredients, except the spinach, in a food processor until smooth.
2. Squeeze the water out of the spinach and add it to the food processor *(if the batter is too thick add more milk).*
3. **To cook the crêpes**, warm some vegetable oil in a small frying pan and spoon in a little of the batter, tilting the pan so it covers the base evenly. Cook for a minute or two and then turn to cook the other side *(in-between each crêpe you may need to add a little more oil to the pan. Notice that one side of the crêpe is greener in colour).*
4. **To make the filling**, melt the butter in a pan and cook the mushrooms and the garlic for a few minutes.
5. Stir in the flour and gradually add the milk and sherry, stirring continually to keep the sauce smooth. Season to taste. *
6. Fill crêpes with the mushroom mixture, roll up, making sure the greener side is on the outside and place in a shallow baking dish.
7. Sprinkle with cheese * and bake for 15 minutes. With the left over crêpe mixture you can make Spinach Whirls *(see canapé section).*

Potato Baskets with Oyster Mushrooms, Artichokes & Sun-dried Tomatoes

VEGETARIAN

INGREDIENTS ££

Baskets
400g (14 oz) peeled baking potatoes
1 tbsp fresh rosemary, *chopped*
2 tbsp olive oil

Filling
1 tbsp vegetable oil
100g (3½ oz) tinned artichoke hearts, *drained and sliced*
150g (5¼ oz) oyster mushrooms, *roughly chopped*
50g (2 oz) sun-dried tomatoes, *roughly chopped*
1 garlic clove, *crushed*
8 tsp cranberry sauce or redcurrant jelly
25g (1 oz) Gruyere cheese, *grated*
25g (1 oz) Stilton cheese, *grated*

METHOD

SERVES 8

Preheat the oven to 180°C / 350°F / gas mark 4

1. **To make the baskets**, grease a muffin tin with butter and line 8 wells with greaseproof paper.
2. Coarsely grate the potatoes and squeeze out the liquid. Sandwich the potato between a double layer of kitchen paper and press to thoroughly dry.
3. Put the potato into a bowl, stir in the olive oil, rosemary and season generously with salt and pepper.
4. Line the muffin tin with the potato mixture, pressing it up the sides and into the base to make baskets *(keep the base very thin so that it cooks)*. Cover the whole tray with a layer of greaseproof paper.
5. Bake in the oven for 30-40 minutes until crisp, then remove the paper from the top and allow the baskets to cool in the tray.
6. **To make the filling**, warm the oil in a frying pan, add the artichokes, mushrooms, garlic and tomato and fry over a medium heat for about 5 minutes until the mushrooms are soft. Season to taste.
7. Spoon a teaspoon of cranberry sauce, or redcurrant jelly, into each basket and top with the filling, then sprinkle with the cheese. *
8. Carefully remove the baskets from the tray, peel off the paper, place on a lined baking tray and cook for a further 10-15 minutes.

Red Onion, Courgette & Goats' Cheese Tart

INGREDIENTS ££

1 red onion, *finely sliced*
15g (½ oz) **butter**
1 tsp sugar
Puff pastry
Egg, *to glaze*
1 courgette, *finely sliced*
5 thin slices of **goats' cheese**
Pinch of thyme

METHOD

SERVES 4

Preheat the oven to 180°C / 350°F / gas mark 4

1. Fry the onion in the butter for about 5 minutes. Sprinkle with the sugar and cook for a further 5 minutes.
2. Add the courgettes and continue to cook until they have softened slightly. *
3. Roll out the puff pastry.
4. Using a pastry cutter, cut out a circle about 15 cm (6 inch) in diameter. Using a pastry cutter 2 cm (¾ inch) smaller in diameter, make an imprint in the circle of pastry. *(If you do not have a pastry cutter, cut out a square about 14 x 14 cm / 5½ x 5½ inch and make an imprint using a knife about 1 cm / ½ inch from the edge, being very careful not to cut right through the pastry).*
5. Prick the centre with a fork, brush the outer edge with beaten egg and arrange the onions, courgettes and cheese in the middle *(the outer edge should be left completely clear so that it is free to rise in the oven).* Sprinkle with thyme, season * and bake for about 20-25 minutes until golden.

VEGETARIAN

POTATOES, RICE, PASTA & BREAD

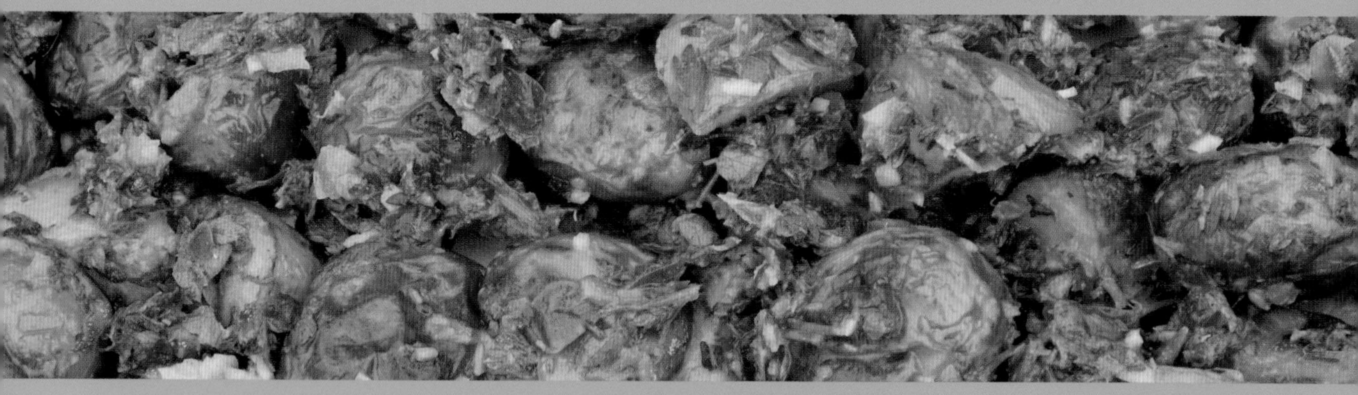

POTATOES, RICE, PASTA & BREAD

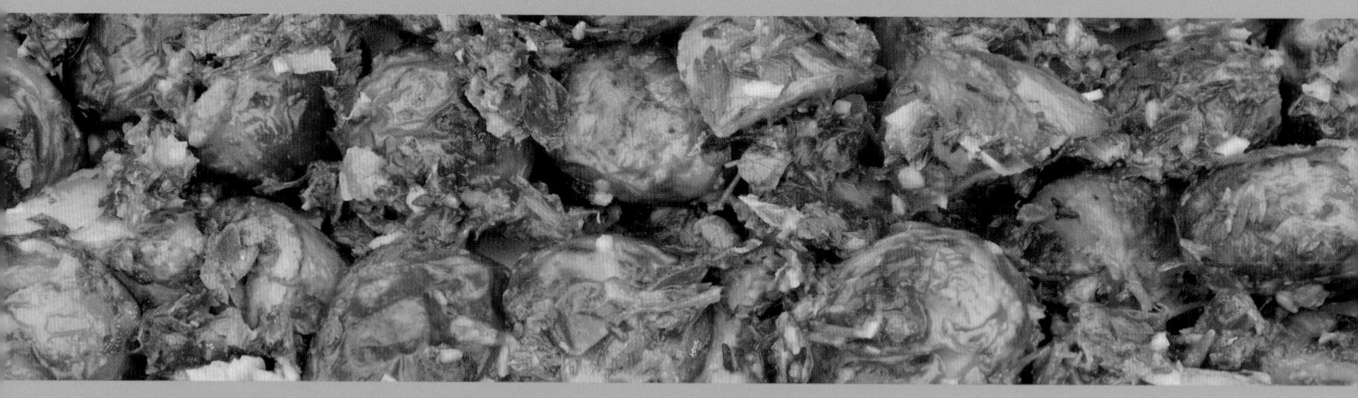

POTATOES, RICE, PASTA & BREAD

POTATOES, RICE, PASTA & BREAD

Buttered New Potatoes with Mint, Parsley & Chives

INGREDIENTS ££

900g (2 lbs) potatoes
Sprig of fresh mint
3 tbsp fresh mixed herbs; parsley, mint & chives, *chopped*
45g (1½ oz) **butter**

METHOD

SERVES 8

1. Put the potatoes, with a sprig of mint, in a saucepan of salted water and bring to the boil. Simmer for approx 25 minutes until cooked. *(To test, stab a potato with a paring knife and if it is cooked it will begin to slide off the knife).*
2. Drain the potatoes and add the butter and chopped herbs to the hot saucepan.
3. Return the potatoes to the saucepan, season and swirl the pan around to coat them in the butter, serve immediately.

Mustard or Garlic Mashed Potato

INGREDIENTS £

900g (2 lbs) peeled potatoes
5 tbsp **cream**
45g (1½ oz) **butter**
2-3 tbsp wholegrain **mustard** or
2-3 garlic cloves, *crushed*

METHOD

SERVES 8

1. Quarter the potatoes and cook for 25 minutes in salted water until very soft.
2. Drain and mash in the saucepan with the butter, cream, wholegrain mustard or crushed garlic *(if using garlic add a little to start with)* plenty of seasoning and taste *(add more garlic if necessary).* *

Dauphinoise Potatoes

POTATOES, RICE, PASTA & BREAD

INGREDIENTS ££

675g (1½ lbs) peeled potatoes
570ml (20 fl oz / 1 pt) double cream
4 tbsp milk
1 garlic clove, *crushed*

METHOD

SERVES 8

Preheat the oven to 180°C / 350°F / gas mark 4

1. Slice the potatoes *(approx 2 mm / 1/8 inch thick).*
2. Rinse the slices and roughly dry with a tea towel.
3. Put all ingredients into a large saucepan adding lots of seasoning and bring to the boil.
4. Transfer the potato mixture to an ovenproof dish keeping the better shaped potato pieces to decorate the top. *(Use a dish that when filled has about 1 cm / 3/8 inch space between the mixture and the top).*
5. Bake for 1 hour. *(If the top starts to brown too quickly cover in foil. If preparing the dish in the morning, bake for 1/2 hour and then reheat when required for 40 minutes).*

The dish retains its heat and remains very hot having left the oven. Extra thick table mats are required to protect your table.

Rösti Potatoes

INGREDIENTS £

900g (2 lbs) peeled potatoes
1 onion
1 **egg**, *beaten*
55g (2 oz) **butter**

METHOD

SERVES 8

1. Peel the onion and grate the onion and potato together in a food processor *(apple can be added if serving with pork).*
2. Add the egg with plenty of seasoning and combine ingredients with your hands.
3. Melt half the butter in a non-stick frying pan and empty the mixture into the pan, pressing down to flatten and compact it.
4. Cover with a light baking tray and cook for about 10 minutes over a low to medium heat, shaking the pan occasionally to prevent it from sticking.
5. Turn the potato *(away from the heat, place the base of a light baking tray over the frying pan and turn the pan holding the tray firmly to it, protecting your hand with an oven cloth).*
6. Melt the remaining butter in the pan, slide the potato back into it and cook for a further 15 minutes, cover to keep the heat in for the first 5 minutes. * *(If the cooked side of the potato is not browned to your liking, cook the other side for a little longer and then turn the potato again to finish).*

This dish can be reheated, either in the frying pan over a low heat *(uncovered)* or, on a baking tray in a preheated oven at 180°C / 350°F / gas mark 4 for about 20-25 minutes.

Hasselback Potatoes

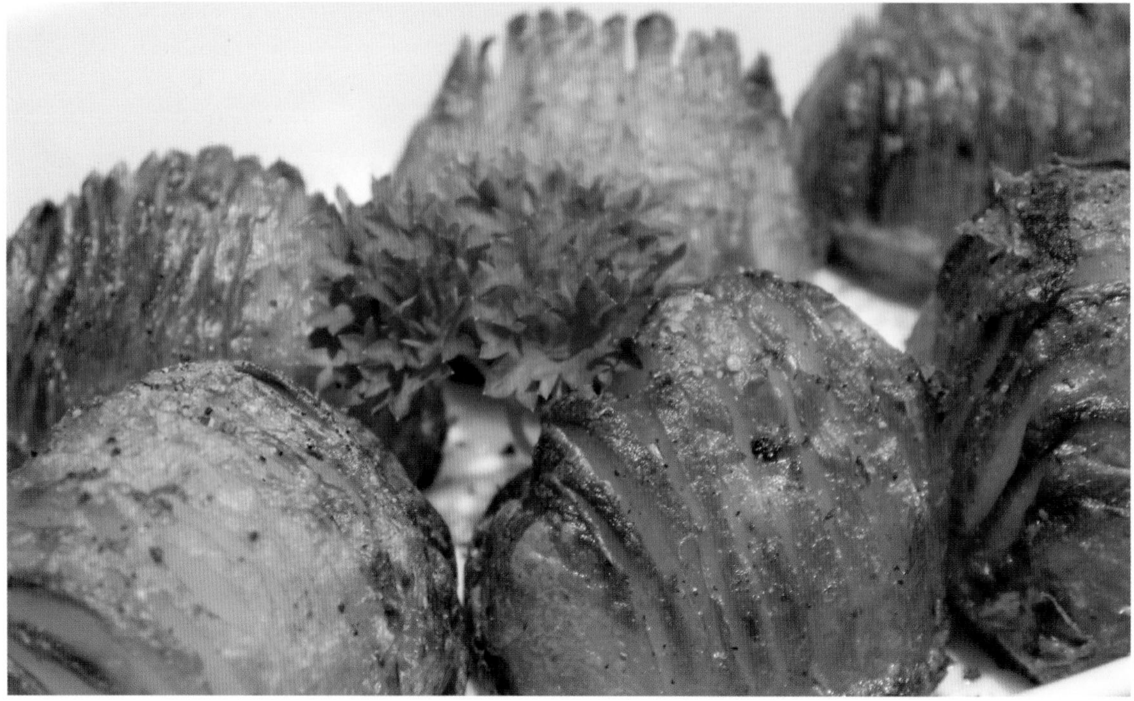

INGREDIENTS £

900g (2 lbs) potatoes
8 tbsp vegetable oil *(goose or duck fat makes tasty potatoes)*

METHOD

SERVES 8

Preheat the oven to 180°C / 350°F / gas mark 4

1. You can peel the potatoes, or leave them with the skins on. Cut them into quarters, place flat side down and slice three quarters of the way down through each potato at approximately 2 mm (1/8 inch) intervals. *(This can be done by placing the potatoes in a gap between two chopping boards and slicing down to the boards).*
2. Bring the potatoes to the boil in salted water * and simmer for 4 minutes.
3. Put the oil in a baking tray and warm in the oven.
4. Drain the potatoes and add to the hot oil, *(take care not to allow water into the tray because it will cause the oil to spit)* season, toss to coat them in fat and bake for 1-1½ hours, turning occasionally until crisp and brown.

Mini Roasties with Rosemary

POTATOES, RICE, PASTA & BREAD

INGREDIENTS £

900g (2 lbs) peeled potatoes
1-2 tsp rosemary *(dried or fresh)*
8 tbsp vegetable oil

METHOD

SERVES 8

Preheat the oven to 180°C / 350°F / gas mark 4

1. Cut the potatoes into small pieces *(approximately 3 cm / 1¼ inch squares).* *
2. Bring the potatoes to the boil in salted water and simmer for 4 minutes.
3. Put the oil in a baking tray and warm in the oven.
4. Drain the potatoes, put them back in the saucepan, cover with a lid and shake vigorously to roughen the edges.
5. Add them to the hot oil *(take care not to allow water into the tray because it will cause the oil to spit),* season, add the rosemary and turn to coat in oil.
6. Bake for an hour, turning occasionally until crisp and brown.

Amandine Potatoes

INGREDIENTS ££

675g (1½ lbs) peeled potatoes
45g (1½ oz) **butter**
1 **egg**, *beaten*
Plain **flour**
35g (1¼ oz) **almonds**, *chopped or flaked (could use* **breadcrumbs** *& chopped parsley)*

METHOD

SERVES 8

Preheat the oven to 180°C / 350°F / gas mark 4

1. Quarter the potatoes and cook for 25 minutes in salted water until very soft.
2. Drain, then mash in the saucepan with the butter and plenty of seasoning, allow to cool.
3. Using two dessert spoons, make small rounded shapes of potato, roll them in flour, then in the beaten egg and finally in the almonds. *
4. Bake on a lined baking tray for 20-30 minutes until golden brown, turning occasionally

Sweet Potato Dauphinoise

INGREDIENTS ££

675g (1½ lbs) peeled sweet potatoes
570ml (20 fl oz / 1 pt) double cream
4 tbsp milk
1 garlic clove, *crushed*

METHOD

SERVES 8

Preheat the oven to 180°C / 350°F / gas mark 4

1. Slice the potatoes *(approx 2 mm / 1/8 inch thick).*
2. Rinse the slices and roughly dry with a tea towel.
3. Put all ingredients into a large saucepan adding lots of seasoning and bring to the boil.
4. Transfer the potato mixture to an ovenproof dish keeping the better shaped potato pieces to decorate the top *(the dish used should allow about 1 cm of clearance between the mixture and the top of the dish, otherwise it will overflow during cooking).*
5. Bake for 1 hour. *(If the top starts to brown too quickly cover in foil). If preparing the dish in the morning, bake for 1/2 hour and then reheat for 30 minutes when required.*

The dish retains its heat and remains very hot having left the oven. Extra thick tablemats are required to protect your table.

Sautéed Potatoes

INGREDIENTS £

900g (2 lbs) peeled potatoes
55g (2 oz) butter

METHOD

SERVES 8

1. Cut the potatoes into small pieces *(approx 3 cm / 1¼ inch squares).*
2. Bring to the boil in salted water and simmer for 4 minutes.
3. Drain the potatoes and put back in the saucepan, replace the lid and shake vigorously to roughen the edges.
4. Melt the butter in a large frying pan and fry the potatoes with lots of salt, stirring occasionally until golden brown *(for about 25 minutes).* *

Potato Wedges

INGREDIENTS £

900g (2 lbs) potatoes
8 tbsp olive oil *(approx)*

METHOD

SERVES 8

Preheat the oven to 180°C / 350°F / gas mark 4

1. Cut the potatoes into wedges, place in a saucepan of salted water, * bring to the boil and simmer for 5 minutes.
2. Put the oil in a baking tray and warm in the oven.
3. Drain the potatoes and add them to the hot oil *(take care not to allow water into the tray because it will cause the oil to spit),* season and turn to coat in oil.
4. Bake for about 1-1¼ hours, turning occasionally until crisp and brown.

Horseradish Potatoes

INGREDIENTS ££

1 kg (2 lb 4 oz) new potatoes, *cut into bite size chunks*
3 tbsp **horseradish sauce**
3 tbsp **soured cream**
3 tbsp fresh chives, *finely chopped*
2 tbsp rapeseed oil

METHOD

SERVES 8

1. Put the potatoes in a saucepan of salted water, bring to the boil and simmer for 20 minutes.
2. Mix together the horseradish, soured cream and chives.
3. Drain the potatoes really well.
4. Warm the oil in a frying pan and fry the potatoes for approximately 5 minutes until golden brown.*
5. Stir in the horseradish mixture and serve immediately.

Byron Potatoes

INGREDIENTS ££

900g (2 lbs) peeled potatoes
45g (1½ oz) **butter**
110ml (4 fl oz) double **cream**
Pinch of ground nutmeg
150g (5¼ oz) **cheese**, *grated*

METHOD

SERVES 8

Preheat the oven to 180°C / 350°F / gas mark 4

1. Quarter the potatoes and cook for 25 minutes in salted water until very soft.
2. Drain, then mash in the saucepan with the butter, just over half the cream, a pinch of nutmeg and plenty of seasoning.
3. Transfer the potato to a greased ovenproof dish and smooth over the top.
4. Make wells in the potato with a spoon and pour in remaining cream.
5. Cover with cheese * and bake for 15-20 minutes. *(If heating from cold, bake for 30-45 minutes, keeping an eye on the top. If the cheese browns too quickly cover with foil).*

Spicy Roasted Sweet Potatoes & Carrots

INGREDIENTS £

¼ tsp coriander seeds
¼ tsp fennel seeds
2 garlic cloves, *peeled*
Pinch of salt
1 tsp ground cumin
2 tbsp olive oil
4 carrots, *peeled and chopped into approx 2 cm chunks*
3 sweet potatoes, *peeled, halved lengthways and cut into 1 cm slices*

METHOD

SERVES 8

Preheat the oven to 180ºC / 350ºF / gas mark 4

1. Gently dry fry the coriander and fennel seeds in a small frying pan for about 1-2 minutes until you can really smell their aroma.
2. Meanwhile, place the garlic and a pinch of salt in a pestle and mortar and crush into a paste.
3. Add the coriander seeds, fennel seeds, cumin and some black pepper to the garlic and crush together.
4. Put the carrots and sweet potatoes on a baking tray, sprinkle the spice mixture over and toss in the oil.
5. Bake for 40-60 minutes until tender and golden in colour.

Hot Potato Wedges

INGREDIENTS £

900g (2 lbs) potatoes
8 tbsp olive oil
½ tsp chilli powder

METHOD

SERVES 8

Preheat the oven to 180°C / 350°F / gas mark 4

1. Cut the potatoes into wedges, place in a saucepan of salted water, * bring to the boil and simmer for 5 minutes.
2. Warm the oil in a lined baking tray.
3. Drain the potatoes and add them to the hot oil *(take care not to allow water into the tray because it will cause the oil to spit),* sprinkle over the chilli powder, season and turn to coat in oil.
4. Bake for about 1-1½ hours, turning occasionally, until crisp and brown.

Sweet Potato Purée

INGREDIENTS ££

900g (2 lbs) peeled sweet potatoes
45g (1½ oz) **butter**

METHOD

SERVES 8

1. Cut the potatoes into small pieces and cook for 25 minutes in salted water until very soft.
2. Drain and mash in the saucepan with the butter and plenty of seasoning. *

Baked Mustard or Garlic Mashed Potato

INGREDIENTS £

900g (2 lbs) peeled potatoes
5 tbsp cream
45g (1½ oz) butter
2-3 tbsp wholegrain mustard
or 2-3 garlic cloves, *crushed*

METHOD

SERVES 8

Preheat the oven to 180°C / 350°F / gas mark 4

1. Quarter the potatoes and cook for 25 minutes in salted water until very soft.
2. Drain and mash in the saucepan with the butter, cream, wholegrain mustard or crushed garlic and plenty of seasoning.
3. Put in an ovenproof serving dish, fork the top * and bake for 40 minutes until golden brown on top.

Sun-Dried Tomato & Chive Mashed Potato

INGREDIENTS ££

900g (2 lbs) peeled potatoes
6 tbsp milk
45g (1½ oz) butter
2 tbsp tomato purée
6 pieces of sun-dried tomatoes, *finely chopped*
Fresh chives, *finely chopped*

METHOD

SERVES 8

1. Quarter the potatoes and cook for 25 minutes in salted water until very soft.
2. Drain the potatoes and mash in the saucepan with the milk, butter and tomato purée.
3. Stir in the sun-dried tomatoes and plenty of seasoning. * Stir in the chives just before serving.

Boulangere Potatoes

INGREDIENTS £

30g (1 oz) butter
675g (1½ lb) peeled potatoes
1 onion, *thinly sliced*
290ml (10 fl oz / ½ pt) vegetable stock (use 1 cube)

METHOD

SERVES 8

Preheat the oven to 180°C / 350°F / gas mark 4

1. Use half of the butter to grease the inside of an ovenproof baking dish.
2. Slice the potatoes in a food processer using the fat blade so that the potatoes are about ½ cm (3/16 inch) thick.
3. Arrange the potatoes in layers putting the onion and seasoning between the layers *(do not add much salt as the stock is salty).*
4. Pour over the stock and dot with the remaining butter.
5. Press the potatoes down firmly *(they should be fully submerged in the stock).*
6. Cover the top in foil and bake for 45 minutes, then remove the foil and bake for a further 45 minutes. *

Roasted New Potatoes with Red Onion & Rosemary

INGREDIENTS ££

900g (2 lbs) new potatoes
2 red onions, *divided into 8ths*
Rosemary *(dried or fresh)*
4-5 tbsp olive oil

METHOD

SERVES 8

Preheat the oven to 180°C / 350°F / gas mark 4

1. Quarter the potatoes and put them in to a saucepan of salted water. Bring to the boil and simmer for 4 minutes.
2. Drain the potatoes and transfer them to a lined baking tray. Scatter over the red onion, rosemary, olive oil, season and bake for 1 hour, turning occasionally.

Duchesse Potatoes

INGREDIENTS £

675g (1½ lbs) peeled potatoes
30g (1 oz) butter
1 egg yolk
2 tbsp cream

METHOD

SERVES 8

Preheat the oven to 180°C / 350°F / gas mark 4

1. Quarter the potatoes and cook for 25 minutes in salted water until very soft.
2. Drain and mash in the saucepan with the butter, egg yolk, cream and plenty of seasoning. *
3. Use a piping bag with a star shaped nozzle and pipe "Walnut Whip" shaped mounds on to a greased baking tray.
4. Bake for 20-25 minutes until golden brown.

Sage & Onion Mashed Potato

INGREDIENTS £

900g (2 lbs) peeled potatoes
45g (1½ oz) **butter**
2 onions, *finely chopped*
2 tbsp **milk**
2 tbsp fresh sage leaves, *chopped*

METHOD

SERVES 8

1. Quarter the potatoes and cook for 25 minutes in salted water until very soft.
2. Warm the butter in a frying pan and cook the onion over a very low heat until soft.
3. Drain the potatoes and mash in the saucepan with the milk.
4. Stir in the onion and plenty of seasoning. * Stir in the sage leaves just before serving.

Crushed Mint Potatoes with Broad Beans & Peas

INGREDIENTS ££

500g (1 lb 2 oz) new potatoes
Sprigs of mint
200g (7 oz) frozen broad beans, *defrosted*
200g (7 oz) peas, *defrosted*
15g (½ oz) **butter**

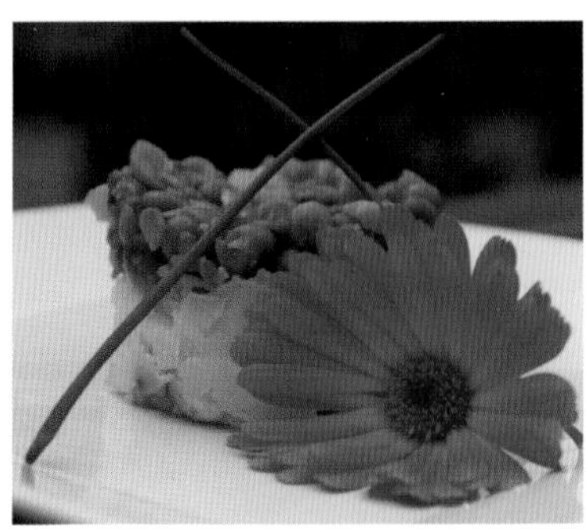

METHOD

SERVES 8

1. Quarter the potatoes and put them in to a saucepan of salted water with a sprig of mint. Bring to the boil and simmer for approximately 25 minutes until cooked *(to test, stab a potato with a paring knife and if it is cooked the potato will begin to slide off the knife).*
2. Meanwhile, skin the beans by squeezing the bean to remove it from the shell *(discard the skins).*
3. Drain the potatoes and then break up with a fork. Season and add the butter.
4. Put 8 lined mousse rings on a lined baking tray and spoon the potato into the rings. Press in place, cover with foil and keep warm in the oven.
5. Melt the butter in a frying pan and sauté the peas and beans for a few minutes until cooked. Season to taste and gently break up with a fork.
6. Place the potato and mousse ring on the plate, top with the peas and beans and remove the ring.

Apple & Potato Rösti

INGREDIENTS ££

510g (1 lb 2 oz) potatoes, *peeled*
2 onions, *peeled*
2 apples, *peeled and cored*
2 tbsp plain **flour**
2 **eggs**, *beaten*
55g (2 oz) **butter**

METHOD

SERVES 8

Preheat the oven to 180°C / 350°F / gas mark 4

1. Grate the potato, onion and apple in the food processor *(use the fat grating disc)*.
2. Empty into a bowl and mix together using your hands, squeezing out any excess liquid.
3. Sprinkle the flour over the potato, add the egg, season generously and mix together.
4. Shape into 8 even size patties *(fat burger shapes)*.
5. Melt half the butter in a frying pan over a low heat and gently fry the patties until golden, adding the rest of the butter to brown the other side.
6. Place on a lined baking tray * and bake in the oven for 20-25 minutes.

Crushed New Potatoes with Mint, Parsley & Chives

INGREDIENTS ££

900g (2 lbs) new potatoes
Sprig of fresh mint
45g (1½ oz) **butter**
3 tbsp fresh mixed herbs; parsley, mint & chives, *chopped*

METHOD

SERVES 8

1. Put the potatoes, with a sprig of mint, in a saucepan of salted water and bring to the boil. Simmer for approximately 25 minutes until cooked *(to test, stab a potato with a paring knife and if it is cooked the potato will begin to slide off the knife).*
2. Drain the potatoes, then transfer them back to the saucepan. Add the butter, season and using a potato masher gently break up the potatoes *(do not mash them, you only want to break them up a little).*
3. Transfer the potatoes to a warm serving dish, sprinkle over the chopped herbs and serve immediately.

Jacob's Jackets

INGREDIENTS £

900g (2 lbs) potatoes
75ml (2½ fl oz) **crème fraîche**
1½ tbsp fresh chives, *chopped*
2 tbsp olive oil

METHOD

SERVES 8

Preheat the oven to 180°C / 350°F / gas mark 4

1. Put the oil in a baking tray and warm in the oven.
2. Cut the potatoes in half, place flat side down and cut a cross in the top, cutting almost half way through the flesh.
3. Add them to the hot oil and turn so they get coated in oil, ensuring they all finish up flat side down.
4. Season with salt and bake for about 1–1¼ hours until the potatoes are soft and the skins crisp.
5. Mix the chives and crème fraîche.
6. To serve the potatoes, squeeze them open and dollop a spoonful of crème fraîche and chives on top.

Potato & Celeriac Quenelles

INGREDIENTS ££

½ celeriac (225g / 8 oz), *peeled and diced*
2 tsp lemon juice
500g (16 oz) potatoes, *peeled and quartered*
30g (1 oz) butter
2 tsp horseradish sauce
1 egg yolk
30g (1 oz) butter, *melted to glaze*

METHOD

SERVES 8

Preheat the oven to 180°C / 350°F / gas mark 4

1. Put the celeriac and lemon juice in a saucepan, cover with cold water, bring to the boil and simmer until tender *(approximately 25 minutes).* Drain, put back in the saucepan and allow to cool slightly.
2. Cook the potatoes in salted water until very tender. Drain and allow to cool slightly.
3. Add the butter, horseradish and plenty of seasoning to the potatoes and mash until smooth.
4. Purée the celeriac using a hand blender and stir into the potato with the egg yolk and allow to cool completely.
5. Shape the mash into 24 quenelles using a dessert spoon and place on a lined baking tray.*
6. Brush with melted butter and bake in the oven for 25-30 minutes until golden.

Baby New Potatoes with Salsa Verde

INGREDIENTS

Salsa Verde
7g (¼ oz) fresh mint, *coarsely chopped*
20g (¾ oz) fresh parsley, *coarsely chopped*
7g (¼ oz) fresh thyme leaves
2 garlic cloves, *crushed*
2 tsp Dijon **mustard**
1 lemon, *juiced*
2 tbsp olive oil
½ tsp of sugar

Potatoes
900g (2 lb) baby new potatoes
2 garlic cloves, *crushed*
4 tbsp olive oil

METHOD

SERVES 8

Preheat the oven to 180°C / 350°F / gas mark 4

1. Cut the potatoes in half or into quarters, so that they are all similar size.
2. Put them in a saucepan of salted water, bring to the boil and simmer for 4 minutes, then drain.
3. Return the potatoes to the pan, add the garlic and olive oil and mix together. Transfer to a lined baking tray and cook for about 25-30 minutes until cooked.
4. **To make the salsa verde,** blend all the ingredients in a food processor *(only to combine, not to make into a purée).*
5. When the potatoes are cooked, toss them in the salsa verde and serve immediately.

Tommy Tatties

INGREDIENTS ££

1 kg (2 lb 4 oz) new potatoes
6 tbsp rapeseed oil
2 tsp turmeric
2 tbsp black onion seeds or poppy seeds
2 tsp honey *(optional)*
4 tomatoes, *finely diced*
6 tbsp fresh coriander, *chopped*

METHOD

Serves 8

1. Cut the potatoes into quarters and cook in salted water until cooked. Drain well. *
2. Warm the rapeseed oil in a large frying pan and fry the potatoes until golden. *
3. Sprinkle over the turmeric and onion or poppy seeds and cook for a further 4-5 minutes then stir in the honey.
4. Stir in the tomatoes and cook for a further 2-3 minutes.
5. Season to taste, stir in the coriander and serve immediately.

Evelyn's Couscous Salad

INGREDIENTS ££

500ml (17½ fl oz) chicken **stock**
280g (10 oz) **couscous**
4 tbsp vegetable oil
2 red onions, *finely chopped*
1 red pepper, *finely chopped*
1 yellow pepper, *finely chopped*
1 courgette, *finely chopped*
2 garlic cloves, *crushed*
1 lemon, *juiced*
3-4 tomatoes, *deseeded and finely chopped*
2 Pepperdews (optional), *finely chopped*
2 tbsp fresh mint, *chopped*
200g (7 oz) **feta cheese**, *cubed*

METHOD

SERVES 8

1. Pour boiling stock over the couscous, season, stir with a fork and leave for about 5 minutes until all the liquid has been absorbed. Leave to cool.
2. Warm the vegetable oil in a frying pan and cook the red onion until soft.
3. Add the peppers, courgette, garlic and seasoning and cook for a further 5 minutes.
4. Add to the couscous with all the other ingredients and season to taste. *

Can be served hot or cold.

Tabbouleh Salad

POTATOES, RICE, PASTA & BREAD

INGREDIENTS

70g (2½ oz) couscous or bulgur wheat
Vegetable stock - 125ml (4½ fl oz) if using couscous or 170ml (6 fl oz) if using bulgur wheat
15g (½ oz) fresh flat leaf parsley, *chopped*
15g (½ oz) fresh mint, *chopped*
100g (3½ oz) tomatoes, *deseeded and finely chopped*
1-2 spring onions, *finely sliced*
1 tbsp lemon juice
1½ tbsp olive oil
15g (½ oz) pine nuts, *toasted*

METHOD

SERVES 8

1. **If using couscous;** put the couscous into a bowl and pour over the boiling stock. Season, stir with a fork and leave to cool for about 5 minutes until all the liquid has been absorbed.

   If using bulgur wheat; put the bulgur wheat and stock in a saucepan, bring to the boil, cover and simmer for about 12 minutes, or until the liquid has been absorbed.

2. Mix together the parsley, mint, tomatoes, spring onions, lemon juice and olive oil.

3. Stir in the couscous or bulgur wheat and pine nuts, season and serve.

Basmati Onion Rice

INGREDIENTS £

55g (2 oz) butter
1 shallot, *diced*
570ml (20 fl oz / 1 pt) basmati rice *(measured in volume rather than weight)*
1 chicken stock cube
1.1 L (40 fl oz / 2 pts) boiling water

METHOD

SERVES 8

1. Melt the butter in a large saucepan, add the shallots, cook for a couple of minutes and then stir in the rice.
2. Break up the stock cube, add it to the rice with some salt and pour the boiling water into the pan. Bring to the boil, cover with a lid and simmer gently for 15 minutes, then test the rice to see if it is cooked to your liking. *(Check the rice packet for guidelines on cooking time).*
3. Drain, pour over boiling water *(to wash away the starch)* and serve.

Boiled Rice

INGREDIENTS £

570ml (20 fl oz / 1 pt) long grain rice *(measured in volume rather than weight) (½ a cup of rice per person)*
1 L (40 fl oz / 2 pts) boiling water

METHOD

SERVES 8

1. Pour the boiling water into a pan, add the rice and a good pinch of salt and bring to the boil.
2. Cover with a lid and simmer gently for 10 minutes, then taste the rice to see if it is cooked to your liking. *(Check the rice packet for guidelines on cooking time).*
3. Drain, pour over boiling water *(to wash away the starch)* and serve.

Bulgur Wheat with Lemon & Thyme / Parsley

POTATOES, RICE, PASTA & BREAD

INGREDIENTS £

300g (11 oz) **bulgur wheat**
900ml (30 fl oz / 1½ pts) chicken **stock**
5 tbsp fresh parsley, *chopped*

METHOD

SERVES 8

1. Put the bulgur wheat into a large saucepan and pour over the stock.
2. Season and cook over a low heat until it is tender *(approx 12 minutes),* stirring regularly so that it does not stick to the bottom of the saucepan *(add more water if necessary).*
3. Just before serving stir in the parsley and season to taste.

Variation: instead of adding parsley, add the zest of 1½ lemons and ¾ tbsp fresh thyme.

Three Grain or Long Grain Rice with Fennel Seeds

INGREDIENTS £

340g (12 oz) three grain rice *(or long grain rice)*
2 tsp fennel seeds

METHOD

SERVES 8

1. Put the rice, fennel seeds and a good pinch of salt into a large saucepan. Pour over boiling water, bring to the boil, cover and simmer gently for approx 25 minutes *(half way through cooking check to see there is enough water in the saucepan as the rice will absorb lots of water),* test the rice to see if it is cooked to your liking *(check the rice packet for guidelines on cooking time).*
2. Drain, pour over boiling water *(to wash away the starch)* and serve.

Pasta

INGREDIENTS £

100g (3½ oz) **pasta**
Vegetable oil
Knob of **butter**

METHOD

SERVES 1

1. Fill a pan with boiling water from the kettle, add a good pinch of salt and a few drops of oil *(the oil prevents the pasta from sticking together).*
2. Add the pasta and cook for the length of time recommended on the back of the packet *(you often have to cook it for longer!).*
3. When the pasta is cooked drain it in a colander and pour over boiling water.
4. Return the pasta to the pan, add a knob of butter and stir to coat the pasta in butter *(to prevent it from sticking together on the plate).*

Yorkshire Puddings

INGREDIENTS £

85g (3 oz) plain **flour**
1½ **eggs**
225ml (7½ fl oz) **milk**
Salt
Lard

METHOD

SERVES 8

Preheat the oven to 210°C / 410°F / gas mark 6-7

1. Beat the flour, egg, and milk in a bowl, add a pinch of salt and leave to stand for 1 hour. *
2. Coat each well of a muffin tin with a little lard and put the tin in the oven to warm for about 5 minutes.
3. Remove the tin from the oven. Transfer the batter mix into a jug and pour a little of the mixture into each well *(the mixture should not come more than half way up the sides of each well, otherwise they will be too big)*.
4. Bake for 12-15 minutes until golden and then transfer onto a cooling rack. *

Oriental Soba Noodle Salad

INGREDIENTS £

Salad
85g (3 oz) soba noodles
1 large carrot, *grated*
½ large courgette, *deseeded and grated*
¼ large cucumber, *deseeded and grated*
½ chilli, *deseeded and very thinly sliced into long strips*
15g (½ oz) fresh coriander, *including stalks, finely chopped*
7g (¼ oz) fresh ginger, *thinly sliced*
½ tbsp peanut butter or finely chopped roasted peanuts, *(optional)*

Dressing
2 tbsp rapeseed oil
1 tbsp soy sauce
1 tbsp rice wine vinegar
½ garlic clove, *crushed*
½ tbsp fish sauce
½ tbsp sesame seeds, *toasted*
½ tsp sesame seed oil

METHOD

SERVES 8

1. **To make the dressing** put all the ingredients in a jar, season and shake to combine. Leave to infuse for an hour. *
2. Plunge the noodles into a pan of boiling water and cook for about 7 minutes. Drain then refresh in cold water to stop them from cooking any further.
3. In a large bowl mix together the carrot, courgette, cucumber, chilli, coriander, ginger and peanut butter / roasted peanuts. *
4. Add the dressing, stir in the noodles and serve immediately.

Serve cold with citrus marinated salmon.

Cheese Polenta

INGREDIENTS ££

255g (9 oz) polenta
1¼ tsp salt
750ml (26 fl oz) boiling water
170g (6 oz) Cheddar cheese, *grated*
30g (1 oz) Parmesan, *grated*

METHOD

SERVES 8

1. Put the polenta and salt in a saucepan and pour over the boiling water.
2. Cook for about 10 minutes, stirring regularly *(so that it does not stick to the bottom of the saucepan)* until it reaches a mash consistency.
3. Stir in the Cheddar and Parmesan, season to taste and serve immediately.

Fig & Walnut Bread

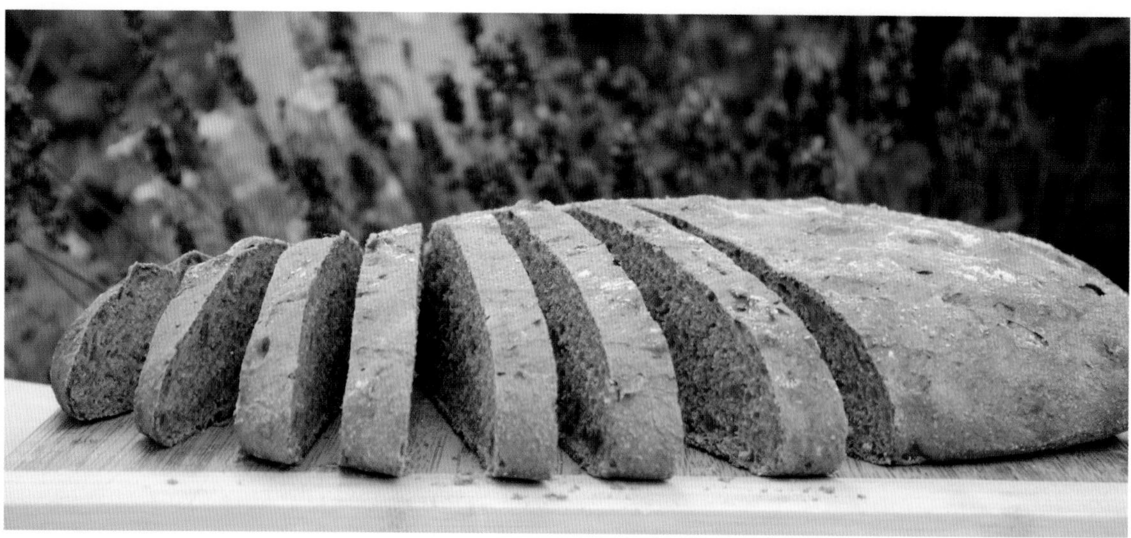

INGREDIENTS

2 tsp dried **yeast**
Tepid water
100g (3½ oz) **dried figs**, *chopped*
50g (1¾ oz) **walnuts**, *chopped*
4 tbsp orange juice
500g (1 lb 2 oz) wholegrain spelt **flour**
1 tsp sugar
1 tsp salt
1 tbsp olive oil

METHOD

1. Mix together the yeast and 3 tbsp of tepid water and leave for 15 minutes.
2. Put the figs, walnuts and orange juice into a bowl, stir to coat the fruit in the juice and set aside until you need it.
3. Mix together the flour, sugar and salt in a large bowl and then stir in the yeast and 300ml (10½ fl oz) of tepid water. While the mix is still lumpy, add the oil and knead for a few minutes until smooth and pliable. *Kneading – using the heel of one hand, push out from the middle of the dough (pulling down with the other hand) and then with clenched knuckles fold the outside edge into the middle. Give it a quarter turn and repeat the process.*
4. Leave the dough to prove for 30 minutes in a bowl covered with a tea towel.
5. Turn the dough out onto a floured surface, add the soaked figs and walnuts and knead firmly for a few minutes.
6. Shape the dough in to a round and place on a lined baking tray.
7. Cover and leave to prove in a warm place for a further 40 minutes.
8. Bake in a preheated oven (200°C / 400° F / gas mark 6) for 45-50 minutes *(when it is cooked, it will sound hollow when tapped on the base).*

Bread

INGREDIENTS £

1kg (2 lbs 4 oz) strong white plain flour *(or ½ white ½ wholemeal / granary)*
21g (¾ oz) dried yeast
2 tbsp caster sugar
1 tbsp salt
Olive oil
570ml (20 fl oz / 1 pt) tepid water, *approx*

METHOD

1. Put all dry ingredients into a large bowl, make a well in the centre and pour in the water. Combine and then knead until firm and elastic. *Kneading – using the heel of one hand, push out from the middle of the dough (pulling down with the other hand) and then with clenched knuckles fold the outside edge into the middle. Give it a quarter turn and repeat the process.*
2. Scrape the bowl clean, place the dough in the bowl, score the top, brush with oil, cover in cling film and leave in a warm place until risen to twice its size *(approx 1 hour).*
3. "Knock down" the dough and knead into shape *(buns or a loaf).*
4. Brush with olive oil and leave to prove for 1 hour.
5. Bake in a preheated oven (180°C / 350°F / gas mark 4) for approximately 35 minutes until cooked *(cooking time depends on whether you have made buns or a loaf. When it is cooked, it will sound hollow when tapped on the base).*

Variations: add any of the following to the dough at stage 1; rosemary, sage, olives, raisins, garlic, tomatoes, nuts, poppy seeds, sesame seeds, pumpkin seeds, sunflower seeds, onion, cheese.

Focaccia (Italian Bread)

INGREDIENTS ££

Bread
7g (¼ oz) dried yeast
15g (½ oz) sugar
290ml (10 fl oz / ½ pt) tepid water
250g (9 oz) strong flour
250g (9 oz) plain flour
1 tsp salt

Red onion topping
2 red onions, *chopped*
2 garlic cloves, *crushed*
2 tbsp olive oil
2 tbsp red wine vinegar

Sun-dried tomato topping
2 pieces of sun-dried tomatoes, *chopped*
½ tsp dried basil
2 tbsp olive oil
30g (1 oz) cheese, *grated*

Olive topping
2 tbsp black or green olives, *sliced*
1 tsp fresh rosemary
2 tbsp olive oil

METHOD

Preheat the oven to 200°C / 400°F / gas mark 6

1. Dissolve the yeast and sugar in half the tepid water.
2. Put the flours and salt in a large mixing bowl, make a well in the centre and pour in the yeast mixture. Combine the mixture, adding the remaining water to make a dough *(if you need to, add water or flour to get the correct dough consistency).*
3. Transfer the dough on to a floured surface and knead for 5 minutes until firm and elastic. *Kneading – using the heel of one hand, push out from the middle of the dough (pulling down with the other hand) and then with clenched knuckles fold the outside edge into the middle. Give it a quarter turn and repeat the process.*
4. Scrape the bowl clean. Place the dough in the bowl, score the top, brush with oil, cover in cling film and leave in a warm place until it has risen to twice its size *(approx 1 hour).*
5. "Knock down" the dough and knead for about a minute, then shape into a rectangle slightly smaller than an A4 sheet of paper *(so that the dough is about 1½ cm / ½ inch thick).* Place on a lined baking tray.
6. To make the red onion topping, fry the onion and garlic in the olive oil until soft. Add the vinegar and simmer to reduce the liquid. To prepare the sun-dried tomato topping, combine the tomatoes, basil and oil, sprinkle over the bread and top with cheese.
7. Sprinkle over your chosen topping and, using your fingers, push some of the topping down into the bread.
8. Leave to prove for 45 minutes and then carefully place in the oven. Bake for 15-20 minutes.
9. Drizzle with olive oil, salt and pepper and serve warm.

Cranberry and Pine Nut Soda Bread

INGREDIENTS £££

½ lemon, *juiced*
290ml (½ pt / 10 fl oz) whole **milk**
340g (12 oz) plain wholemeal **flour**
50g (1¾ oz) **dried cranberries**, *roughly chopped*
50g (1¾ oz) **pine nuts**
¾ tsp bicarbonate of soda
¾ tsp salt

METHOD

Preheat the oven to 200°C / 400°F / gas mark 6

1. Put the lemon juice into a measuring jug and add milk to make it up to 290ml (10 fl oz / ½ pt) of liquid *(this makes sour milk)*.
2. Mix together the dry ingredients in a large bowl.
3. Make a well in the centre and pour in the milk. Mix together to make a soft dough.
4. Transfer the mixture on to a floured surface and roll it into a ball.
5. Place on a lined baking tray and flatten the dough slightly. Using a knife cut a cross into the top of the bread mix.
6. Bake for 30 minutes then remove from the oven. Wrap the bread in a damp tea towel and leave to cool.

Louis' Best Bread

INGREDIENTS

300g (11 oz) very strong Canadian wholemeal flour or white Spelt flour
½ tbsp brown sugar
14g (½ oz) dried yeast
1 tsp of salt
15g (½ oz) sesame seeds, plus a few extra for the top
15g (½ oz) poppy seeds, plus a few extra for the top
200ml (7 fl oz) tepid water
½ tbsp clear honey
½ tbsp sunflower oil

METHOD

1. Mix all the dry ingredients together, make a well in the centre and pour in the water, honey and oil.
2. Mix together then turn out onto a floured surface. Knead for 5-10 minutes, until smooth and elastic. *Kneading – using the heel of one hand, push out from the middle of the dough (pulling down with the other hand) and then with clenched knuckles fold the outside edge into the middle. Give it a quarter turn and repeat the process.*
3. Place on a baking tray, cut a small cross on the top and sprinkle over some poppy and sesame seeds.
4. Cover with lightly greased cling film and leave in a warm place for 1 hour to prove.
5. Preheat the oven to 220°C / 425°F / gas mark 7 and bake for 35 minutes *(cooking time depends on whether you have made buns or a loaf. When it is cooked, it will sound hollow when tapped on the base).*

Brioche Bread

INGREDIENTS £ £

300g (10½ oz) plain flour
14g (½ oz) dried yeast
¼ tsp salt
50g (2 oz) sugar
170g (6 oz) soft unsalted butter
4 eggs

Glaze
1 egg, *beaten*
2 tsp water
50g (2 oz) icing sugar

METHOD

SERVES 8

Preheat the oven to 180°C / 350°F / gas mark 4

1. Put the flour, yeast, salt and sugar into a bowl, add the butter and rub together in your fingertips until it resembles breadcrumbs *(you can do this stage in the food processor).*
2. Add the eggs and stir using a fork to combine together.
3. Turn out onto a floured surface and knead for 10 minutes. You will need to keep adding flour to stop it sticking. The longer you knead it, the less sticky it will become. *Kneading - using the heel of one hand, push out from the middle of the dough (pulling down with the other hand) and then with clenched knuckles fold the outside edge into the middle. Give it a quarter turn and repeat the process.*
4. Put the dough into a clean bowl, cover with cling film and leave in a warm place to prove for 2 hours, or until doubled in size. *
5. Knock the dough down and shape. Here are two suggestions for shaping the bread:

   Method 1: *Braid*: divide the dough into 3 equal-sized balls and roll each ball into a 25 cm (10 inch) long rope. Join one end of each rope together and plait, turning the ends under.

   Method 2: *Oval Loaf:* shape it into an oval.
6. Put onto a lined baking tray and allow to prove for a further 45 minutes. *
7. Glaze with the egg, bake for 20 minutes until golden brown.
8. Mix together the water and icing sugar and brush over loaf as soon as it comes out of the oven.

Quick Malt Loaf

INGREDIENTS £

100g (3½ oz) Kellogg's All Bran
275g (9¾ oz) mixed fruit
100g (3½ oz) sugar
300ml (10½ fl oz) semi-skimmed milk
100g (3½ oz) self raising flour

METHOD

1. Mix together the bran, dried fruit and sugar in a large bowl.
2. Pour the milk over the mixture and leave to stand for 40 minutes.
3. Add the flour and mix well.
4. Line a loaf tin with greased baking paper and pour in the mixture.
5. Preheat the oven to 180°C / 350°F / gas mark 4 and bake for 50-60 minutes then turn out of the tin immediately and allow to cool.
6. Slice thinly and butter one side.

Garlic Bread

INGREDIENTS £

French **baguette**
2 garlic cloves, *crushed*
110g (4 oz) **butter**
1 tsp herbes de Provence

METHOD

SERVES 4-8

Preheat the oven to 180°C / 350°F / gas mark 4

1. Mix together the garlic, herbs and butter, with a fork.
2. Slice the baguette, at an angle, into pieces about 2½ cm (1 inch) thick.
3. Butter both sides of the bread and rebuild the baguette on a sheet of foil.
4. Wrap the bread in foil and bake for 20 minutes.

VEGETABLES

VEGETABLES

VEGETABLES

VEGETABLES

Roast Swede in a Parmesan Shell

INGREDIENTS ££

1 large swede, *peeled and cut into 5 cm (2 inch) chip-like wedges*
6 tbsp groundnut oil *(this is peanut oil)*
110g (4 oz) plain flour
45g (1½ oz) fresh Parmesan, *very finely grated*

METHOD

SERVES 8

Preheat the oven to 180°C / 350°F / gas mark 4

1. Put the swede wedges in a saucepan, pour over boiling water, add salt, bring back to the boil and simmer for 3 minutes.
2. Put the oil in a baking tray and warm in the oven.
3. Combine the flour, Parmesan and seasoning in a large mixing bowl.
4. Drain the swede and immediately add it to the flour mixture *(the flour mixture will only stick while the wedges are hot and steamy).* Toss the wedges in the flour so that all sides are coated.
5. Put the swede in the hot baking tray, season, toss it in the oil and bake in the oven for about 40 minutes, until crisp and golden. *(Do not cover with foil as they will become soggy).*

Bevington Parsnip Bake

VEGETABLES

INGREDIENTS ££

900g (2 lbs) parsnips
5 tbsp olive oil
55g (2 oz) butter
3 tbsp soft brown sugar
450g (1 lb) tomatoes, *skinned, de-seeded & sliced*
170g (6 oz) Gruyère or Cheddar cheese, *grated*
290ml (10 fl oz / ½ pt) double cream
2 slices of bread, *made into breadcrumbs*

METHOD

SERVES 8

Preheat the oven to 180°C / 350°F / gas mark 4

1. Peel the parsnips, top and tail, then finely slice.
2. Heat the oil in a frying pan and lightly fry the parsnips for 8-10 minutes until slightly soft.
3. Grease a 1.1 L (40 fl oz / 2 pts) ovenproof dish with half the butter and add half the parsnips to cover the base.
4. Sprinkle with half the sugar, tomatoes, cheese, cream and seasoning.
5. Add the remaining parsnips, followed by the sugar, tomatoes, cheese, cream and seasoning.
6. Top with breadcrumbs, dot the remaining butter over the top * and bake for 50 minutes. *(You may need to loosely cover in foil for the last 15 minutes to prevent the top from browning too much).*

Savoy Cabbage with Wholegrain Mustard

INGREDIENTS £

½ savoy cabbage, *finely sliced*
15g (½ oz) **butter**
1½ tbsp wholegrain **mustard**

METHOD

SERVES 8

1. Plunge the cabbage into boiling, salted water. When the water comes to the boil simmer for approximately 3 minutes until cooked and then drain thoroughly.
2. Melt the butter in the hot saucepan, add the wholegrain mustard and toss in the cabbage. Season with plenty of salt.

Carrot & Swede Purée

INGREDIENTS £

5 carrots, *peeled and roughly chopped*
1 swede, *peeled and roughly chopped*
30g (1 oz) **butter**
2-4 tbsp **cream**

METHOD

SERVES 8

1. Cook the carrots and swede in a saucepan of salted water for about 30 minutes, until very soft.
2. Drain, mash with the butter and cream and season to taste. *

VEGETABLES

Cabbage with Caraway

VEGETABLES

INGREDIENTS £

30g (1 oz) **butter**
2 onions, *sliced*
½ savoy / white cabbage
1 tsp caraway seeds
1 tsp lemon juice

METHOD

SERVES 4-8

1. Melt the butter in a frying pan and soften the onions.
2. Add the caraway seeds, lemon juice and seasoning and cook for a further minute. *
3. Finely slice the cabbage *(about 3 mm / 1/2 inch thick - discarding the centre core and outer ribs)* * and plunge into a saucepan of salted boiling water. When the water comes back to the boil simmer for 3 minutes, until cooked.
4. Drain the cabbage well, put back in the saucepan, stir in the onions and season to taste with plenty of salt.

Braised Red Cabbage

INGREDIENTS £££

30g (1 oz) **butter**
500g (1 lb 2 oz) onion, *chopped*
1 red cabbage, *finely sliced (about 3 mm / 1/8 inch thick)*
500g (1 lb 2 oz) apple, *peeled, cored and diced*
1 orange, *zest & juice*
30g (1 oz) **sultanas**
2 tbsp brown sugar
3 tbsp red currant jelly
85ml (3 fl oz) **red wine**
85ml (3 fl oz) **malt vinegar**
175ml (6 fl oz / 0.3 pt) water

METHOD

SERVES 8

1. Melt the butter in a large saucepan and soften the onions.
2. Add the rest of ingredients, season, cover with a lid and simmer until cooked to your liking *(for at least 1 hour)*, stirring occasionally. * *(If it becomes a little dry add more water).*

Roast Mediterranean Vegetables

INGREDIENTS £££

1 aubergine, *diced into 2½ cm (1 inch) cubes*
2 courgettes, *cut into chunky batons*
1 red pepper, *cut into 8ths*
2 onions, *divided into 8ths*
4 tomatoes, *skinned, de-cored and quartered*
2 garlic cloves, *crushed,*
Olive oil

METHOD

SERVES 8

Preheat the oven to 180°C / 350°F / gas mark 4

1. Put the aubergine and courgette pieces into a colander, sprinkle generously with salt. Put a plate on top, weight it down and leave for ½ hour, *(the salt draws out liquid removing bitterness).* Rince then dab dry.
2. Put all the ingredients in a roasting tray, season, drizzle with olive oil, toss to coat in the oil and roast for about 40-50 minutes until browned. *

French Beans with Roasted Baby Tomatoes

INGREDIENTS ££

85g (3 oz) baby tomatoes, *halved in the same way as you cut a grapefruit*
450g (1 lb) French beans, *topped and tailed*
15g (½ oz) **butter**

METHOD

SERVES 8

Preheat the oven to 180°C / 350°F / gas mark 4

1. Place the tomatoes on a lined baking tray, sprinkle with salt and roast for about 10 minutes. *
2. Plunge the beans into salted, boiling water and cook until just tender.
3. Drain the beans, put them back in the saucepan, add the butter and stir in the tomatoes.

Peas & Leeks

INGREDIENTS £

1 leek, *sliced*
30g (1 oz) **butter**
450g (1 lb) frozen peas
1 tsp sugar

METHOD

SERVES 8

1. Fry the leek in half the butter, until soft. *
2. Empty the peas into a saucepan, pour over boiling water, add the sugar and cook until tender.
3. Drain the peas and return them to the saucepan. Add the remaining butter and leeks, gently stir, season to taste and serve immediately.

Cauliflower & Parsley Mash

INGREDIENTS £

1 cauliflower
3 tbsp fresh parsley, *finely chopped*
30g (1 oz) **butter**

METHOD

SERVES 8

1. Roughly chop the cauliflower and cook in salted water for approximately 15 minutes, until it is just soft enough to mash but will retain some texture.
2. Drain well, add the butter and parsley and roughly mash, season to taste * *(if there is too much moisture in the mash, cook away the liquid).*

Celeriac Purée

INGREDIENTS ££

2 **celeriacs**
1 lemon, *juiced*
4-6 tbsp **cream**
Pinch of cayenne pepper
Pinch of paprika

METHOD

SERVES 8

1. Peel the celeriac and chop roughly into small pieces.
2. Cook in a saucepan of salted water, with ½ the lemon juice, for about 20 minutes until very soft.
3. Drain well and blend in a food processor with the cream, cayenne pepper, paprika and remaining lemon juice. *
4. Heat and season to taste.

VEGETABLES

Creamed Spinach

INGREDIENTS £

1 packet of frozen spinach, *thawed and drained*
30g (1 oz) **butter**
4-6 tbsp **cream**
Pinch of ground nutmeg

METHOD

SERVES 8

1. Squeeze the water out of the spinach *(if the spinach is not already finely chopped, purée it in a food processor).*
2. Melt the butter in a saucepan, add the spinach and warm through.
3. Add some cream and nutmeg and season to taste. *

Buttered Leeks

INGREDIENTS £

8 leeks
55g (2 oz) butter
Mustard seeds *(optional)*

METHOD

SERVES 8

1. Prepare the leeks by trimming the roots, removing all but about 4 cm (1½ inch) of the green end and slice.
2. Melt the butter in a saucepan, add the leeks with plenty of seasoning, cover and cook for about 15 minutes until soft, stirring occasionally.
3. Add the mustard seeds * and serve.

Sautéed Courgettes & Thyme

INGREDIENTS £

4 courgettes, *cut into batons*
30g (1 oz) butter
Thyme
1 garlic clove, *crushed*

METHOD

SERVES 8

1. Melt the butter in a frying pan, add the courgettes, garlic, thyme and seasoning and fry until browned. *

Braised Leeks

INGREDIENTS ££

4 leeks
175ml (6 fl oz / 1/3 pt) stock *(dissolve 1/2 a stock cube in boiling water)*
3 tbsp cream
2-3 tbsp fresh Parmesan cheese

METHOD

SERVES 8

1. Prepare the leeks by trimming the roots, removing all but about 4 cm (1½ inch) of the green end, cut into 2½ cm (1 inch) chunks.
2. Plunge into a saucepan of boiling water for a couple of minutes to blanch and then drain.
3. Return the leeks to the pan, pour over the stock, season, cover with a lid * and cook over a gentle heat until soft, basting the leeks two or three times during cooking.
4. Drain and transfer leeks to a hot serving dish, pour over the cream and sprinkle with Parmesan cheese.

Beetroot Bake

INGREDIENTS ££

450g (1 lb) fresh beetroot (or 225g / 8 oz cooked beetroot)
1 tbsp **malt vinegar**
2 garlic cloves, *crushed*
215ml (7½ fl oz) **cream** or **crème fraîche**
1½ tsp wholegrain **mustard**
45g (1½ oz) grated **cheese**

METHOD

SERVES 8

Preheat the oven to 180°C / 350°F / gas mark 4

1. Put the beetroot in a saucepan of water, so the water covers the beetroot, add the vinegar and cook for about 20 minutes until cooked *(to see if they are cooked, stab the beetroot with a paring knife and if it is cooked it will slide off the knife).*
2. Allow to cool then peel and finely slice.
3. Arrange the beetroot in an ovenproof dish.
4. Add the garlic to the cream, together with the mustard and seasoning, stir once and pour over the beetroot.
5. Sprinkle with grated cheese * and bake for 35-40 minutes.

Sautéed Baby Spinach

INGREDIENTS ££

30g **butter**
360g (13 oz) bag of pre-washed spinach

METHOD

SERVES 8

1. Melt the butter in a large saucepan and when it starts bubbling add all of the spinach, pushing it down into the pan. Cover with a saucepan lid and shake the pan to coat in the butter.
2. Stir and as soon as all the spinach has wilted drain, season and serve immediately.

Runner Beans with Buttered Almonds

INGREDIENTS ££

900g (2 lbs) runner beans
50g (2 oz) **butter**
30g (1 oz) flaked **almonds**

METHOD

SERVES 8

1. Top and tail, remove the edges from the beans using a potato peeler and slice diagonally into 2½ cm (1 inch) pieces. *
2. Plunge the beans into salted, boiling water and cook until tender.
3. Melt the butter in a saucepan and lightly brown the almonds.
4. Drain the beans, place in a warmed serving dish and pour over the buttered almonds.

Pea Purée

INGREDIENTS ££

500g (1 lb 2 oz) frozen peas
250ml (9 fl oz) dry white wine
150ml (5 fl oz) chicken stock *(dissolve 1 stock cube in the water)*
150ml (5 fl oz) double cream

METHOD

SERVES 8

1. Put the stock and wine in a saucepan and bring to the boil.
2. Add the peas and simmer for about 3-4 minutes.
3. Drain the peas over a bowl to reserve the liquid *(as you may need some of it)*.
4. Blend the peas with the cream until smooth, adding some of the reserve liquid to get the right consistency. Season to taste.

Creamed Pea Purée

INGREDIENTS £

500g (1 lb 2 oz) frozen peas
290ml (10 fl oz / ½ pt) chicken stock *(use 1 stock cube)*

METHOD

SERVES 8

1. Put the stock in a saucepan and bring to the boil.
2. Add the peas and simmer for about 3-4 minutes.
3. Drain the peas over a bowl to reserve the liquid *(as you may need some of it)*.
4. Blend the peas until smooth, adding some of the reserve liquid to get the right consistency. Season to taste.

Sautéed Courgette Ribbons & Baby Sweetcorn

INGREDIENTS £££

4 courgettes
8 baby sweetcorn, *cut into quarters, lengthways*
45g (1½ oz) butter
2 tsp lemon juice

METHOD

SERVES 8

1. Warm the butter in a large frying pan and cook the sweetcorn until it starts to brown. *
2. To prepare the courgettes, use a potato peeler and peel off long strips of courgette.
3. Add the courgette ribbons and cook for about 5 minutes *(be careful not to over cook the courgettes or stir them too much, otherwise they become mushy).*
4. Add the lemon juice and season to taste.

Brussel Sprouts & Almonds

INGREDIENTS £££

1.35kg (3 lbs) small Brussel sprouts
30g (1 oz) butter
30g (1 oz) flaked almonds

METHOD

SERVES 8

1. Prepare the sprouts by trimming the stalks and outside leaves if necessary and cut a cross in the bottom of each one. *
2. Plunge the sprouts into salted boiling water and cook until just tender *(to test, stab a sprout with a paring knife and if it is cooked it will begin to slide off the knife).*
3. Melt the butter in a saucepan and lightly brown the almonds.
4. Drain the sprouts and put them back in the saucepan, pour over the almonds and toss.

Tomato & Basil Salad

INGREDIENTS ££

Tomatoes, *skinned & sliced*
Fresh basil, *roughly torn*
Olive oil

Variations:
Red onion / **mozzarella** / **feta** / chives etc.

METHOD

1. Layer the tomato and basil in a serving dish, sprinkle each layer lightly with olive oil and black pepper.
2. Cover in cling film and refrigerate. Remove from the fridge 20 minutes before serving and season with salt.

Carrot & Chervil Purée

VEGETABLES

INGREDIENTS ££

1.35 kg (3 lbs) carrots, *peeled & roughly chopped*
1.1 L (40 fl oz / 2 pts) chicken or vegetable **stock**
1 cardamom pod, *crushed (seeds only)*
2 bay leaves
4 tbsp **crème fraîche** or **cream**
1 tbsp fresh chervil (½ tbsp of dried), *chopped*

METHOD

SERVES 8

1. Cook the carrots in the stock with the cardamom seeds, bay leaves and salt for about 20 minutes until very soft.
2. Drain really well, remove the bay leaves and blend, or mash with the crème fraîche. *(If the consistency is too wet, return to the heat to cook away some of the moisture, stirring continuously).*
3. Add the chervil and season to taste. *

Glazed Carrots

INGREDIENTS £

6-8 carrots
2 tsp sugar
45g (1½ oz) **butter**

METHOD

SERVES 8

1. Peel the carrots and cut into batons.
2. Put about 1 cm of water in a saucepan, add the carrots, sugar, butter and salt, cover * and simmer for about 6 minutes.
3. Add a little butter to glaze and serve immediately.

French Beans with Sesame Seeds

INGREDIENTS ££

450g (1 lb) French beans, *topped and tailed*
1 tbsp **sesame seeds**
30g (1 oz) **butter**
½ tbsp lemon juice

METHOD

SERVES 8

1. Plunge the beans into salted, boiling water and cook until just tender.
2. Brown the sesame seeds in the butter and add the lemon juice.
3. Drain the beans, put them back in the saucepan, pour over the sesame seeds, toss and season to taste.

Roasted Red Onions

INGREDIENTS ££

Red onions *(1 per person)*
Olive oil

METHOD

Preheat the oven to 180°C / 350°F / gas mark 4

1. Cut a cross into the top of each onion, cutting a third of the way down.
2. Coat the skins in olive oil and salt. Roast for 1½ hours.

Serve in their skins.

Honey Glazed Courgettes

VEGETABLES

INGREDIENTS £

30g (1 oz) butter
5-6 courgettes, *sliced at an angle ¾ cm (¼ inch) thick*
2 tbsp honey
2 tsp fresh mint, *finely chopped*

METHOD

SERVES 8

1. Melt the butter in a frying pan and cook the courgettes over a gentle heat for 8-10 minutes, until the courgettes are slightly brown *(be careful not to overcook them, or stir them too much otherwise they will become mushy).*
2. Stir in the honey* and mint and cook for a further minute. Season to taste.

Red Cabbage with Blueberries

INGREDIENTS ££

1 tbsp vegetable oil
½ onion, *chopped*
100ml (3½ fl oz) red wine
100ml (3½ fl oz) vegetable stock
½ red cabbage, *finely sliced (about 3 mm thick)*
1 tbsp Port
50g (2 oz) frozen blueberries, *thawed*

METHOD

SERVES 8

1. Warm the oil in a saucepan and cook the onions over a gentle heat until soft.
2. Add the stock, red wine and cabbage and bring to the boil.
3. Season, add the Port and simmer for 1 hour. *
4. Stir in the blueberries and cook for another minute or so to bring them up to temperature.
5. Season to taste then drain really well.

Braised Carrots with Tarragon

VEGETABLES

INGREDIENTS £

675g (1½ lbs) carrots, *peeled*
30g (1 oz) butter
1½ tbsp olive oil
3 tbsp white wine
2 tsp sugar
½ large lemon *(or 1 small), juiced*
2 tbsp fresh tarragon, *chopped*

METHOD

SERVES 8

1. Grate the carrots in a food processor.
2. Warm the butter and the olive oil in a saucepan, add the grated carrots, white wine, sugar, lemon juice, tarragon and seasoning and cook for 8 minutes over a medium to high heat, stirring occasionally.

Provincial Tomatoes

INGREDIENTS ££

1½ slices of **bread**, *made into breadcrumbs*
2 garlic cloves, *crushed*
2 tbsp fresh parsley, *finely chopped*
4 tbsp olive oil
4-8 tomatoes *(depending on size)*
1½ tsp sugar

METHOD

SERVES 8

Preheat the oven to 180°C / 350°F / gas mark 4

1. Blend the bread, garlic and parsley in a food processor to make a breadcrumb mixture, then stir in the olive oil.
2. Halve the tomatoes in the same way as you would cut a grapefruit and place on a lined baking tray, season and sprinkle with sugar.
3. Spoon the breadcrumb mixture on to the tomatoes, press in place * and bake for 15 minutes until the breadcrumb mixture browns and the tomatoes are cooked.

Mushrooms with Parsley

INGREDIENTS ££

900g (2 lb) button mushrooms, *halved*
150ml (5 fl oz / ¼ pt) **stock**
1 tbp fresh parsley, *chopped*

METHOD

SERVES 8

1. Cook the mushrooms in the stock in a covered saucepan for a few minutes until tender.
2. Transfer the mushrooms to a warmed serving dish and simmer the remaining liquid until it has reduced to a few tablespoons.
3. Add the parsley and pour over the mushrooms.

VEGETABLES

Mangetout Peas

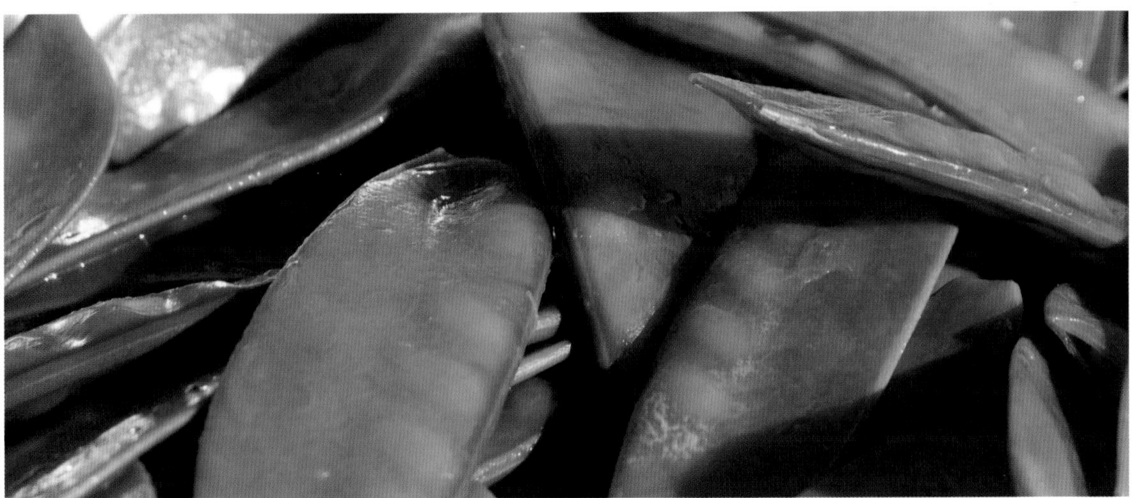

INGREDIENTS ££

450g (1 lb) mangetout peas, *topped & tailed*
1 tsp sugar
15g (½ oz) butter

METHOD

SERVES 8

1. Plunge the mangetout and the sugar into a pan of boiling water and simmer for about 4 minutes until the mangetout are cooked, but still retain their crunchiness.
2. Drain, add the butter and serve immediately.

Baked Butter Beans with Leeks & Parmesan

INGREDIENTS £

3 leeks, *finely sliced*
2 garlic cloves, *crushed*
15g (½ oz) butter
1 tin (410g) butter beans, *drained and washed*
110ml (4 fl oz) cream
2 tbsp Parmesan cheese, *grated*

METHOD

SERVES 8

Preheat the oven to 180°C / 350°F / gas mark 4

1. Fry the leeks and garlic in the butter until soft.
2. Stir in the butter beans, add the cream and season.
3. Transfer to an ovenproof dish, sprinkle with Parmesan * and bake for 15-20 minutes until golden.

Red Cabbage with Walnuts

VEGETABLES

INGREDIENTS ££

½ cabbage, *finely sliced (about 3 mm thick)*
45g (1½ oz) **butter**
30g (1 oz) **walnuts**, *chopped*
1 orange, *grated zest*
2 tsp marmalade
2 tsp **balsamic vinegar**

METHOD

SERVES 8

1. Blanch the cabbage in salted boiling water for 2 minutes, then drain really well.
2. Melt the butter in the same saucepan, then add the remaining ingredients.
3. Stir in the cabbage and cook over a gentle heat for a few minutes. Season to taste.

Crunchy Baked Fennel

INGREDIENTS £

3 fennel bulbs, *trimmed and cut into quarters, lengthways*
1½ - 2 slices of wholemeal **bread**
1 garlic clove, *crushed*
2 tbsp fresh parsley
2 tbsp olive oil

METHOD

SERVES 8

Preheat the oven to 180°C / 350°F / gas mark 4

1. Place the fennel in a saucepan, pour over boiling water, season with salt and bring back to the boil. Simmer for 10 minutes.
2. Blend the bread, garlic and parsley in a food processor.
3. Drain the fennel and place on a lined baking tray.
4. Drizzle with the olive oil, season and sprinkle over the breadcrumbs.
5. Bake for 35 minutes until the fennel is tender and the breadcrumbs are crisp.

Roasted Courgettes & Onion

INGREDIENTS £

3 medium onions, *divided into 8ths*
4 courgettes, *cut into thick batons*
Vegetable oil

METHOD

SERVES 6-8

Preheat the oven to 180°C / 350°F / gas mark 4

1. Put the onions and courgettes in a roasting tray, season, drizzle with oil and toss.
2. Roast for 40 minutes, tossing occasionally, until the vegetables are browned. *

Sautéed Grated Courgette with Lemon

INGREDIENTS £

4-5 courgettes
30g (1 oz) **butter**
½ lemon, *juice and grated zest*

METHOD

SERVES 8

1. Grate the courgettes in a food processor using the thick grating blade.
2. Melt the butter in a large frying pan, add the lemon zest and cook it for a minute, add the courgette and a little lemon juice and cook over a high heat until soft.
3. Season to taste, adding more lemon juice if you like *(you may have to drain some liquid away before serving).*

Cauliflower with Garlic & Parsley

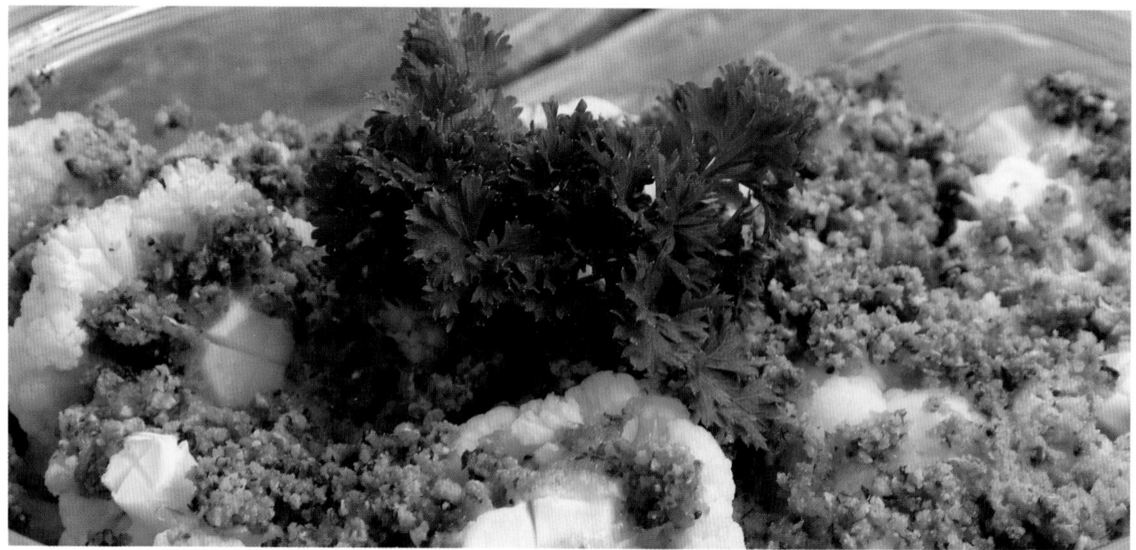

INGREDIENTS £

1½ slices of brown **bread**, *made into breadcrumbs*
1½ garlic cloves
1½ tbsp fresh parsley, *chopped*
1 cauliflower, *cut into small florets*
45g (1½ oz) **butter**

METHOD

SERVES 8

Preheat the oven to 180°C / 350°F / gas mark 4

1. Blend the bread, garlic and parsley in a food processor.
2. Prepare the cauliflower by dividing into florets and cut a cross into the end of each floret.
3. Plunge into salted boiling water and simmer for about 4 minutes until cooked *(to test, stab a floret with a paring knife and if it is cooked it will begin to slide off the knife).*
4. Drain really well and leave to cool in the colander.
5. Put the cauliflower into an ovenproof dish, season, sprinkle over the breadcrumbs, cut up the butter and place on top. *
6. Bake in the oven for 30 minutes or until golden in colour.

Stir Fried Sugar Snap Peas with Red Peppers

INGREDIENTS £££

1 tbsp sesame seeds
2 tsp soy sauce
1 tbsp honey
½ red pepper, *thinly sliced*
450g (1 lb) sugar snap peas

METHOD

SERVES 8

1. Toast the sesame seeds in a dry frying pan until golden. *
2. Add the soy sauce and honey and stir in the vegetables.
3. Cook for just a few minutes until the peas are cooked, but still retain their crunchiness.
4. Strain off excess liquid retaining the sesame seeds and serve immediately.

Tangy Tomatoes

INGREDIENTS £

4-8 tomatoes *(depending on size)*
2-3 tbsp tomato ketchup
1 tbsp English mustard
¼ tsp chilli powder
Dash of Tabasco
1 tbsp olive oil

METHOD

SERVES 8

Preheat the oven to 180°C / 350°F / gas mark 4

1. Halve the tomatoes in the same way as you would cut a grapefruit. Cut a cross in the flesh and seeds of the tomato being sure not to cut through the skin.
2. Combine all the other ingredients to make a paste and spoon a little on top of each tomato.
3. Place on a lined baking tray, season * and bake for 15 minutes.

Caramelised Shallots

INGREDIENTS ££

20-30 shallots
50g (1¾ oz) butter
50g (1¾ oz) brown sugar

METHOD

SERVES 8

1. Put the shallots in a saucepan of water, bring to the boil, simmer for 12 minutes and then peel. *
2. Melt the butter and sugar in a frying pan, add the shallots and cook for 8 minutes, until soft, turning occasionally. *(If the sugar starts to brown too much add a little water and cook until the water has evaporated).*

Asparagus

INGREDIENTS £££

500g (1 lb 2 oz) asparagus
55g (2 oz) **butter**

METHOD

SERVES 6-8

1. Trim the stalks to remove the woody part, so you are left with about 20-23 cm (8-9 inch) lengths of asparagus.
2. Using a potato peeler, remove a fine layer of stalk *(about 4 cm / 1½ inch in length)* from the cut end.
3. Cook in a saucepan of salted boiling water for about 8-10 minutes until the stalk is tender half way down *(cooking time depends on the thickness of the asparagus).*
4. Drain well, coat in butter and serve immediately.

Cauliflower Cheese

INGREDIENTS ££

1 cauliflower, *cut into small florets*
170g (6 oz) Cheddar cheese, *grated*
Paprika

White Sauce
55g (2 oz) butter
70g (2½ oz) plain flour
570ml (20 fl oz / 1 pt) milk
1 tsp Dijon mustard

METHOD

SERVES 8

Preheat the oven to 180°C / 350°F / gas mark 4

1. Plunge the cauliflower into salted boiling water and simmer for about 4 minutes until cooked *(to test, stab a floret with a paring knife and if it is cooked it will begin to slide off the knife).*
2. Drain **really well** and arrange the florets in a serving dish.
3. **To make the white sauce**, melt the butter over medium heat, remove from the heat and stir in the flour to make a roux.
4. Return to the heat and gradually add the milk, stirring until all the liquid has been incorporated and the sauce is smooth and glossy.
5. Add the mustard, season and pour over the cauliflower.
6. Sprinkle with the cheese * and bake for 15 minutes.

Dust with paprika and serve.

Peperonata

INGREDIENTS £££

1½ tbsp olive oil
4 onions, *sliced*
4 garlic cloves, *crushed*
2 red peppers, *thinly sliced*
2 yellow peppers, *thinly sliced*
1 green pepper, *thinly sliced*
4 tsp capers
8 whole anchovy fillets *(optional), chopped*
2 tbsp white wine vinegar
2 tbsp fresh parsley and / or basil *(optional)*

METHOD

SERVES 8

1. Warm the oil in a frying pan and cook the onions and garlic over a gentle heat until the onion is soft.
2. Add the peppers and cook for 30 minutes until soft. *
3. Add the capers, anchovy fillets and vinegar and cook for a further 5 minutes.
4. Adjust seasoning, add fresh parsley and / or basil, if using, and serve hot.

Savoy Cabbage with Chestnuts, Bacon & Nutmeg

INGREDIENTS £££

½ tbsp vegetable oil
½ shallot, *finely diced*
½ garlic clove, *crushed*
1 rasher bacon, *chopped*
30ml (1 fl oz) chicken **stock**,
use half a stock cube
⅛ tsp ground nutmeg
25g (1 oz) tinned cooked
chestnuts, *roughly chopped*
50ml (2 oz) **cream**
½ savoy cabbage, *shredded*
15g (½ oz) **butter**
½ tbsp fresh parsley, *chopped*
½ tbsp fresh chives, *chopped*

METHOD

SERVES 8

1. Warm the vegetable oil and cook the shallot, garlic and bacon in a frying pan over a gentle heat until soft. Drain off any excess oil when cooked.
2. Add chicken stock, nutmeg and chestnuts and simmer to cook the liquid away.
3. Add cream, bring to the boil and simmer for 2 minutes to reduce. *
4. Plunge the cabbage into a saucepan of boiling salted water. When the water comes to the boil simmer for approximately 3 minutes until cooked, then drain thoroughly.
5. Put the cabbage back in the saucepan and pour over the hot cream mixture.
6. Stir in the butter, parsley and chives and serve immediately.

Courgettes with Chilli & Ginger

INGREDIENTS £

30g (1 oz) **butter**
1-2 tbsp olive oil
4 tsp chilli, *deseeded and finely chopped*
4 tsp fresh ginger, *finely grated*
2 garlic cloves, *crushed*
5-6 courgettes *cut into juliennes (fine sticks) about 2 mm (¼ inch) wide*

METHOD

SERVES 8

1. Melt the butter with the oil in a frying pan over a gentle heat.
2. Add the chilli, ginger and garlic and gently cook for 2 minutes.*
3. Add the courgettes and cook over a medium high heat for about 8-10 minutes until the courgettes start to become translucent *(be careful not to overcook the courgettes or stir them too much, as they will break up and become mushy).* Season to taste.

White Bean & Rosemary Purée

INGREDIENTS £

1 tbsp olive oil
1½ onion, *chopped*
1-2 garlic cloves, *crushed*
1 sprig of fresh rosemary, *stalk removed and finely chopped*
2 x 400g tins of white beans *(flageolet, cannellini, butter or haricot)*
100ml (4 fl oz) vegetable **stock**

METHOD

SERVES 8

1. Warm the oil in a small frying pan and cook the onion, garlic and rosemary over a low heat until the onions are soft.
2. Drain the beans and rinse them in cold water.
3. Put all the ingredients into a food processor and blend until smooth.
4. Warm and season to taste.

Herby Lentils

INGREDIENTS £

340g (12 oz) lentils
1 bay leaf
1 lemon, *juiced*
2 tbsp olive oil
2 tbsp fresh parsley, *chopped*
2 tbsp fresh basil, *chopped*
2 tbsp fresh mint, *chopped*

METHOD

SERVES 8

1. Rinse the lentils in cold water and put them in a saucepan with the bay leaf, pour over boiling water, bring to the boil and simmer until tender.
2. Drain, remove the bay leaf and add the lemon juice and olive oil. *

Just before serving stir in the fresh herbs and season to taste.

Artichokes with Bacon & Tarragon

INGREDIENTS £

½ tbsp vegetable oil
1 onion, *finely chopped*
2 rasher's bacon, *chopped*
100ml (3½ oz) white wine
2 tbsp cream
½ tsp dried tarragon
1 x 390g tin artichokes, *washed and drained*
10g (¼ oz) Parmesan, *finely grated*

METHOD

SERVES 6

1. Warm the oil in a frying pan and cook the onion and bacon over a low heat until onion is soft.
2. Add the white wine, cream and tarragon and season.
3. Cut the artichokes in to quarters and arrange in an ovenproof dish.
4. Pour over the wine mixture, sprinkle with Parmesan * and bake for 20 minutes.

Broccoli with Almonds

VEGETABLES

INGREDIENTS £

2 heads of broccoli
30g (1 oz) **butter**
30g (1 oz) flaked **almonds**, *toasted*

METHOD

SERVES 8

1. Prepare the broccoli by separating into florets, cut a cross in the end of the stalk of each floret.
2. Plunge into salted, boiling water and simmer for 4 minutes until cooked *(to test, stab a floret with a paring knife and if it is cooked it will begin to slide off the knife).*
3. Drain the broccoli, return to the pan, add the butter and the almonds and toss.
4. Place in a warmed serving dish *(turn any florets that are sitting stalk up).*

Lentil Dhal

INGREDIENTS £

½ tbsp olive oil
½ onion, *finely chopped*
1 garlic clove, *crushed*
1 carrot, *peeled and finely chopped*
150g (5½ oz) dried puy **lentils** *(dark speckled) washed and drained*
290ml (10 fl oz / ½ pt) vegetable **stock**
1 tbsp **garam masala**
¼ tsp turmeric
¼ a 400g tin chopped tomatoes

METHOD

SERVES 8

1. Warm the olive oil in a frying pan and cook the onion, garlic and carrot over a gentle heat until soft.
2. Stir in the lentils and cook for a further 2 minutes.
3. Add the stock, bring to the boil, cover and simmer until the lentils are just tender *(you may need to turn up the heat to reduce some of the liquid).*
4. Add the garam masala, turmeric and chopped tomato and simmer for about 5 minutes until you have a good consistency. Season to taste. *

Roast Parsnips

INGREDIENTS £

5-6 parsnips, *peeled*
4-5 tbsp vegetable oil

METHOD

SERVES 8

Preheat the oven to 180°C / 350°F / gas mark 4

1. Cut the parsnips in half and then into wedges, place in a saucepan of salted water, * bring to the boil and simmer for 5 minutes.
2. Warm the oil in a lined baking tray.
3. Drain the parsnips and add them to the hot oil *(take care not to allow water into the tray because it will cause the oil to spit),* season and turn to coat in oil.
4. Bake for about 1 hour, turning occasionally until crisp and slightly brown.

Ratatouille

INGREDIENTS ££

3 tbsp olive oil
1 onion, *diced*
2 garlic cloves, *crushed*
½ red pepper, *diced*
½ green pepper, *diced*
½ yellow pepper, *diced*
2 courgette, *sliced*
½ aubergine, *diced*
1 tsp herbes de Provence
2 x 400g tins of chopped tomatoes

METHOD

SERVES 8

1. Warm the oil in a frying pan and cook the onion until soft.
2. Add the garlic and peppers and cook for about 5 minutes until the peppers start to soften.
3. Add the courgette and aubergine and fry for a further 5 minutes.
4. Add the dried herbs and tomatoes, season and simmer uncovered for 30 minutes, or until all the vegetables are soft *(stir occasionally)*.

Lemon & Herb Dressed Broccoli

INGREDIENTS £

2 heads of broccoli

Dressing
4 garlic cloves
2 tbsp fresh parsley
4 sprigs of fresh thyme
1 lemon, *juice and grated zest*
100ml (3½ oz) olive oil

METHOD

SERVES 8

1. **To make the dressing**, blend the garlic, parsley and thyme in the small bowl of a food processor until smooth. Stir in the juice, zest and olive oil.
2. Prepare the broccoli by dividing into florets and cut a cross into the end of each floret.
3. Plunge into salted boiling water and simmer for 4 minutes until cooked *(to test, stab a floret with a paring knife and if it is cooked it will begin to slide off the knife).*
4. Drain the broccoli, put back into the saucepan, add most of the dressing and toss. Add more dressing if required and then place in a warmed serving dish *(turn any florets that are sitting stalk up)* and serve.

Creamed Sweetcorn

INGREDIENTS £

500g (1 lb 2 oz) frozen sweetcorn, *thawed*
1 tbsp vegetable oil
1 onion, *chopped*
2 garlic cloves, *crushed*
Pinch of nutmeg
3 tbsp double **cream**
2 tbsp **Parmesan**, *grated*

METHOD

SERVES 8

1. Cook the sweetcorn in boiling water for about 5 minutes, then drain.
2. Warm the oil in a saucepan and cook the onions and garlic until soft.
3. Add the sweetcorn and the rest of ingredients, season and blend until smooth *(add a splash of milk if it seems too dry)*. Season to taste. *

PUDDINGS

PUDDINGS

PUDDINGS

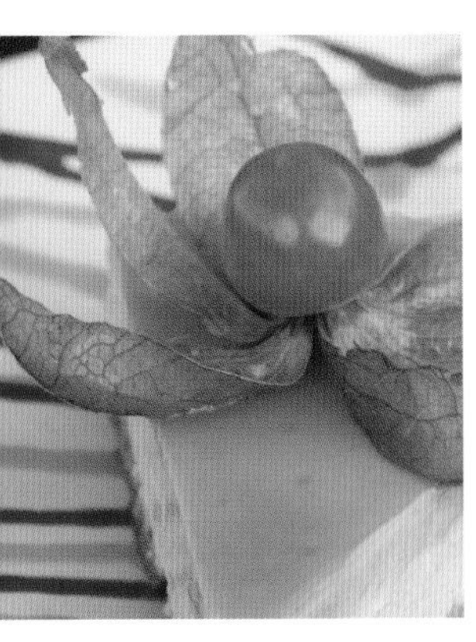

PUDDINGS

PUDDINGS

Brandy Snap Baskets

INGREDIENTS £

120g (4¼ oz) unsalted **butter**
90g (3 oz) caster sugar
120g (4¼ oz) golden syrup
Pinch of ground ginger
100g (3½ oz) plain **flour**

Fill with **ice cream**, **sorbet** or **syllabub**

METHOD

SERVES 8

Preheat the oven to 180°C / 350°F / gas mark 4

1. Melt the butter and sugar with the golden syrup and ground ginger, allow to cool a little, then stir in the flour.
2. Line a couple of baking trays and drop a heaped teaspoonful of the mixture on to the tray *(allowing enough room between them as they will expand in the oven, 2 per tray works well).*
3. Bake in the oven for approximately 6 minutes until the biscuit darkens in colour.
4. Meanwhile, grease the outsides of two small water glasses with butter.
5. Remove from the oven, allow to cool for about 1½ minutes and shape each one over a glass, allow to cool. *

They will keep in an airtight container for a month.

Chocolate & Hazelnut Ice Cream with Chocolate Sauce

INGREDIENTS £

40g (1½ oz) hazelnuts
4 tbsp Nutella
1 large tin (397g) condensed milk
570ml (20 fl oz / 1 pt) whipping cream
6 whole hazelnuts, *for garnish*

Chocolate Sauce *(makes lots but you can freeze it)*
100g (3¾ oz) butter
70g (2½ oz) cocoa
Small tin (170g) evaporated milk
285g (10 oz) icing sugar, *sieved*

METHOD

SERVES 8

Preheat the oven to 180ºC / 350ºF / gas mark 4

1. Roast 40g (1½ oz) of hazelnuts in the oven for about 5 minutes. Allow to cool slightly and remove the skins by rubbing them between the palms of your hands. Roughly chop.
2. Mix together the Nutella and condensed milk.
3. Whip the cream until stiff, add the chocolate mixture and combine with the whisk on a low speed, then stir in the nuts.
4. Pour into a serving dish and freeze.*
5. **To make the chocolate sauce**, melt the butter in a large saucepan, stir in the cocoa and cook for 1 minute. Remove from the heat and stir in the evaporated milk and sieved icing sugar.

Serve with chopped hazelnuts and warm chocolate sauce.

The ice cream will keep for 10 days.

Honeycomb Ice Cream with Raspberry Coulis

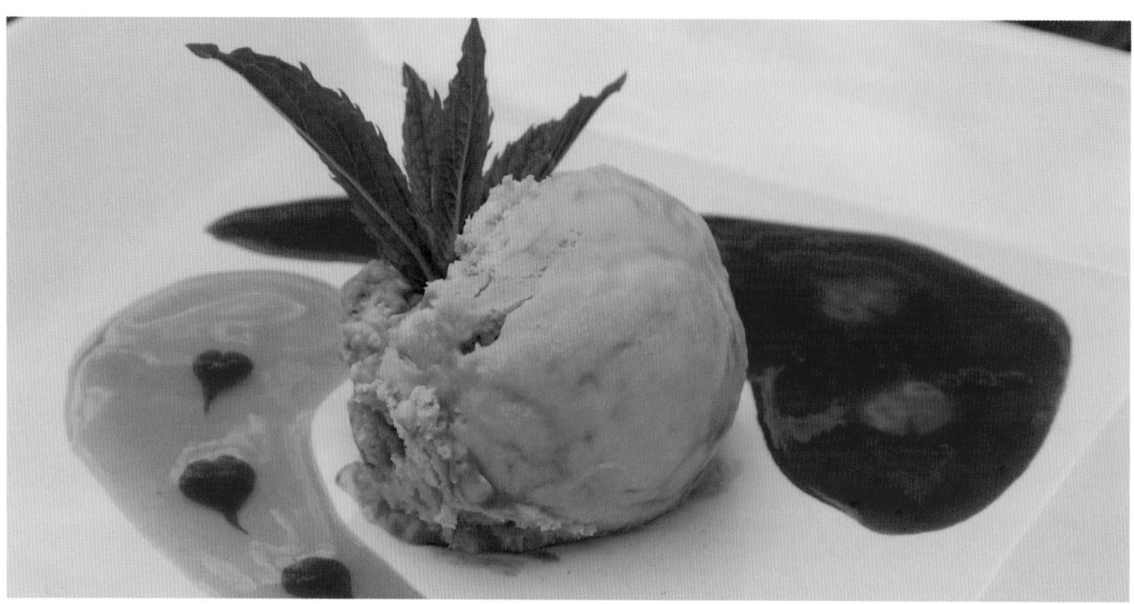

INGREDIENTS ££

Honeycomb
5 tbsp caster sugar
2 tbsp golden syrup
1 tsp bicarbonate of soda

Ice Cream
570ml (20 fl oz /1 pt) whipping cream
1 large tin condensed milk *(397g)*

Raspberry Coulis
Frozen raspberries, *thawed*

METHOD

SERVES 8-12

1. **To make the honeycomb**, put the sugar and syrup into a non-stick frying pan and cook over low heat until the sugar melts.
2. Increase the heat and boil rapidly until mid golden in colour *(watch carefully because it turns dark brown very quickly).*
3. Sift bicarbonate of soda into it, stir well and pour on to a lined baking tray. Do not spread the mixture out as you will break down the air *(put a mat under the baking tray as the honeycomb is very hot and could burn the worktop).* Allow to cool.
4. **To make the ice cream**, whip the cream until stiff, add the condensed milk and combine with the whisk on a low speed.
5. Break the honeycomb into small pieces and add to the cream mixture.
6. Freeze for 8 hours or, ideally, leave overnight.
7. **To make the raspberry coulis**, simply push the raspberries through a sieve. * The ice cream will keep for 10 days and the raspberry coulis for 3 days in the fridge.

Poached Pears in Red Wine

INGREDIENTS ££

8 pears, *peeled*
100g (3½ oz) caster sugar
900ml (30 fl oz / 1½ pt) **red wine**
Strip of lemon peel
1 cinnamon stick (5 cm / 2 inch)
1 tsp black peppercorns
Double **cream**, *whipped (for decoration)*
Fresh mint, *for garnishing*

METHOD

SERVES 8

1. Put all the ingredients, except for the pears, in a large saucepan and slowly bring to the boil.
2. Add the pears and poach for about 30 minutes until tender *(add a little extra wine to completely cover the pears if needed).*
3. Remove the pears from the wine and allow it to cool.
4. Return the pears to the wine and leave them to absorb the colour. *
5. Remove the pears and reduce the red wine to a syrupy sauce. Allow to cool.
6. Serve cold - cut each pear in half and core with the help of a melon baller. Slice through the fat end of each pear *(leaving the stalk end whole),* holding the knife at a 45° angle and fan out the slices. Arrange two halves on the plate to make a butterfly, joining with a blob of whipped cream. Spoon the red wine syrup around the pears and garnish with mint.

Coffee Éclairs filled with Tia Maria Cream / Chocolate Profiteroles filled with Ice Cream

INGREDIENTS £

Choux Pastry
50g (2 oz) unsalted butter or margarine
150ml (5 fl oz / ¼ pt) water
70g (2½ oz) plain flour
2 eggs

Coffee Topping
110g (4 oz) icing sugar, *sieved*
2 tsp coffee essence
1 tbsp water *(approx)*

or

Chocolate Topping
100g (3¾ oz) unsalted butter
70g (2½ oz) cocoa
1 tin of evaporated milk (170g)
285g (10 oz) icing sugar, *sieved*

Tia Maria Cream Filling
2 tbsp Tia Maria
2 tbsp icing sugar, *sieved*
150ml (5 fl oz / ¼ pt) double cream

or

Vanilla Ice Cream Filling

METHOD

SERVES 6-8

Preheat the oven to 200°C / 400°F / gas mark 6

1. **To make the choux pastry**, melt the butter in a saucepan, add the water and bring to the boil.
2. Remove from the heat, add flour and stir hard with a wooden spoon until the mixture leaves the side of the pan clean *(a little more heat may be needed).*
3. Cool for a minute or two and add the eggs, one at a time, beating well until smooth.
4. If making profiteroles, put individual teaspoonfuls of the mixture on a greased baking tray *(the mixture should make 24) or, using a piping bag, pipe out the éclairs* and bake for 15-20 minutes until golden.
5. Immediately transfer the profiteroles or éclairs to a cooling rack and pierce the side of each one to allow the steam to escape. *
6. When cool, fill with whipped cream or ice cream and top with coffee icing, or pour over the chocolate sauce:
    a. **To make the coffee topping:** mix all ingredients together and adjust the consistency *(needs to be a thick pouring consistency)* and coffee strength accordingly.
    b. **To make the chocolate topping:** melt the butter in a large saucepan, stir in the cocoa and cook for 1 minute. Remove from heat and stir in the evaporated milk and sieved icing sugar.
    c. **To make the Tia Maria cream filling:** whip the cream, then add the icing sugar and Tia Maria to taste.
    d. **Vanilla ice cream filling:** the ice cream can be prepared in advance. Use a teaspoon or melon baller to shape the ice cream and refreeze until required.

Lime & Mascarpone Cheese Cake

INGREDIENTS ££

340g (12 oz) hobnobs, ginger or digestive biscuits *(plain or chocolate covered)*
100g (3½ oz) unsalted butter, *soft*
500g (1lb 2 oz) mascarpone
85g (3 oz) icing sugar
3 limes, *finely grated zest and juice*
Chocolate, *grated (for decoration)*
Fresh mint, *for garnishing*

METHOD

SERVES 8

1. Combine the biscuits and the butter in a food processor.
2. Grease the base and sides of a 25 cm (10 inch) round tin and press the biscuit mixture into the base.
3. Using a wooden spoon, beat together the mascarpone, sieved icing sugar, zest and juice of the limes until smooth.
4. Spoon on to the biscuit base, smooth over the top and refrigerate. *

Serve from the fridge and decorate with grated chocolate and a sprig of mint.

Iced Lemon Tart with Winter Berries

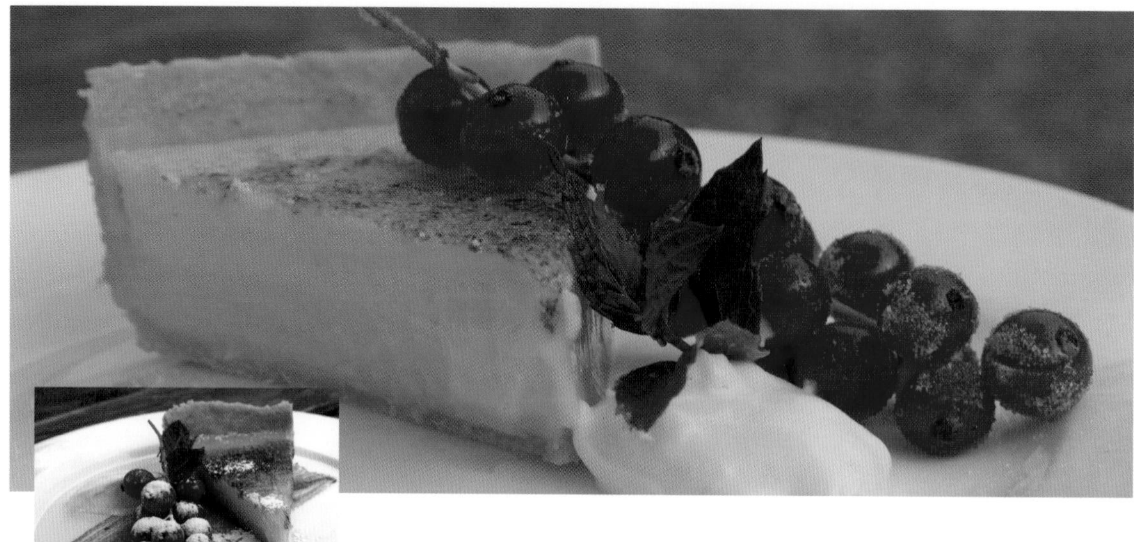

METHOD

SERVES 8

INGREDIENTS £

Pastry
110g (4 oz) plain flour
55g (2 oz) butter
Vanilla essence
2 tbsp icing sugar
¼ lemon, *finely grated zest*
½ egg

Filling
4 eggs
½ lemon, *finely grated zest*
3 lemons, *juiced*
200g (7 oz) caster sugar
150ml (5 fl oz / ¼ pt) double cream

Garnish
Icing sugar
Fresh red currants, *on stalks*
Caster sugar

Preheat the oven to 140°C / 285°F / gas mark 1

1. **To make the pastry**, mix all the pastry ingredients in food processor, gather into a ball and then roll out to fit the flan tin.
2. Grease and flour an 18 cm (7 inch) loose bottomed tin, then line it with the pastry.
3. Blind bake the pastry for 15 minutes *(put a layer of greaseproof paper over the pastry and weigh it down with baking beans or rice. This prevents the pastry base from ballooning)*. Remove the baking beans or rice and greaseproof paper and cook for a further 5 minutes.
4. **To make the filling**, combine all ingredients and pour into the hot pastry case.
5. Bake for 30 minutes or until set. *
6. Allow to cool, dust heavily with icing sugar and caramelise the top *(under a hot grill or with a chef's blow torch)*.

Serve chilled. To decorate with red currants, wet the fruit, roll the berries in caster sugar and serve immediately.

Chocolate / Raspberry Meringue Roulade

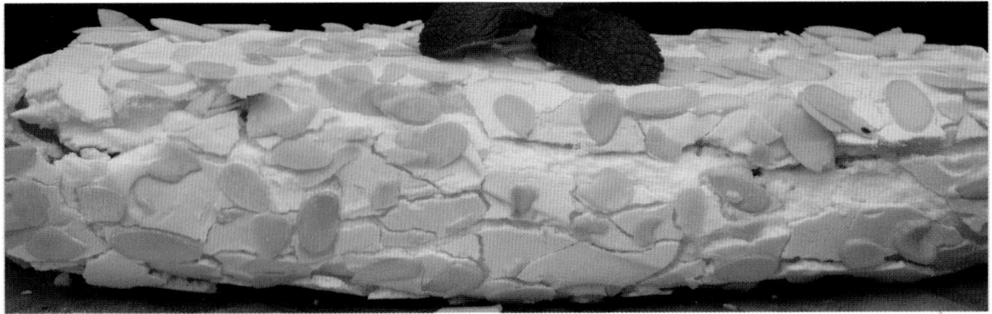

INGREDIENTS £

3 egg whites
170g (6 oz) caster sugar
30g (1 oz) flaked almonds

Chocolate filling
3 egg yolks
200g (7 oz) Bournville chocolate
425ml (15 fl oz / ¾ pt) double cream

or

Raspberry filling
310g (11 oz) raspberries *(fresh or frozen)*
290ml (10 fl oz / ½ pt) double cream

METHOD

SERVES 8

Preheat the oven to 120°C / 240°F / gas mark 1

1. Line a large baking tray with greased baking paper.
2. Whisk the egg whites in a large bowl until stiff *(when you have whipped them enough you will be able to hold the bowl upside down without the mixture falling out).*
3. Add the sugar gradually, a spoonful at a time to start with, while whisking on a low speed, until all the sugar has been incorporated.
4. Spoon the meringue on to the lined tray, level *(creating a rectangle about 23 x 30 cm / 9 x 12 inch)* and sprinkle with flaked almonds, bake for 1 hour.
5. Turn out on a cooling rack covered with a sheet of baking paper, carefully peel off the paper that lined the tray and leave to cool. *
6. The fillings:
   a) **Raspberry filling** - whip the cream until stiff and spread evenly over the meringue. Sprinkle over the fruit and roll the meringue.

   b) **Chocolate filling** - melt the chocolate in a bain-marie. Stir in the egg yolks and allow to cool slightly. Stir in 2 tbsp double cream to stop the chocolate from setting. Whip the remaining cream until stiff and gradually fold in the chocolate mixture, refrigerate to set. Spoon the chocolate on to the meringue forming a line down the centre.
7. To roll the meringue, hold the long sides of the baking paper and lift, curling the edges of the meringue upwards and inwards *(unlike a traditional roulade you are not rolling it up, just rolling it so the ends meet).* Shape with your hands and roll the meringue over so that the two edges that meet are hidden underneath. *

Chill and serve from the fridge, dust with icing sugar just before serving.

PUDDINGS

Raspberry Soufflé

INGREDIENTS ££

3 eggs
110g (4 oz) caster sugar
340g (12 oz) frozen raspberries, *thawed*
3 tbsp water
1 sachet of powdered gelatine *Check manufacturer's instructions as you need enough gelatine to set 570ml (20 fl oz /1 pt) of liquid.*
150ml (5 fl oz / ¼ pt) double cream

For presentation

Frozen raspberries, *thawed (to make a coulis)*
8 whole raspberries
Double cream, *whipped*
Fresh mint leaves *(4 leaves)*
8 rings, 7 cm (2¾ inch), lined with baking paper *(ramekins can be used).*

METHOD

SERVES 8

1. Separate the eggs and blend the egg yolks and the sugar in a food processor.
2. Push the raspberries through a fine sieve, discard the seeds. Add the raspberries to the food processor and blend to combine.
3. Put the water in a saucepan, sprinkle in the gelatine and warm, stirring briskly until the gelatine has completely dissolved. *(Do not allow it to boil).*
4. Turn on the food processor and pour the gelatine in to combine it with the raspberry mixture.
5. Whip the cream and gradually fold in the raspberry mixture. *(Taste, if it is too sour you can add sieved icing sugar to sweeten it).*
6. Whisk the egg whites to soft peaks and fold in the raspberry mixture.
7. Place the lined rings on a lined baking tray and pour the mixture into them. Refrigerate to set. *
8. To make the raspberry coulis, simply push the raspberries through a fine sieve, discarding the seeds.

To serve, place each pudding on a plate using a spatula, carefully remove the rings and peel off the paper. Top with a little whipped cream, a raspberry and a mint leaf and circle with raspberry coulis.

Banoffee Pie

INGREDIENTS ££

Topping
1 tin condensed milk (397g)
3 large bananas
290ml (10 fl oz / ½ pt) double cream

Base
225g (8 oz) digestive biscuits, *crushed*
125g (4½ oz) butter

METHOD

SERVES 8-10

1. Place the tin of condensed milk in a saucepan, fill the pan with hot water and cover with a lid.
2. Bring to the boil and simmer for 3 hours, topping up with water when necessary. Remove the tin from the saucepan and leave to cool. *
3. **To make the base**, melt the butter in a saucepan and add the biscuits.
4. Transfer into a 25 cm (10 inch) greased flan dish, press firmly into place and allow to cool.
5. When the tin of condensed milk is cool, peel and slice the bananas and arrange the pieces over the biscuit base.
6. Open the tin of condensed milk and stir to loosen. Spoon over the bananas and smooth over the top.
7. Whip the cream until just thick, spread over the top and decorate with grated chocolate.

Chocolate & Grand Marnier Mousse

This mousse needs time to set, so ideally make it the day before you want to serve it.

INGREDIENTS £££

100g (3½ oz) caster sugar
100ml (3½ fl oz) water
400g (14 oz) plain chocolate
2 eggs, *beaten*
150ml (5 fl oz / ¼ pt) double cream
4 tbsp Grand Marnier

For presentation
200g (7 oz) plain chocolate
Frozen raspberries, *thawed (to make a coulis)*
8 whole raspberries, *for decoration*
Double cream, *whipped*
Fresh mint leaves

METHOD

SERVES 8

1. Heat the sugar and water in a pan over a low heat until the sugar has dissolved. Increase the heat and simmer for a few minutes to reduce the liquid *(this is how you adjust the consistency of the mousse, the more you reduce it the firmer the mousse sets).*
2. Take off the heat, stir in the chocolate, then the beaten eggs.
3. Whip the cream so that it is very stiff and fold into the chocolate mixture, together with the Grand Marnier.
4. Cover and refrigerate, preferably overnight, to set the mousse.
5. To make the chocolate discs, melt the chocolate in a bain-marie and, using the back of a spoon, paint circular discs about 8 cm in diameter on a lined baking tray. You will need two per person. *

To serve, spoon a dollop of the mousse on to a plate, place a chocolate disc on top, followed by a second dollop of mousse and another chocolate disc. Top with a little whipped cream, a raspberry and a mint leaf and circle with raspberry coulis. *(To make the raspberry coulis, push the raspberries through a sieve).*

Plum Fool

INGREDIENTS £

400g (14 oz) plums, *washed and stalks removed*
100ml (3½ fl oz) water
2 tbsp golden syrup
½ sachet powdered gelatine *(check manufacturer's instructions as you need enough gelatine to set 255ml (8 fl oz / ½ pt) of liquid)*
150ml (5 fl oz / ¼ pt) double cream
Icing sugar *(optional)*
Mint leaves *(optional), for garnishing*

METHOD

SERVES 4-6

1. Count the plums into a saucepan *(so that you know how many stones you need to remove later)*, add the water and golden syrup, sprinkle in the powdered gelatine, cover and simmer gently for about 5 minutes.
2. Squash the plums down into the juice and continue to simmer, stirring occasionally, until the plums are really soft and the stones have come away from the fruit. Remove from the heat and allow to cool slightly.
3. Remove the stones and blend the mixture in a food processor until light, fluffy and completely smooth.
4. Whip the cream until just thick and gradually fold it into the plum mixture *(if it is too sour you can fold in sieved icing sugar to sweeten it).*
5. Pour into a bowl or individual dishes, cover and refrigerate to set.

Mango, Peach & Lime Sorbet

INGREDIENTS ££

200ml (7 fl oz) water
3 limes, *grated zest of 1 lime and the juice of 3 limes*
250g (9 oz) caster sugar
2 tins mangoes (approx 425g tin), *drained*
2 tins of peaches (approx 410g tin), *drained*
1 egg white
Fresh mint, *for garnishing*
Langues de Chat, *for serving* *(see page 378)*

METHOD

SERVES 8

1. Place the water, lime zest, lime juice and sugar in a small saucepan, bring to the boil and simmer for about 5 minutes to make a syrup.
2. Blend the fruit in a food processor until smooth, while the food processor is blending pour in the syrup through the feeding tube.
3. Transfer the blended mixture into a serving dish, cover with cling film and freeze. *
4. Once frozen, remove the sorbet from the freezer, allow to thaw for about 20 minutes and then spoon into a food processor.
5. Add the egg white and blend until smooth. Refreeze immediately.

Remove from the freezer 10 minutes before you want to serve. Serve with Langues de Chat and fresh mint.

Coconut Panna Cotta with Summer Fruits

INGREDIENTS £££

1 x 400ml tin of coconut milk
300ml (10½ fl oz) double cream
50g (2 oz) sugar
1 vanilla pod
3 tbsp water
½ sachet powdered gelatine
Check manufacturer's instructions as you need enough gelatine to set 290ml (10 fl oz / ½ pt) of liquid

Sauce
250g (9 oz) frozen summer fruits, *thawed*
2 tbsp sugar

METHOD

SERVES 8

1. Put the coconut milk, cream and sugar in a saucepan.
2. Place the vanilla pod on a chopping board and slice lengthwise through the middle so that you can open the pod and remove the seeds. Scrape the seeds out with the tip of the knife and add both the pod and the seeds to the saucepan.
3. Warm over a medium heat to dissolve the sugar *(do not allow to boil, otherwise it will separate).* Remove from the heat and leave to infuse for 5 minutes. *
4. Measure the water into a saucepan, sprinkle in the gelatine and warm, stirring briskly, until the gelatine has completely dissolved *(do not allow to boil).*
5. Lightly grease 8 ramekins with vegetable oil.
6. Remove the empty vanilla pod from the saucepan and mix in the gelatine.
7. Pour the mixture into the ramekins, making sure the seeds that fall to the bottom are evenly distributed between the ramekins. Refrigerate to set and serve straight from the fridge.
8. **To make the sauce**, put the summer fruits and sugar in a saucepan, bring to the boil and simmer gently for 5 minutes. Remove from the heat and allow to cool. *
9. Turn each panna cotta out on to a plate *(place a plate upside down on a ramekin, hold the plate and ramekin tightly together, turn them over so the plate is the right way up, shake and carefully remove the ramekin. If they do not come out, slide a knife down the side of the ramekin to release the pudding).*

Spoon the fruit around the plate and serve.

Figs in Red Wine Syrup with Mascarpone Cheese

INGREDIENTS ££

24 dried figs
290ml (1/2 pt / 10 fl oz) red wine
120g (4 1/4 oz) sugar
4 sprigs of fresh rosemary
2 x 5 cm cinnamon sticks
4 strips lemon zest
8 tbsp mascarpone

Fresh mint leaves, *for garnishing*

METHOD

SERVES 8

1. Place the figs in a saucepan, pour over the red wine and leave to soak for at least 2 hours. *
2. Add the sugar, rosemary, cinnamon and lemon zest, bring to the boil and simmer for 15 minutes.
3. Transfer the figs to a medium sized bowl and sieve the red wine mixture into the same bowl. Allow to cool. *

To serve, place 3 figs on each plate, pour over the red wine syrup, spoon 1 tbsp of mascarpone on to each plate and garnish with a mint leaf.

Blueberry Soufflé

INGREDIENTS ££

3 eggs
110g (4 oz) caster sugar
300g (10 oz) frozen blueberries, *thawed*
3 tbsp water
1 sachet powdered gelatine *(3 leaves). Check manufacturers instructions as you need enough gelatine to set 570ml (20 fl oz / 1 pt) of liquid*
150ml (5 fl oz / ¼ pt) double cream

For presentation
55g (2 oz) blueberries, *for decoration*
Double cream
8 rings, 7 cm (2¾ inch) lined with baking paper *(ramekins can be used).*

METHOD

SERVES 8

1. Separate the eggs and blend the yolks and the sugar in a food processor.
2. Add the blueberries to the food processor to combine and roughly blend.
3. Measure the water into a saucepan, sprinkle in the gelatine and warm, stirring briskly, until the gelatine has completely dissolved. *(Do not allow it to boil).*
4. Turn the food processor on and add the gelatine to combine with the blueberry mixture.
5. Whip the cream and gradually fold in the blueberry mixture. *(Taste, if it is too sour you can add sieved icing sugar to sweeten it).*
6. Whisk the egg whites to soft peak and fold in the blueberry mixture.
7. Place the lined rings on a lined baking tray and pour the mixture into them. Refrigerate to set. *

To serve, place each pudding on a plate. Using a spatula, carefully remove the rings and peel off the paper. Top with three blueberries and circle the plate with cream.

PUDDINGS

Exotic Oranges with Chilli & Ginger Syrup

INGREDIENTS £

4-6 oranges
150ml (5 fl oz / ¼ pt) water, *approx*
100ml (3½ fl oz) orange juice, *approx*
100g (3½ oz) caster sugar
1 lime, *zested*
¼ tsp chilli, *deseeded and finely chopped*
5g (¼ oz) fresh ginger, *sliced*

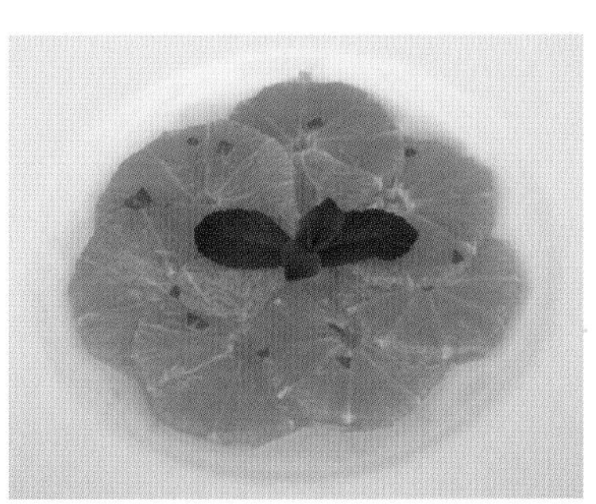

METHOD

SERVES 8

1. Remove the skin and pith from the oranges using a knife.
2. Finely slice the oranges *(cutting across the segments)* and pour the juices that come out into the measuring jug.
3. Top up the measuring jug with orange juice to make 400ml (14 fl oz) of liquid.
4. Pour the liquid into a saucepan, add the sugar, lime zest, chilli and ginger and bring to the boil.
5. Simmer for 10-15 minutes until the liquid has reduced to a syrup.
6. Remove from the heat and allow to cool. Remove the ginger from the syrup before serving.

To serve, arrange the orange slices on a plate and pour over the syrup.

Chocolate Meringue Torte

INGREDIENTS ££

4 **eggs**, *separated*
225g (8 oz) sugar
225g (8 oz) **Bournville chocolate**
425ml (15 fl oz / ¾ pt) double **cream**
Chocolate, *grated (to decorate)*

METHOD

SERVES 8

Preheat the oven to 120°C / 240°F / gas mark 1

1. Line and lightly grease a large baking tray with baking paper.
2. Whisk the egg whites in a large bowl until stiff.
3. Add the sugar gradually, starting with a spoonful at a time while whisking on a low speed, until all the sugar has been incorporated.
4. Spoon the meringue on to the lined tin and make into a birds nest shape.
5. Bake for 1½ hours *(this could vary depending on the thickness of the meringue)*, allow to cool slightly, then peel off the paper. Leave to cool completely. *
6. Melt the chocolate in a bain-marie and paint the inside of the nest with a thin layer of chocolate.
7. Stir the egg yolks into the remaining chocolate and allow to cool slightly. Stir in 2 tbsp double cream to stop the chocolate setting.
8. Whip the remaining cream until stiff and spread half of it over the base of the meringue.
9. Fold the chocolate mixture into the remaining cream and carefully spread over the cream.
10. Decorate with grated chocolate.

Summer Fruits Sorbet

INGREDIENTS £

1 kg (2 lb 4 oz) frozen summer fruits, *thawed*
250g (9 oz) caster sugar
250ml (9 fl oz) water
1 **egg white**
Fresh mint, *for garnishing*
Langues de Chat, *for serving* *(see page 378)*

METHOD

SERVES 8

1. Put the fruit, sugar and water in a small saucepan, bring to the boil and simmer gently for 7 minutes.
2. Push the mixture through a fine sieve and discard the seeds.
3. Cover with cling film and freeze. *
4. Once frozen, remove the sorbet from the freezer, allow to thaw for about 20-30 minutes and then spoon into a food processor.
5. Add the egg white to the food processor and blend until light and fluffy. Refreeze immediately.

Remove from the freezer 10 minutes before you want to serve.

Serve with Langues de Chat and fresh mint.

Hazelnut Cream Roll

INGREDIENTS ££

3 eggs
85g (3 oz) plus 3 tbsp caster sugar
85g (3 oz) hazelnuts, *ground*
2 tbsp wholemeal flour
3 tbsp caster sugar
290ml (10 fl oz / ½ pt) double cream
255g (9 oz) raspberries plus 8, *for decoration*

PUDDINGS

METHOD

SERVES 8

Preheat the oven to 180°C / 350°F / gas mark 4

1. Grease and line a 30 x 20 cm (12 x 8 inch) tin. Whisk the eggs and the 85g (3 oz) of sugar in a bain-marie for about 5 minutes until thick and pale in colour.
2. Remove from the heat, fold in the hazelnuts and flour, spread the mixture evenly in the baking tin and bake for about 12 minutes until firm and golden in colour.
3. Sprinkle a large piece of greaseproof paper with 2 tbsp of caster sugar. Turn the hazelnut cake on to the paper, carefully peel off the paper that lined the tray and, starting at a short end, roll up the cake with the greaseproof paper inside it. Allow to cool on a cooling rack until completely cold.
4. Whip the cream and place a quarter of the cream in a piping bag fitted with a star nozzle.
5. Unroll the cake carefully, remove the paper and spread with the remaining cream. Arrange the raspberries *(except for the 8 being used for decoration)* on top and roll up again. Sprinkle with 1 tbsp sugar. Transfer to a serving plate.

Decorate with piped cream and the remaining raspberries.

Variations: blackberries / chocolate and orange / strawberries.

Crème Brûlée

INGREDIENTS £

570ml (1 pt / 20 fl oz) double cream
150ml (¼ pt / 5 fl oz) milk
1 vanilla pod
6 egg yolks
70g (2½ oz) caster sugar

METHOD

SERVES 8

Preheat the oven to 160°C / 315°F / gas mark 2-3

1. Put the cream and milk in a saucepan.
2. Place the vanilla pod on a chopping board and slice lengthwise through the middle so you can open the pod and remove the seeds. Scrape the seeds out with the tip of the knife and add both the pod and the seeds to the saucepan.
3. Gently heat the cream mixture and remove from the heat just before it boils. Set aside to infuse for 30 minutes.
4. Using an electric whisk, whisk the egg yolks and sugar together until creamy and pale in colour *(be careful not to over whisk).*
5. Add the cream mixture to the egg mixture and combine using a hand whisk *(try not to add air to the mixture).*
6. Pour the mixture through a sieve *(discard the pod but push all the seeds through as you need them to flavour the pudding).*
7. Pour the mixture into 8 ramekins, making sure the seeds that fall to the bottom are evenly distributed between the ramekins.
8. Set aside for 30 minutes to allow the bubbles on the top of each ramekin to disappear.
9. Place the ramekins in a deep baking tray, fill the baking tray with warm water so that the water comes ¾ of the way up the sides of the ramekins.
10. Stir the mixture in each ramekin just before cooking and bake for 25-30 minutes.
11. Remove from the oven and carefully remove the ramekins from the tin *(otherwise they will overcook).* Allow to cool and refrigerate until ready to serve.

To serve, dust the tops with a generous portion of icing sugar and, using a chef's blowtorch, gently melt the sugar until caramelised. Place each ramekin on a plate, dust the plate with icing sugar and serve immediately.

Chocolate Meringue Roulade with Morello Cherries

INGREDIENTS ££

Filling
270g (9½ oz) morello cherries
1 tbsp brandy
290ml (½ pt / 10 fl oz) double cream
55g (2 oz) Bournville chocolate

Meringue
3 egg whites
170g (6 oz) caster sugar
30g (1 oz) cocoa, *sieved*

METHOD

SERVES 8

Preheat the oven to 120°C / 240°F / gas mark 1

1. Drain all the liquid from the cherries and remove any stones. Pour over the brandy and leave to marinade for 1 hour, stirring occasionally. *
2. Line a large baking tray with greased baking paper.
3. **To make the meringue**, whisk the egg whites in a large bowl until stiff *(when you have whipped them enough you will be able to hold the bowl upside down without them falling out).*
4. Add the sugar gradually, starting with a spoonful at a time, while whisking on a low speed, until all the sugar has been incorporated.
5. Carefully fold in the cocoa.
6. Spoon the meringue on to the lined tray, level *(creating a rectangle about 23 x 30 cm / 9 x 12 inch)* and bake for 1 hour.
7. Turn out on to a cooling rack covered with a sheet of baking paper, carefully peel off the paper that lined the tray and leave to cool. *
8. Melt the chocolate in a bain-marie, allow to cool slightly.
9. Whip the cream until just stiff *(be very careful not to over whip)*, add the melted chocolate, mixing together with the whisk on low speed.
10. Spread the chocolate cream evenly over the meringue, spoon the cherries over the meringue *(discard the brandy)* forming a line down the centre. To roll the meringue, hold the long sides of the baking paper and lift, curling the edges of the meringue upwards and inwards. *(Unlike a traditional roulade you are not rolling it up, just rolling it so the ends meet).* Shape with your hands and roll the meringue over so that the two edges that meet are hidden underneath. *

Chill and serve from the fridge, dust with icing sugar just before serving.

Ice Cream & Chocolate Sauce

INGREDIENTS £

Chocolate Sauce
100g (3¾ oz) unsalted butter
70g (2½ oz) cocoa
170g tin of evaporated milk
285g (10 oz) icing sugar, *sieved*

Vanilla ice cream

METHOD

This makes a lot of sauce. It freezes well and you can spoon it out of the freezer and use immediately.

1. **To make the chocolate sauce**, melt the butter in a large saucepan, stir in the cocoa and cook for a couple of minutes.
2. Remove from the heat, stir in the evaporated milk and sieved icing sugar and beat until smooth.
3. Decorate the plate with the sauce *(as above)* or pour over balls of ice cream.

Queen of Puddings

INGREDIENTS £

570 ml (20 fl oz / 1 pt) milk
110g (4 oz) fine breadcrumbs
2 egg yolks
1 orange or lemon, *grated zest (optional)*
1 tbsp caster sugar
3 tbsp strawberry jam

For the Meringue Topping
2 egg whites
45g (1½ oz) caster sugar

METHOD

SERVES 4-6

Preheat the oven to 180°C / 350°F / gas mark 4

1. Heat the milk in a pan and pour over the breadcrumbs. Allow to stand for 10 minutes.
2. Stir in the egg yolks, zest and sugar, pour into a greased ovenproof dish and bake for about 25 minutes until it is just firm to touch.
3. Melt the jam in a saucepan and spread evenly over the bread base.
4. **To make the topping**, whisk the egg whites until stiff.
5. Gradually add the sugar, a spoonful at a time to start with, while whisking on a low speed, until all the sugar has been incorporated. Increase the speed and whisk until stiff.
6. Spread the mixture over the base and bake for approximately 15 minutes until the top is golden. Serve immediately.

Greek Raspberry / Grape Cocktail

INGREDIENTS ££

290ml (10 fl oz / ½ pt) double cream
570ml (20 fl oz / 1 pt) natural yoghurt
Grapes, *washed and dried* or raspberries *(fresh or frozen)*
3-4 tbsp soft brown sugar

METHOD

SERVES 8

1. Whip the cream until stiff, add the yoghurt and combine with the whisk on a low speed.
2. If using grapes, add the grapes to the cream mixture, mix well and spoon into ramekin dishes or a large pudding dish. If using raspberries, serve in a wine glass and layer the raspberries and yoghurt, sprinkling a little sugar after each layer of raspberries.
3. Sprinkle with a layer of brown sugar and refrigerate for a few hours to allow the sugar to dissolve. *

Serve straight from the fridge.

Cappuccino Cheesecake

INGREDIENTS ££

300g (10½ oz) hobnobs, ginger or digestive biscuits *(plain or chocolate covered)*
85g (3 oz) unsalted butter, *soft*
500g (1lb 2 oz) mascarpone
85g (3 oz) icing sugar, *sieved*
2½ tbsp coffee essence
8 tbsp soured cream
Cocoa, *for decoration*

METHOD

SERVES 8

1. Combine the biscuits and the butter in a food processor.
2. Grease the base and sides of a 25 cm (10 inch) round tin and press the biscuit mixture into the base.
3. Using a wooden spoon, beat together the mascarpone, icing sugar and coffee essence until smooth.
4. Spoon on to the biscuit base, smooth over the top and refrigerate. *

To serve, spoon over the soured cream and dust with cocoa.

PUDDINGS

Strawberry Cheesecake

INGREDIENTS ££

300g (10½ oz) hobnobs, ginger or digestive biscuits *(plain or chocolate covered)*
85g (3 oz) unsalted butter, *soft*
500g (1 lb 2 oz) mascarpone
85g (3 oz) icing sugar, *sieved*
8 tbsp strawberry jam

METHOD

SERVES 8

1. Combine the biscuits and the butter in a food processor.
2. Grease the base and sides of a 25 cm (10 inch) round tin and press the biscuit mixture into the base.
3. Using a wooden spoon, beat together the mascarpone and icing sugar until smooth.
4. Spoon on to the biscuit base, smooth over the top and refrigerate. *
5. Just before serving, or once it has had time to chill, carefully spoon over the strawberry jam.

Chocolate Almond Pudding (Gluten free)

INGREDIENTS ££

Knob of unsalted butter
250g (9 oz) Bournville chocolate
3 eggs
1 tbsp brandy
85g (3 oz) ground almonds
125ml (4½ fl oz) double cream
Icing sugar, *to dust*
Vanilla ice cream, *to serve*

METHOD

SERVES 8

Preheat the oven to 150°C / 300°F / gas mark 2

1. Grease a small round ovenproof dish with butter.
2. Melt the chocolate in a bain-marie, remove from the heat and allow to cool slightly.
3. Place a medium sized bowl over a saucepan of warm water and whisk the eggs and brandy until light and foamy *(make sure the bottom of the bowl is not touching the water or you will end up scrambling the egg).* Remove from the heat.
4. Fold in the chocolate and ground almonds.
5. Whip the cream, fold it into the mixture and pour into an ovenproof dish.
6. Place the dish in a deep baking tray and fill the tray with water, so that the water comes ¾ of the way up the sides of the dish, creating a bain-marie.
7. Bake in the oven for 35-40 minutes * then allow to cool.

To serve, slice, dust with icing sugar and serve with ice cream.

Dark Chocolate & Pecan Tart

INGREDIENTS ££

Pastry
100g (3¾ oz) plain flour
45g (1½ oz) unsalted butter
2 tbsp icing sugar
2 tbsp Demerara sugar
2 drops vanilla essence
½ egg, *beaten*

Filling
200g (7 oz) Bournville chocolate
100ml (3½ oz) milk
150ml (5 fl oz / ¼ pt) double cream
2 eggs
45g (1½ oz) pecans, *roughly chopped (save 8 whole halves for presentation)*
Crème fraîche, *for serving*

METHOD

SERVES 8

Preheat the oven to 140°C / 285°F / gas mark 1

1. Grease and flour an 18 cm (7 inch) flan tin.
2. **To make the pastry**, blend the flour, butter, icing and Demerara sugar in the food processor.
3. Add the vanilla essence and egg and pulse until just combined. Flour your hands, gather into a ball and roll out to fit the flan tin *(you will need to use lots of flour when rolling).*
4. Blind bake the pastry for 15 minutes *(put a layer of greaseproof paper over the pastry and weigh it down with baking beans or rice. This prevents the pastry base from ballooning).* Remove the baking beans and greaseproof paper and cook for a further 5 minutes.
5. Turn the oven temperature up to 190°C / 375 °F / gas mark 5.
6. **To make the filling**, melt the chocolate in a bain-marie.
7. Bring the milk to the boil *(be very careful not to over boil)* and add it to the chocolate. Stir until it is smooth then remove from the heat.
8. Stir in the cream, then the egg and chopped pecans and pour the mixture into the pastry case.
9. Decorate with the remaining whole pecans, put in the oven and turn the oven off. Leave for an hour without opening the oven door *(or cook it in the oven for 20 minutes)* then chill in the fridge for at least 2 hours.

Serve with crème fraîche.

White Chocolate, Cardamom & Bay Leaf Panna Cotta

INGREDIENTS

6 cardamom pods
500ml (17½ fl oz) double **cream**
200ml (7 fl oz) **milk**
60g (2 oz) caster sugar
2 large bay leaves
1 sachet **gelatine** *(enough gelatine to set 570ml / 20 fl oz / 1 pt)*
150g (5½ oz) white **chocolate**
Strawberries, *for presentation*

METHOD

SERVES 8

1. Squash the cardamom pods with the side of a chef's knife, being careful not to crush the seeds inside.
2. Put the cardamom pods and seeds, double cream, milk, sugar and bay leaves in a saucepan, slowly bring to the boil, then remove from the heat.
3. Remove the bay leaves then whisk in the gelatine.
4. When the gelatine has completely melted, sieve the mixture to remove the cardamom pods and seeds.
5. Melt the chocolate in a bain-marie then slowly stir in the milk mixture, a little at a time.
6. Grease 8 timbales with vegetable oil then pour in the mixture. Refrigerate to allow to set.

Turn out on to a plate and serve with strawberries.

Passion Fruit Bavarois

INGREDIENTS

6 egg yolks
100g (3½ oz) caster sugar
200ml (7 fl oz) milk
200ml (7 fl oz) double cream
1 sachet of powdered gelatine
Check manufacturer's instructions as you need enough gelatine to set 570ml (20 fl oz /1 pt) of liquid.
3 tbsp water
200ml (7 fl oz) passion fruit purée (or blackcurrant or raspberry coulis / purée)
Kiwi, *peeled and sliced, for serving*
Passion fruit purée, *for decoration*
Grenadine, *for presentation*

METHOD

SERVES 8

1. Put the egg yolks and the sugar in a food processor and blend until pale and creamy
2. Gently warm the milk and cream in a saucepan. When it comes to the boil take off the heat and slowly add to the yolk and sugar mixture while the food processor is on.
3. Pour into a bain-marie and heat until the mixture thickens *(to a thick custard consistency)* and coats the back of the spoon *(stir continuously so that it does not scramble).* Remove from the heat to stop it cooking.
4. Measure the water into a small saucepan, sprinkle in the gelatine and warm, stirring briskly until completely dissolved *(do not allow it to boil).*
5. Add the creamy mixture to the pan and then stir in the passion fruit purée.
6. Pour into ramekins greased with vegetable oil and refrigerate to set.

Serve in the ramekins or turn out on to a plate. Serve with slices of kiwi and passion fruit purée with dots of grenadine through the purée.

Coconut Ice Cream

PUDDINGS

INGREDIENTS ££

570ml (20 fl oz / 1 pt) whipping cream
1 large tin condensed milk
180ml (6 fl oz) coconut purée
6 tbsp desiccated coconut
55g (2 oz) dark chocolate, *grated*

METHOD

SERVES 8

1. Whip the cream until stiff, add the condensed milk, coconut purée, desiccated coconut and grated chocolate and combine with the whisk on a low speed.
2. Pour into a serving dish and freeze. *

Serve with chocolate shavings or warm chocolate sauce *(see page 289)*.

The ice cream will keep for 10 days.

Passion Fruit & Hazelnut Cheesecake

INGREDIENTS

30g (1 oz) hazelnuts
100g (3½ oz) digestive biscuits
30g (1 oz) unsalted butter
500g (1 lb 2 oz) cream cheese
6 tbsp (90 ml) passion fruit purée
85g (3 oz) icing sugar
1 egg
1 lemon, *grated zest*
1 passion fruit

Passion fruit coulis
100ml (3½ oz) passion fruit purée
2 tbsp sugar
1 tsp lemon juice
½ tsp cornflour, *diluted in a little water*

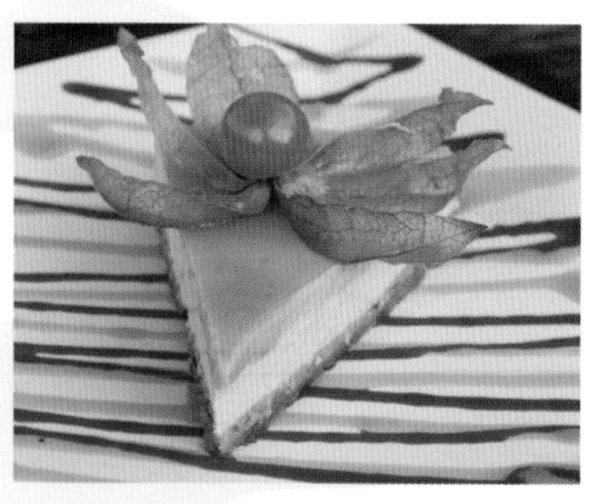

METHOD

SERVES 8

Preheat the oven to 160°C / 320°F / gas mark 2-3

1. Roast all the hazelnuts in the oven for about 5 minutes. Allow to cool slightly and remove the skins by rubbing them between the palms of your hands. Roughly chop.
2. To make the base, blend the hazelnuts, biscuits and butter in a food processor.
3. Grease a loose bottomed tin (18 cm / 7 inch) and press the biscuit mixture firmly on to the base and then chill.
4. Blend the cream cheese in a food processor until smooth. Then add the passion fruit purée, icing sugar, egg and lemon zest and blend just enough to combine.
5. Pour the mixture over the biscuit base and bake in the oven for 25 minutes *(it will still be very wobbly in the centre but should be just set when cool)*. When it comes out of the oven, carefully run a knife around the edge of the cheesecake to help reduce cracking as it cools. Allow to cool and refrigerate.
6. **To make the coulis**, put all the ingredients in a saucepan, bring to the boil and simmer for about 2 minutes until slightly thickened. Allow to cool, then pour into a squeezy bottle.

Slice the cheesecake, plate and then carefully cover the top of each slice of cheesecake with the coulis. Spoon some passion fruit seeds over the top and serve.

Champagne Jelly with Strawberries, Blueberries, & Pomegranate

INGREDIENTS

225ml (8 fl oz) water
1½ sachet powdered gelatine or 6 leaves *(check manufacturer's instructions, you need enough gelatine to set 900ml (30 fl oz / 1½ pts) of liquid*
195g (7 oz) caster sugar
1½ vanilla pods
425ml (15 fl oz / ¾ pt) Champagne or sparkling wine
225g (8 oz) fresh fruit: blueberries, strawberries and a few pomegranate seeds
Crème fraîche, *to decorate*
Fresh mint, *to garnish*

METHOD

SERVES 8

1. Put the water in a saucepan, sprinkle over the gelatine, stir to combine and warm over a gentle heat until the gelatine has disolved.
2. Add the sugar and vanilla pod and continue to heat until almost boiling *(do not allow to boil)*.
3. Remove from the heat and allow to stand for 30 minutes to allow the vanilla pod to infuse.
4. To prepare the fruit, cut most of the blueberries in half horizontally, slice the strawberries and spoon out a few pomegranate seeds. Divide the fruit between the glasses.
5. Remove the vanilla pod from the jelly and gently pour in the Champagne.
6. Carefully pour into 8 presentation glasses, cover with cling film and refrigerate to set. (If you want to remove the fizzy taste and prevent bubbles from setting around the edge of the glass, reheat the jelly, allow to cool and then pour into the presentation glasses). *

Serve with crème fraîche and a sprig of fresh mint.

Pear & Frangipane Tart

INGREDIENTS ££

250ml (9 fl oz) water
½ tbsp lemon juice
50g (2 oz) sugar
Pinch of saffron strands *(optional)*
4 pears
1½ tbsp apricot jam

Frangipane
65g (2¼ oz) unsalted butter
65g (2¼ oz) sugar
1 egg
15g (½ oz) flour
60g (2¼ oz) ground almonds
1 tbsp white rum

Pastry
150g (5¼ oz) plain flour
75g (2¾ oz) unsalted butter
75g (2¾ oz) icing sugar
½ egg
3-4 drops vanilla essence

Ice cream or crème fraîche, *for serving*

METHOD

SERVES 6

Preheat the oven to 160°C / 320°F / gas mark 2-3

1. Put the water, lemon juice, sugar and saffron *(if using)* in a saucepan.
2. Peel, quarter and remove the core of the pears and put them straight into the saucepan *(otherwise they will go brown)*.
3. Bring to the boil and simmer for about 10-15 minutes until tender.
4. Carefully remove pears with a slotted spoon and leave them to drain.
5. Add the apricot jam to the water and simmer for 30 minutes to reduce it to a syrup.
6. Grease and flour an 18 cm (7 inch) loose bottomed flan tin.
7. **To make the pastry**, blend the ingredients in a food processor then make into a ball using your hands.
8. Roll out the pastry on a sheet of baking paper and line the tin. Neaten up the edges using the back of a knife.
9. Blind bake for 8 minutes *(put a layer of greaseproof paper over the pastry and weigh it down with rice or baking beans. This prevents the pastry base from ballooning). Remove the rice or baking beans and greaseproof paper and cook for a further 4 minutes to dry it out a bit.* Allow to cool.
10. **To make the frangipane**, blend all the ingredients in the processor until smooth.
11. Spread the frangipane over the base of the pastry.
12. Dry the pears and arrange them on top, pressing them down into the frangipane.
13. Bake for 30 minutes, remove from the oven, baste with the syrup then return to oven for 5 minutes.

Serve warm or at room temperature with crème fraîche or ice cream.

Lemon Posset

INGREDIENTS £

2 lemons, *finely grated zest and juice*
570ml (20 fl oz / 1 pt) double cream
120g (4¼ oz) caster sugar
8 tbsp lemon curd
4 tsp orange juice
Plain chocolate *(high cocoa content)*

METHOD

SERVES 8

1. Put the lemon zest, lemon juice, cream and sugar in a saucepan. Bring to the boil and simmer for 5 minutes, stirring occasionally. Allow to cool for a few minutes.
2. Mix together the lemon curd and orange juice and pour into 8 small presentation glasses.
3. Pour the cream mixture through a fine sieve and then carefully spoon it in to the presentation glasses. Refrigerate to set.
4. Melt some chocolate in a bain-marie and pipe shapes, designs or names onto a piece of baking paper. Refrigerate until just before serving, then top each pudding with your decoration.

Profiteroles (Gluten & Lactose free)

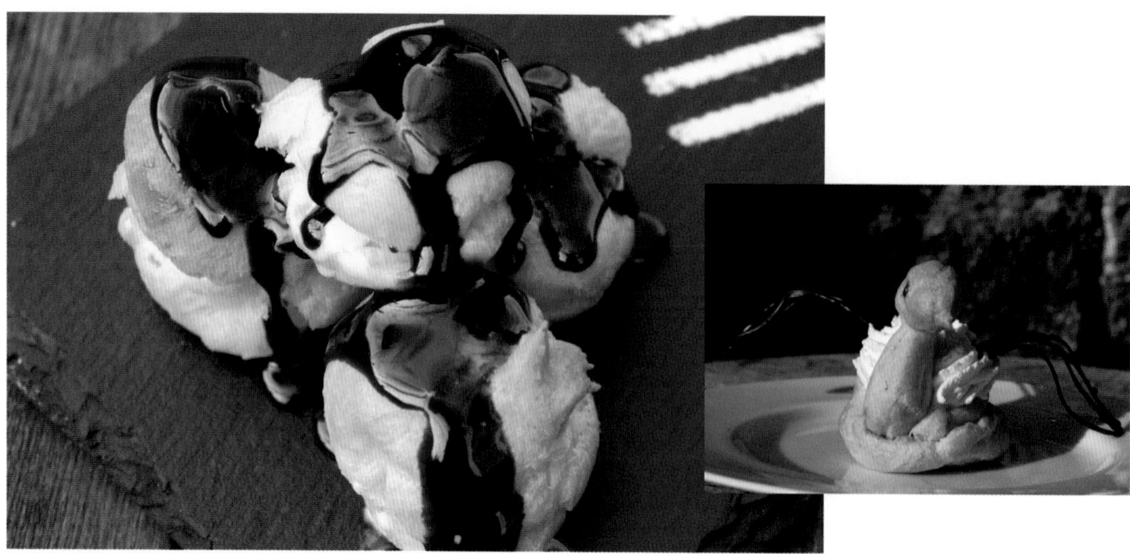

PUDDINGS

INGREDIENTS £

Pastry
300ml water
100g (3½ oz) unsalted butter or sunflower spread
140g (5 oz) gluten-free white bread flour
3 large eggs, *lightly beaten*

Sauce
100g (3½ oz) dairy free chocolate
4 tbsp brandy

Filling
400ml (14 oz) goats', buffalo, soya or rice milk
20g (¾ oz) cornflour
70g (2½ oz) dairy free chocolate
2 tbsp Grand Marnier

METHOD

SERVES 8

Preheat the oven to 200°C / 400°F / Gas mark 6

1. **To make the pastry** melt the butter in a saucepan, add the water and bring to the boil.
2. Remove from the heat, add the flour and stir hard until the mixture leaves the sides of the pan *(a little more heat may be needed).*
3. Cool for a minute or two. Add the eggs, one at a time, beating until smooth and shiny.
4. Put individual teaspoonfuls of the mixture on a greased baking tray and bake for 35-40 minutes until golden.
5. Immediately transfer the profiteroles to a cooling rack and pierce the side of each to allow the steam to escape.*
6. When cool, cut in half and remove any uncooked dough from inside.
7. **To make the filling**, put the milk and cornflour into a saucepan, stir until smooth and cook over a gentle heat to thicken.
8. And the chocolate and Grand Marnier and stir until smooth. Allow to cool, then fill the profiteroles.
9. **To make the sauce**, melt the chocolate in a bain-marie, stir in the brandy and spoon over the profiteroles.

Chocolate & Orange Posset

INGREDIENTS ££

570ml (20 fl oz / 1 pt) double cream
120g (4½ oz) caster sugar
1½ oranges *(keep a few slices aside for decoration)*
200g (7 oz) **Bournville chocolate**
8 tsp orange maramalade

METHOD

SERVES 8

1. Put the cream, sugar, 1 tsp finely grated orange zest and 4 tbsp orange juice in a saucepan, bring to the boil and simmer for 5 minutes, stirring occasionally.
2. Melt the chocolate in a bain-marie, then stir into the cream mixture.
3. Put 1 tsp of marmalade in the bottom of 8 presentation glasses.
4. Carefully spoon the cream mixture on top and refrigerate. Leave to infuse for as long as possible before serving.

Garnish with slices of orange.

Chocolate & Kahlúa Croissant Pudding

Ideally this dish needs to be made the day before you serve it.

INGREDIENTS ££

85g (3 oz) unsalted **butter**
140g (5 oz) plain **chocolate**
110g (4 oz) caster sugar
425ml (15 fl oz / ¾ pt) double **cream**
4 tbsp Kahlúa *(Rum or* **Baileys Cream** *can be used)*
2 pinches of ground cinnamon
3 **eggs**, *beaten*
6 **croissants**, *sliced in half as for a sandwich*

METHOD

SERVES 6

1. Put the butter, chocolate, sugar, cream, alcohol and cinnamon in a bain-marie and warm until the butter, sugar and chocolate have melted.
2. Beat the eggs into the chocolate mixture.
3. Arrange the bases of the croissants in an ovenproof dish and pour over half of the mixture.
4. Decorate with the top halves of the croissants, pour over the remaining chocolate mixture and refrigerate for at least 10 hours, so the croissants absorb the chocolate. *
5. Bake in a preheated oven for 25-30 minutes at 180°C / 350°F / gas mark 4.

Dust with icing sugar and serve with cream.

Fruit Tarts

INGREDIENTS ££

Pastry
225g (8 oz) plain flour
110g (4 oz) unsalted butter
80g (3 oz) sugar
1 egg, *beaten*
1 egg yolk, *to glaze*

Crème Patissiere
4 egg yolks
65g (2¼ oz) caster sugar
1 tbsp cornflour
1 tbsp plain flour
350ml (12 fl oz) milk
½ vanilla pod

Strawberries, raspberries
and /or blueberries

METHOD

SERVES 8

Preheat the oven to 160°C / 310°F / gas mark 2-3

1. **To make the pastry**, put the flour into a bowl and rub in the butter, using your fingertips, until it is a bread crumb like consistency.
2. Stir in the sugar, then add the beaten egg and mix to form a ball.
3. Put the pastry onto a floured chopping board and roll it out thinly.
4. Using a crinkle edged cutter, cut out circles *(the size depends on the tin size)* and place the circles into a greased and floured tartlet tin.
5. Blind bake for 6-8 minutes *(put a layer of greaseproof paper over the pastry and weigh it down with baking beans or rice. This prevents the pastry base from ballooning).*
6. Remove the greaseproof paper and baking beans or rice and glaze the inside and the crinkly edge with the egg yolk. Return to the oven and bake for a further 2-3 minutes until golden.
7. Transfer to a cooling rack and allow to cool.
8. **To make the crème patissière**, whisk the egg yolks and caster sugar in a bowl until pale and fluffy.
9. Add cornflour and flour and mix until smooth.
10. Put the milk and vanilla seeds in a saucepan *(to remove the seeds from the vanilla pod, slice the pod open lengthways and scrape the seeds out with the tip of the knife)* and simmer for 2 minutes then remove from the heat.
11. Slowly pour the hot milk into the egg mixture, whisking continuously as you pour.
12. Then pour the mixture back into the saucepan and heat *(whisk using a coil whisk until it is the consistency of thick custard).* Allow to cool, stirring occasionally to prevent a skin from forming.
13. Pour the crème patissière into the pastry cases and arrange the fruit over the top. Refrigerate for at least 4 hours before serving.

Baked Bananas with Ice Cream & Butterscotch Sauce

INGREDIENTS £

Butterscotch Sauce
30g (1 oz) unsalted butter
45g (1½ oz) soft brown sugar
30g (1 oz) caster sugar
5 tbsp golden syrup
55ml (2 fl oz) double cream
Vanilla essence, *a few drops*

4 bananas
4 tsp Demerara sugar
Vanilla ice cream

METHOD

SERVES 4

Preheat the oven to 180°C / 350°F / gas mark 4

1. **To make the sauce**, place the butter, both sugars and syrup in a saucepan and cook over a gentle heat. Once the sugar has completely dissolved continue to cook gently for a further 5 minutes.
2. Remove from the heat and gradually stir in the double cream. *
3. Add a few drops of vanilla essence and stir well until the sauce is smooth.
4. Leave the bananas in their skins, place them on a lined baking tray and cut out a small "V" shape along the top.
5. Fill with the Demerara sugar and bake for about 20 minutes until the skins blacken.

Plate up the bananas (in their skins) and pour over the hot sauce. Serve with a couple of balls of vanilla ice cream.

This sauce will keep in the fridge for up to two weeks in a sealed container. You can also add some chocolate to make a chocolate sauce.

Apple Crumble

INGREDIENTS £

675g (1½ lbs) cooking apples, *peeled, cored and chopped*
1 tbsp sugar
½ tsp ground cinnamon

Topping
110g (4 oz) self raising **flour**
55g (2 oz) sugar
55g (2 oz) unsalted **butter**

METHOD

SERVES 4

Preheat the oven to 180°C / 350°F / gas mark 4

1. Put the apples, sugar, cinnamon and a little water in a saucepan and cook over a gentle heat until soft and fluffy.
2. Spoon the mixture into an ovenproof dish and allow to cool slightly.
3. **To make the topping**, mix the flour, sugar and butter together with a fork so that it resembles breadcrumbs.
4. Sprinkle the topping over the fruit and bake for 30 minutes.

Serve with ice cream or Crème Anglaise / Custard *(see below)*.

Crème Anglaise (Custard)

INGREDIENTS £

30g (1 oz) caster sugar
3 **egg yolks**
4-5 drops of vanilla essence
250ml (9 fl oz) **milk**

METHOD

SERVES 8

1. Mix the sugar, egg yolks and vanilla essence in a bowl.
2. Bring the milk to the boil in a saucepan and pour into the mixture.
3. Transfer the mixture to a bain-marie * and heat gently until it coats the back of the spoon *(do not let it boil because it curdles easily)*.

PUDDINGS

Lemon Syllabub

INGREDIENTS £

290ml (10 fl oz / ½ pt) double **cream**
110g (4 oz) caster sugar
1 large lemon, *grated zest and juice*
4 tbsp medium **sherry**

METHOD

SERVES 8

1. Place all the ingredients in a large bowl and whisk until thick and creamy.
2. Pour into wine glasses and refrigerate, or, if serving in Brandy snap baskets, refrigerate until serving *(fill the baskets just before serving, otherwise the baskets will become soft)*. *

Decorate with fresh fruit and grated chocolate.

Chocolate & Mango Fondant

INGREDIENTS ££

150g (5¼ oz) unsalted butter
150g (5¼ oz) dark chocolate
(at least 60% cocoa)
3 egg yolks
3 eggs
75g (2¾ oz) caster sugar
100g (3½ oz) plain flour
Fresh mint, *for garnish*

Mango Curd
150ml (5 fl oz / ¼ pt) mango purée
1 tsp gelatine powder
3 tbsp icing sugar
1 tbsp lemon juice

With thanks to the Watergate Bay Hotel who gave us the inspiration and the recipe which we adapted to use in the school

METHOD

SERVES 8

Preheat the oven to 190°C / 375°F / gas mark 5

1. **To make the mango curd**, warm the mango purée in a small saucepan over a gentle heat. Add the gelatine and stir until it has dissolved *(for about 4 - 5 minutes)*. Do not allow to boil.
2. Pour into a small bowl and allow to set overnight in the fridge.
3. Blend the mango jelly in a food processor *(the consistency will change to a smooth curd)*. Add the icing sugar and lemon to taste. *
4. Melt the butter and chocolate in a bain-marie, stir to combine and allow to cool slightly.
5. Put 8 lined rings on a lined baking tray.
6. Whisk the eggs, egg yolks and caster sugar until light and fluffy.
7. Slowly fold in the chocolate mixture, sieve in the flour and carefully fold it in.
8. Spoon a little of the mixture into each ring so that it is 1 cm (½ inch) high.
9. Carefully place a heaped teaspoon of the mango curd onto the centre of the chocolate, *(the mango curd must not touch the sides of the rings, otherwise the fondant will collapse)*.
10. Spoon the rest of the chocolate mixture around the curd and over the top.
11. Bake for 8-9 minutes, and leave to stand for 1 minute before plating. Be very careful when plating not to damage the bottom otherwise the mango will escape.

Dust with icing sugar and serve immediately with vanilla ice cream and a sprig of mint.

Chocolate Fondant

INGREDIENTS £

125g (4½ oz) unsalted **butter**
125g (4½ oz) plain **chocolate**
(at least 60% cocoa solids)
3 **eggs**
125g (4½ oz) caster sugar
35g (1¼ oz) plain **flour**
Ice cream or **cream**, *to serve*
Fresh mint, *to garnish*

METHOD

SERVES 6

Preheat the oven to 200°C / 400°F / gas mark 6

1. Melt the butter and chocolate in a bain-marie.
2. Grease and flour the insides of the ramekins.
3. Whisk the eggs, sugar and flour in a bowl until smooth.
4. Pour the chocolate into the egg mixture and whisk together.
5. Divide the mixture into 6 ramekins, cover and refrigerate until required. *
6. Bake uncovered for about 12-14 minutes until the top has formed a slight crust.

Serve immediately with a ball of ice cream on top.

Chocolate Moelleux

INGREDIENTS ££

225g (8 oz) plain chocolate
(at least 60% cocoa solids)
110g (4 oz) unsalted butter
110g (4 oz) plain flour
110g (4 oz) caster sugar
2 eggs
3 egg yolks
Ice cream or cream to serve

8 rings, 7 cm (2¾ inch) lined with baking paper *(ramekins can be used)*

METHOD

SERVES 8

Preheat the oven to 190ºC / 375ºF / gas mark 5

1. Melt the butter and the chocolate in a bain-marie and allow to cool for a few minutes.
2. Put the eggs, egg yolks and sugar into a large bowl and whisk until the mixture has doubled in size.
3. Fold in the melted chocolate and then the sieved flour.
4. Place the lined rings on a lined baking tray and spoon the mixture into them. * *(You can chill them in the fridge at this stage until you want to cook them).*
5. Bake for 7 minutes *(you will need to cook them for longer if you are cooking them straight from the fridge).* They are cooked when the top loses its shine.
6. Place each Moelleux on a plate using a spatula, remove the rings *(you may need to slide a knife in between the ring and the paper)* and peel off the paper.
7. Dust with icing sugar and serve immediately with ice cream. *(The centre should ooze out chocolate when broken open).*

Chocolate Moelleux (Gluten free)

INGREDIENTS ££

50g (2 oz) unsalted butter
100g (3½ oz) plain chocolate
(at least 60% cocoa solids)
1 egg yolk
1 egg
2 tbsp caster sugar
1 tbsp ground almonds
3-4 tbsp Baileys Cream
Icing sugar, *for garnishing*
Ice cream or cream, *to serve*

4 rings, 7 cm (2¾ inch) lined with baking paper *(ramekins can be used)*

METHOD

SERVES 4

Preheat the oven to 190°C / 375°F / gas mark 5

1. Melt the butter and the chocolate in a bain-marie and allow to cool for a few minutes.
2. Put the egg, egg yolk and sugar into a large bowl and whisk until light and pale in colour.
3. Fold in the melted chocolate, ground almonds and Baileys.
4. Place the lined rings on a lined baking tray and spoon the mixture into them. * *(You can chill them in the fridge at this stage until you want to cook them).*
5. Bake for approx 9 minutes *(you will need to cook them for longer if you are cooking them straight from the fridge).* They are cooked when the top loses its shine.

Place each Moelleux on a plate using a spatula, remove the rings *(you may need to slide a knife in between the ring and the paper)* and peel off the paper. Dust with icing sugar and serve immediately with ice cream. *(The centre should ooze out chocolate when broken open).*

Coconut & Lime Pancakes (Lactose free)

INGREDIENTS ££

Pancake Mixture
1 egg
85g (3 oz) plain flour
150ml (5 fl oz / ¼ pt) coconut milk
4 tbsp water
1 lime, *grated zest*
(use juice to serve)
1 tsp sugar

METHOD

MAKES 6 PANCAKES

1. Blend all the pancake ingredients in a food processor. *
2. To cook the pancakes, warm some vegetable oil in a small frying pan and spoon in a little of the batter, tilting the pan so that it covers the base evenly. Cook for a minute or two and turn to cook the other side *(you may need to add a little more oil to the pan).*

Serve with lime juice and sugar.

Pancakes

INGREDIENTS £

Batter Mix
1 egg
85g (3 oz) plain flour
200ml (7 fl oz) milk *(approx)*
Vegetable oil

METHOD

SERVES 4

1. **To make the batter**, blend the egg, flour and milk in a food processor *(or put ingredients in a bowl and beat with a balloon whisk)*. If possible allow to stand for at least ½ hour.
2. Heat approximately 1 tbsp of oil in a frying pan until very hot. Tip the excess oil out of the pan into a small bowl, to be used later.
3. Stir the batter, then pour about 2 tbsp into the pan, tilt the pan so that the mixture spreads and covers the base.
4. Cook until the under surface browns, then toss or turn the pancake and cook the other side until golden.
5. Serve immediately, or stack them up and keep them warm in the oven.
6. Continue making the pancakes adding more oil to the pan each time.

Serving suggestions: Sprinkle with lemon juice and sugar / maple syrup / cherry jam and ice cream / Nutella.

Passion Fruit Ice Cream & Raspberry Sherbet Sorbet

INGREDIENTS £££

Passion Fruit Ice Cream

290ml (10 fl oz / ½ pt) whipping cream
½ large tin condensed milk
6 tbsp (90ml / 3¼ oz) passion fruit purée

Raspberry Sherbet Sorbet

340g (12 oz) frozen raspberries, *thawed*
135g (4¾ oz) sugar
240ml (8½ fl oz) milk
120ml (4 fl oz) double cream
1 tsp lemon juice

METHOD

SERVES 8

1. **To make the ice cream**, whip the cream until stiff, add the condensed milk and combine with the whisk on a low speed.
2. Whisk in the passion fruit purée then pour into a serving dish and freeze. *
3. **To make the sorbet**, push the raspberries through a fine sieve and discard the seeds.
4. Stir in the other ingredients, cover with cling film and freeze. *
5. Once frozen remove from the freezer and allow to thaw for about 20 minutes.
6. Blend in a food processer until smooth and refreeze immediately.

Serve together.

Lemon Sorbet

INGREDIENTS £

450g (1 lb) sugar
1.2 L (42 fl oz) water
8 lemons, *zest and juice*
1 **egg white**

METHOD

SERVES 8

1. Put the sugar, water, lemon juice and zest into a saucepan, bring to the boil and simmer to reduce by half.
2. Allow to cool, cover with cling film and freeze.
3. Once frozen remove from the freezer and allow to thaw for about 20 minutes.
4. Blend with the egg white in a food processer until light and fluffy and refreeze immediately.

The sorbet is very light so it melts very quickly.

It can be served as an amuse-bouche.

Sticky Toffee Pudding

INGREDIENTS ££

290ml (10 fl oz / ½ pt) water
170g (6 oz) pitted dates
1 tsp bicarbonate soda
55g (2 oz) unsalted butter
85g (3 oz) soft brown sugar
2 eggs
1 tbsp ground ginger *(optional)*
1 tbsp treacle *(optional)*
170g (6 oz) self raising flour
Crème fraîche or ice cream, *to serve*
Fresh mint, *for decoration*

Toffee Sauce

200g (7 oz) soft brown sugar
125g (4½ oz) unsalted butter
150ml (5 fl oz / ¼ pt) double cream
½ tsp vanillla essence

METHOD

SERVES 8

Preheat the oven to 160°C / 320°F / gas mark 2-3

1. Bring the water to the boil in a saucepan, add the dates and simmer for 5 minutes.
2. Add the bicarbonate of soda then blend in the small bowl of a food processor for about 10 seconds.
3. Beat the butter and sugar in the large bowl of a food processor until pale.
4. In a very large bowl mix the dates, eggs, treacle and the butter / sugar mixture and then stir in the flour and ginger.
5. Line a tin with greaseproof paper approximately 18 x 28 cm (7 x 11 inch), pour in the mixture and bake for 30 minutes.
6. **To make the sauce**: put all the ingredients in a saucepan and cook over a gentle heat until the sugar has dissolved.
7. Using a skewer, make lots of holes in the sponge, pour over about half the sauce and bake for a further 5 minutes. *

To serve, reheat the sponge in a warm oven, cut into square portions and plate. Pour over hot sauce and top with ice cream, or crème fraîche, and a sprig of mint.

French Pear Pie with Grand Marnier Cream

INGREDIENTS £

Pastry
300g (10½ oz) plain flour
150g (5¼ oz) icing sugar
150g (5¼ oz) unsalted butter
1 egg

Vanilla essence
4-5 ripe pears

Grand Marnier Cream
150ml (5 fl oz / ¼ pt) double cream
Grand Marnier

METHOD

SERVES 8

Preheat the oven to 180°C / 350°F / gas mark 4

1. **To make the pastry**, blend the pastry ingredients in a food processor and make into a ball, using your hands.
2. Roll out just over half of the pastry mixture to line a 25 cm (10 inch) flat bottomed flan tin.
3. Peel, quarter and de-core the pears and arrange neatly in the dish, rounded side up *(they will show through).*
4. Roll out the remaining pastry on a floured baking sheet *(large enough to cover the dish)* and slide it on to the pears to completely cover.
5. Tidy the edges and bake for 25 minutes, until pale golden. *
6. **To make the Grand Marnier cream**, whip the cream and add the Grand Marnier to taste.

Dust the pie with icing sugar and serve warm with the cream.

Peach Crumble

INGREDIENTS £

Crumble Topping
110g (4 oz) plain flour
70g (2½ oz) sugar
70g (2½ oz) unsalted butter
40g (1¼ oz) porridge oats

375g (13 oz) tinned peaches *(410g tin), drained and sliced*
1 banana, *finely sliced*

METHOD

SERVES 8

Preheat the oven to 200°C / 400°F / gas mark 6

1. **To make the crumble topping**, blend the flour, sugar and butter in a food processor until it resembles breadcrumbs *(do not over blend).* Remove the blade from the food processor and work in the oats with your hands. *
2. Place 8 lined mousse rings on a lined baking tray and arrange a layer of peaches in each ring.
3. Slice the banana and arrange the slices on top of the peaches.
4. Crumble over the topping * and bake for 25-30 minutes until golden.

Serve with Crème Anglaise *(custard)*, or cream.

Raspberry Sherbet Sorbet

INGREDIENTS ££

675g (1½ lb) frozen raspberries, *thawed*
270g (9½ oz) sugar
480ml (17 fl oz) milk
240ml (8 fl oz) double cream
2 tsp lemon juice
Fresh mint, *for garnish*

METHOD

SERVES 8

1. Push the raspberries through a fine sieve and discard the seeds.
2. Stir in the other ingredients, cover with cling film and freeze. *
3. Once frozen remove from the freezer and allow to thaw for about 20 minutes.
4. Blend in a food processer until smooth and refreeze immediately.

Apricot Ice Cream

INGREDIENTS £

570 ml (20 fl oz / 1 pt) whipping cream
1 large tin (397g) condensed milk
340g (12 oz) apricot jam *(other jams can be used but apricot is especially nice)*

METHOD

SERVES 8

1. Whip the cream until stiff, add the condensed milk and combine with the whisk on a low speed.
2. Whisk in the jam, pour into a serving dish and freeze. *

Serve with langues de chat *(see page 378)*.

The ice cream will keep for 10 days.

Baileys & Sugared Nut Ice Cream

INGREDIENTS ££

110g (4 oz) walnuts, *roughly chopped*
55g (2 oz) soft brown sugar
570ml (20 fl oz / 1 pt) whipping cream
1 large tin condensed milk (397g)
8 tbsp Baileys cream
Coffee beans, *for decoration*
Cream, *whipped (for decoration)*

METHOD

SERVES 8-12

1. Place the sugar and the nuts in a small saucepan and cook over a medium heat, stirring frequently. As soon as the sugar has melted, turn the nuts out on a sheet of baking paper and allow to cool.
2. Whip the cream until stiff, add the condensed milk and combine with the whisk on a low speed.
3. Stir in the Baileys cream and the sugared nuts, pour into a serving dish and freeze. *

Serve with a teaspoon of whipped cream with two coffee beans placed on top.

The ice cream will keep for 10 days.

Chocolate & Orange Ice Cream

INGREDIENTS £

120g (4½ oz) **hazelnuts**
200g (7 oz) **Bournville chocolate**
1 large tin (397g) **condensed milk**
2 oranges, *juice and grated zest of ½ orange*
570ml (20 fl oz / 1 pt) whipping **cream**
Oranges, *for serving*

METHOD

SERVES 8

Preheat the oven to 180°C / 350°F / gas mark 4

1. Roast all the hazelnuts in the oven for about 5 minutes. Allow to cool slightly and remove the skins by rubbing them between the palm of your hands. Roughly chop.
2. Melt the chocolate in a bain-marie and allow to cool slightly.
3. Mix in the condensed milk, nuts, orange juice and zest.
4. Whip the cream until stiff, add the chocolate mixture and combine with the whisk on a low speed.
5. Pour into a serving dish and freeze. *

Serve with fresh oranges.

The ice cream will keep for 10 days.

Chocolate Tart with Orange Pastry

INGREDIENTS £

Orange Pastry *(freezes well)*
75g (2¾ oz) unsalted **butter**
75g (2¾ oz) icing sugar, *sieved*
½ orange, *grated zest*
½ tsp orange flower water *(if not available, use water)*
1 **egg yolk**
125g (4½ oz) plain **flour**

290ml (10 fl oz / ½ pt) double **cream**
2 tbsp clear honey
50g (2 oz) unsalted **butter**
250g (9 oz) plain **chocolate** *(at least 60% cocoa solids)*
1 **egg yolk**, *beaten*
Raspberries, *for garnish*

METHOD

SERVES 8

Preheat the oven to 180°C / 350°F / gas mark 4

1. **To make the pastry**, beat together the butter, icing sugar, zest, 1 yolk and orange flower water *(or water)*.
2. Mix in the flour, draw the mixture together using your hands and knead into a soft dough.
3. Wrap in cling film and leave to rest in the fridge for at least two hours. *
4. Grease and flour an 18 cm (7 inch) loose bottomed flan tin.
5. Knead the dough lightly on a floured surface before rolling *(this helps to prevent it from cracking)* and roll out to fit the tin.
6. Line the tin, trim the edges with a knife and blind bake for 15 minutes *(put a layer of greaseproof paper over the pastry and weigh it down with rice or baking beans. This prevents the pastry base from ballooning)*.
7. Remove the rice and greaseproof paper and brush the pastry with egg yolk. Return to the oven for about 5 minutes until golden, then allow to cool.
8. **To make the chocolate filling**, warm the cream in a saucepan being careful not to boil it. As it starts to simmer reduce the heat and stir in the chocolate.
9. Stir in the honey and the butter and allow to cool.
10. Pour the chocolate mixture into the pastry case and allow to set in the fridge for at least 2 hours or until set.

Decorate with fresh raspberries.

Butterscotch & Apple Panna Cotta

INGREDIENTS £

1 sachet gelatine or 4 leaves *(check manufacturer's instructions as you need enough gelatine to set 570ml (20 fl oz / 1 pt) of liquid*
400ml (14 fl oz) cream
200ml (7 fl oz) milk
1 vanilla pod
200g (7 oz) caster sugar
30g (1 oz) butter
4 apples, *peeled and chopped*
2 tbsp soft brown sugar

Apple Crisps
2 apples
Ground cinnamon

With thanks to The Knoll House Hotel who gave us the inspiration and the recipe which we adapted to use in the school

METHOD

SERVES 8

Preheat the oven to 130°C / 250°F / gas mark 1

1. Measure 2 tbsp of water into a small saucepan, sprinkle in the gelatine and warm, stirring briskly until the gelatine has completely dissolved *(do not allow to boil)*.
2. Put the cream, milk and vanilla pod in to a saucepan and slowly bring to the boil.
3. Put the sugar and 4 tbsp water into another saucepan and heat gently, stirring until the sugar has dissolved. Then boil rapidly, without stirring, until the mixture is a very light brown colour *(for about 2-3 minutes only, otherwise it will burn)* then remove from the heat.
4. Carefully and gradually add the hot milk mixture to the caramel *(it will bubble up)*.
5. Stir in the gelatine mixture.
6. Melt the butter in a frying pan, add the apples and brown sugar and fry for 1-2 minutes.
7. Stir the apples into the caramel mixture, divide into glasses and refrigerate to set.
8. **To make the apple crisps**, slice the apples finely using a mandolin *(so they are about 2 mm thick)* and remove the pips.
9. Dust lightly with cinnamon and then cook in the oven for 20-50 minutes *(depending on the thickness of the slices)*, turning after the first 20 minutes.

Serve the crisps with the caramel pudding.

Rice Pudding with Brandy Spiced Apples

INGREDIENTS ££

180g (6¼ oz) pudding rice
75g (2¾ oz) caster sugar
540ml semi-skimmed **milk**
290ml (½ pt / 10 fl oz) double **cream**
1 large vanilla pod, *halved and seeds scraped out*

Brandy Spiced Apples
2 large apples, *peeled and chopped*
3 tbsp soft brown sugar
60ml (4 tbsp) **brandy**
Pinch of nutmeg
½ star anise
Pinch of ground cinnamon

METHOD

SERVES 8

1. **To make the rice pudding**, put all ingredients into a large saucepan and bring to the boil.
2. Reduce the heat and simmer gently about 1¼ hours with a lid on the pan. Stir every 5-10 minutes *(add a little more milk if it becomes too dry)*.
3. **To make the spiced apples**, put the apples, sugar and brandy in a small saucepan.
4. Bring to the boil and flame *(to flame, turn the extractor fan off and have a saucepan lid to hand. When the liquid is boiling turn off the heat, stand back and put a match to it. Allow it to burn for a few seconds to reduce the alcohol, then cover with the lid to extinguish the flames)*
5. Add the nutmeg, star anise and cinnamon and simmer for 10-15 minutes.

Use a mousse ring to present the rice pudding and decorate the plate with the spiced apples and a pinch of cinnamon.

Key Lime Pie

INGREDIENTS ££

40g (1½ oz) unsalted butter
150g (5 oz) digestive biscuits
2 tsp ground ginger
1 tin (397g) of condensed milk
3 egg yolks
4 limes

METHOD

SERVES 8

Preheat the oven to 160°C / 320°F / gas mark 2-3

1. Melt the butter in a medium sized saucepan over a gentle heat. Remove from the heat.
2. Blend the biscuits and ginger in a food processor until smooth, then add to the saucepan and stir to mix in the butter.
3. Grease a loose bottom 18 cm (7 inch) tin and press the biscuit mixture firmly onto the base.
4. Bake for 10 minutes, then allow to cool completely.
5. Mix together the condensed milk, egg yolks, grated zest of 3 limes and the juice of all 4 limes.
6. Pour onto the base and bake for 15 minutes.

Allow to cool and served chilled.

Christmas Pudding with Brandy Butter

INGREDIENTS

55g (2 oz) plain flour, *sieved*
55g (2 oz) dark soft sugar
55g (2 oz) breadcrumbs
85g (3 oz) suet *(beef or vegetable)* or unsalted butter
1 tsp mixed spice
¼ tsp ground ginger
¼ tsp ground nutmeg
170g (6 oz) sultanas
110g (4 oz) currants
140g (5 oz) raisins, *stoned*
30g (1 oz) candied peel, *chopped*
110g (4 oz) cooking apples, *grated*
55g (2 oz) dried apricots, *chopped*
55g (2 oz) glacé cherries, *chopped*
½ lemon, *grated zest only*
½ orange, *grated zest only*
55g (2 oz) almonds, *chopped*
1 large egg, *beaten*
1 tbsp brandy
110ml (4 fl oz) brown ale

Brandy Butter
250g (9 oz) icing sugar, *sieved*
250g (9 oz) unsalted butter
6-8 tbsp brandy

METHOD

1. Combine the flour, sugar, breadcrumbs, suet *(from the butcher, if unavailable use unsalted butter)* and spices in a large bowl.
2. Mix in the fruits and almonds, then add the egg, brandy and brown ale.
3. Transfer the mixture into a 1.1 L (40 fl oz / 2 pts) bowl *(not one made of plastic)* lined with greaseproof paper, and flatten the top.
4. Cover the bowl with a double layer of greaseproof paper, with a pleat across the middle to allow the pudding to expand during cooking. Hold in place with string or an elastic band.
5. Put the pudding in a large pan, pour in enough water to come ½ way up the basin and bring to the boil. Then cover with a lid and steam for three hours, topping up with water when necessary so that the pan does not dry out.
6. Allow to cool, remove the paper, rewrap in greaseproof paper and store in the fridge or freezer until required.
7. **To make the brandy butter,** beat the butter and icing sugar together with an electric hand whisk. Gradually add the brandy to taste. *(Brandy butter can be made a couple of days in advance and kept in the fridge).*
8. To serve, warm the pudding following stages 4 and 5, but steam for only 2 hours.
9. **To flame the pudding**, heat about 195ml (6½ fl oz / ⅓ pt) of brandy in a saucepan. Just as it comes to the boil, pour over the steaming Christmas pudding and carefully, but quickly, put a match to it.

Mince Pies

INGREDIENTS

Mincemeat

225g (8 oz) apples, *peeled, cored and chopped*
55g (2 oz) almonds, *chopped*
400g (14 oz) mixed fruit
55g (2 oz) candied peel
55g (2 oz) suet *(from butcher), grated (if unavailable use melted unsalted butter)*
225g (8 oz) light brown sugar
1 orange, *zest and juice*
1 lemon, *zest and juice*
1 tsp mixed spice
1 tsp ground cinnamon
¼ tsp ground nutmeg
5 tbsp brandy

Pastry

225g (8 oz) plain flour
110g (4 oz) butter or margarine
4-5 tbsp water
Pinch of salt

Alternative Topping

55g (2 oz) digestive biscuits
55g (2 oz) demerara sugar
55g (2 oz) almonds, *chopped*

METHOD

Preheat the oven to 180°C / 350°F / gas mark 4

1. Mix all mincemeat ingredients together in a large bowl, cover and leave in the fridge overnight. Stir before using.
2. **To make the pastry**, blend all the ingredients in a food processor, gather into a ball, wrap in cling film and chill in the fridge for 15 minutes to make it easier to handle.
3. Roll out the pastry so it is about 3 mm (1/8 inch) thick. Using a crinkled pastry cutter, cut out circles to line a lightly greased bun tin *(about 7½ cm / 3 inch in diameter)* and place in the greased tin.
4. Fill each pastry case with mincemeat *(do not fill above the level of the pastry).*
5. There are two ways in which you can top them:
   1) Cut circles of pastry to fit the top, brush the outside edges with water and position over the mincemeat. Press the edges lightly to seal, glaze with milk and prick the tops with a fork *(to allow the steam to escape).*
   2) Blend the alternative topping ingredients in a food processor and sprinkle a layer over the mincemeat.
6. Bake for 25-30 minutes until lightly golden brown.

To serve, warm and dust with icing sugar.

These can be made in advance and frozen or stored in an airtight tin.

Elderflower Syllabub

INGREDIENTS ££

290ml (10 fl oz / ½ pt) double cream
2 tbsp caster sugar
2 tbsp lemon juice
6 tbsp sweet sherry
4 tbsp elderflower cordial

METHOD

SERVES 8

1. Place all the ingredients in a large bowl and whisk until thick and creamy.
2. Pour into wine glasses and refrigerate,* or, if serving in Brandy snap baskets, refrigerate until serving *(fill the baskets just before serving, otherwise the baskets will become soft).*

Decorate with fresh fruit and grated chocolate.

Apple Art for a Cheese Board

Use a sharp paring knife.

Paint the flesh of the apple with lemon juice to prevent it from going brown.

PETITS FOURS

PETITS FOURS

PETITS FOURS

Chocolate Amaretti Biscuits

INGREDIENTS ££

65g (2¼ oz) icing sugar
½ tbsp cocoa
50g (2 oz) ground almonds
1 egg white
Nutella

METHOD

Makes 15

Preheat the oven to 160°C / 315°F / gas mark 2-3

1. Sieve the icing sugar and cocoa into a bowl and stir in the ground almonds.
2. Whisk the egg white until stiff and then fold in the chocolate mixture.
3. Put the mixture in to a piping bag and pipe rounds, about the size of a 10p piece on to a lined baking tray.
4. Slightly flatten each one with a wet finger and allow to stand for 15 minutes.
5. Bake in the oven for 15-20 minutes *(they need to be firm on the outside but soft on the inside)*. Immediately transfer to a cooling rack and allow to cool. *
6. Sandwich two together, using Nutella, and serve immediately.

Orange Truffles

INGREDIENTS ££

55g (2 oz) unsalted **butter**, *chopped*
70ml (2½ fl oz) double **cream**
200g (7 oz) plain **chocolate**, *chopped*
1 **egg yolk**
2 tsp orange zest, *finely grated and ground into a paste*
2 tbsp Grand Marnier
Cocoa, *sieved*

METHOD

MAKES 40

1. In a small saucepan melt the butter in the cream over a low heat. As the cream begins to bubble around the edges, remove from the heat and add the chocolate, cover and let it stand to allow the chocolate to melt and then stir until smooth.
2. Stir in the egg yolk.
3. Stir in the orange zest and Grand Marnier and chill until firm.
4. Form into small truffle like balls, roll in cocoa and serve from the fridge.

They will keep in the fridge in a sealed container for up to two weeks.

Variations: you can roll the truffles in icing sugar or ground **hazelnuts**.

Chocolate Truffles

INGREDIENTS ££

110g (4 oz) plain chocolate
110g (4 oz) unsalted butter
110g (4 oz) icing sugar, *sieved*
2 tsp white rum
Cocoa powder / icing sugar

METHOD

1. Melt the chocolate in a bain-marie and allow to cool slightly.
2. Beat the butter and icing sugar until pale and fluffy.
3. Stir in the chocolate and rum and refrigerate until firm enough to make into balls.
4. Make into truffle sized balls and roll in cocoa powder / icing sugar.

Variations: roll in finely chopped hazelnuts. Add alcohol eg. Baileys Cream, Rum, Kahlúa.

Lemon / Chocolate Melting Moments

INGREDIENTS £

Lemon Biscuits
85g (3 oz) unsalted butter
20g (¾ oz) icing sugar
1 lemon, *grated zest*
75g (2¾ oz) plain flour
20g (¾ oz) cornflour

Lemon filling for Lemon Biscuits
2 tbsp mascarpone
2 tbsp lemon curd

Chocolate Biscuits
85g (3 oz) unsalted butter
25g (1 oz) icing sugar
10g (¼ oz) cocoa
65g (2¼ oz) plain flour
20g (¾ oz) cornflour

Vanilla filling for Chocolate Biscuits
2 tbsp mascarpone
2 tsp caster sugar
1 drop vanilla essence

METHOD

Preheat the oven to 180°C / 350°F / gas mark 4

1. **To make the biscuits**, combine the ingredients in a food processor.
2. There are two ways in which to divide the mixture into approx 32 *(when putting the mixture on a lined baking tray allow room for them to spread during cooking):*
   a) shape into evenly sized balls, place on the lined baking tray and flatten lightly with a fork dipped into cold water.
   b) pipe on to the lined baking tray, using a piping bag with a star shaped nozzle.
3. Bake for 6-8 minutes and allow to cool on a cooling rack.
4. **To make the filling**, mix the filling ingredients together. *
5. Sandwich two biscuits together using the filling and serve immediately.

Strawberries with White Chocolate

INGREDIENTS ££

White **chocolate**
Fresh strawberries, *with the stalks still on, washed and dried*

METHOD

1. Melt the chocolate in a bain-marie.
2. Dip the pointed end of the strawberry into the melted chocolate to coat only half of it.
3. Place on a sheet of baking paper and refridgerate to set.

Almond Splinters

INGREDIENTS ££

250g (9 oz) plain **chocolate**
15g (½ oz) unsalted **butter**
1-2 tsp grated orange zest *(optional)*
150g (5¼ oz) flaked **almonds**

METHOD

1. Melt the chocolate with the butter in a bain-marie.
2. Remove from the heat and stir in the zest, followed by the almonds.
3. Spoon small, bite sized portions on to a lined baking tray and refrigerate to set.

Vanilla Fudge

INGREDIENTS ££

225g (8 oz) caster sugar
30g (1 oz) unsalted butter
170g tin of evaporated milk
3 drops vanilla essence

METHOD

1. Put everything, except the vanilla essence, into a large heavy saucepan and stir continuously over a gentle heat.
2. Bring to the boil then simmer gently for about 8 minutes test to see if it has reached the 'soft ball' stage *(when a small amount of the fudge mixture is dropped into cold water it forms a soft ball).*
3. Cook for a couple more minutes, remove from the heat and dip the base of the saucepan briefly into cold water to prevent any further cooking.
4. Add the vanilla essence and beat with a wooden spoon.
5. Pour into a baking tin (approx 15 cm / 6 inch) lined with greased baking paper and allow to cool.
6. Cut into squares while the fudge is still warm.

Variations: chopped walnuts / pecans / alcohol / chocolate / raisins etc. *(add ingredients at stage 4).*

Meringue Crunchies

INGREDIENTS £

1 egg white
Pinch of salt
85g (3 oz) caster sugar
55g (2 oz) plain chocolate, *finely chopped*
30g (1 oz) cornflakes, *roughly crushed*

METHOD

Preheat the oven to 150°C / 300°F / gas mark 2

1. Whisk the egg white and salt until stiff *(when you have whipped it enough you will be able to hold the bowl upside down without it falling out).*
2. Add the sugar gradually, starting with a spoonful at a time, while whisking on a low speed, until all the sugar has been incorporated.
3. Gently fold in the chocolate and corn flakes.
4. Drop teaspoonfuls of the mixture on to a baking tray lined with greased baking paper and bake for about 15-20 minutes until firm to touch.
5. Cool on a cooling rack.

They will keep for up to three weeks in an airtight container.

Mocha Creams

INGREDIENTS ££

170g (6 oz) plain chocolate, *chopped*
1 egg yolk
55g (2 oz) unsalted butter
1 tbsp instant coffee powder, *dissolved in a drop of water*
2 tsp white rum
55g (2 oz) white chocolate, *chopped*

METHOD

MAKES 40

1. Melt the plain chocolate in a bain-marie. Stir in the egg yolk and allow to cool.
2. Cream the butter with the coffee until soft, then add the chocolate and rum.
3. Chill slightly until the mixture is of a piping consistency then, using a fluted nozzle, pipe small rounds, with peaks, on to a lined baking tray and refrigerate to set.
4. Melt the white chocolate in a bain-marie, remove from the heat and dip the tops of the mocha creams into the chocolate *(white chocolate must be used as soon as it has melted).* Chill until set.

They will keep in the fridge in a sealed container for up to two weeks.

Lemon Biscotti

INGREDIENTS ££

18g (½ oz) butter
½ lemon, *grated zest*
1 egg
1 egg yolk
100g (3½ oz) sugar
1 tsp baking powder
140g (5 oz) plain flour
30g (1 oz) flaked almonds
60g (2 oz) sultanas

METHOD

Preheat the oven to 150°C / 300°F / gas mark 2

1. Melt the butter in a small saucepan with the lemon zest and leave to infuse.
2. Using an electric whisk mix together the egg, egg yolk and sugar and whisk for about 30 seconds.
3. Sieve the baking powder and flour into the egg mixture and mix in using a spatula.
4. Stir in the butter and lemon mixture, followed by the almonds and sultanas.
5. On a lightly floured surface divide the mixture into two and roll into two fat, sausage shapes.
6. Place on a lined baking tray and bake in the oven for approximately 25 minutes until golden brown.
7. While still warm, slice at an angle (1 cm / 3/8 inch) thick and place on a lined baking tray *(if you allow it to cool completely it will break up when sliced).* *
8. Cook for 5-7 minutes until golden brown.

They can be stored in an airtight container.

Chocolate Fudge

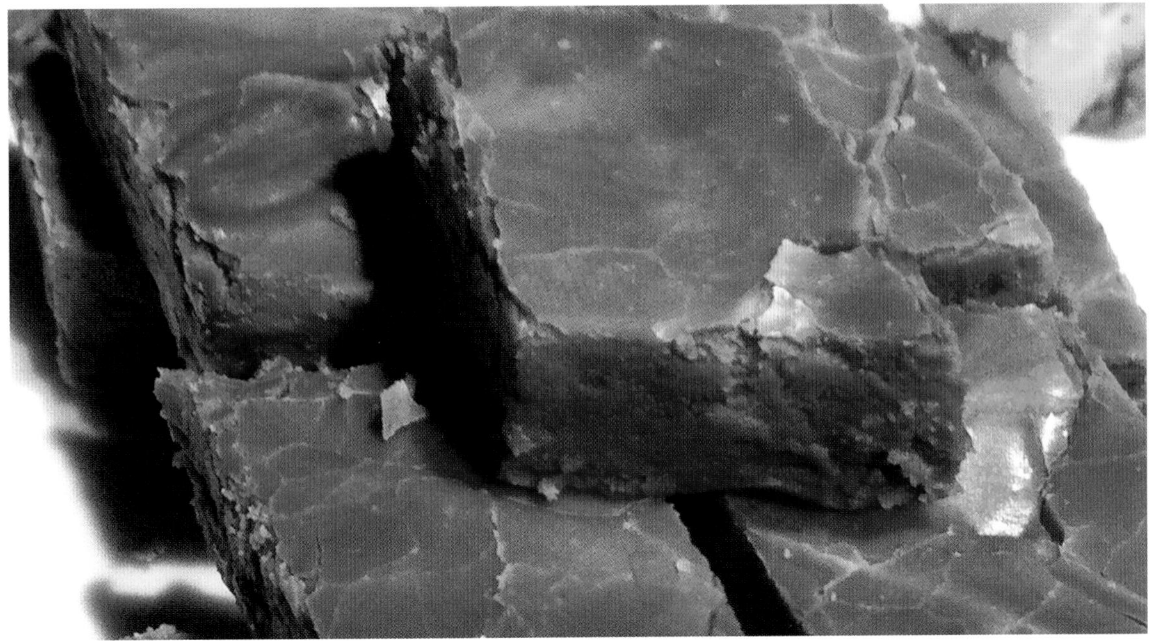

INGREDIENTS £

225g (8 oz) caster sugar
30g (1 oz) butter
170g tin of evaporated milk
100g (3½ oz) high cocoa plain chocolate
3 drops vanilla essence *(optional)*

METHOD

1. Put the sugar, butter and evaporated milk into a large, heavy saucepan and stir continuously over a gentle heat.
2. Bring to the boil and simmer gently for about 8 minutes. Test to see if it has reached the 'soft ball' stage *(when a small amount of the fudge mixture is dropped into cold water it forms a soft ball).*
3. Cook for a couple more minutes, add the chocolate and vanilla essence and beat with a wooden spoon.
4. Pour into a baking tin (approx. 15 cm / 6 inch) lined with a greased baking paper and allow to cool.
5. Cut into squares while the fudge is still warm.

Variations: chopped walnuts / pecans / alcohol / raisins etc.
(add ingredients at end of stage 3).

Nutella & White Chocolate Squares

INGREDIENTS ££

65g (2½ oz) Nutella
100g (3¾ oz) white chocolate
65g (2½ oz) cornflakes, *crushed into small pieces*
White chocolate, *to decorate*

METHOD

1. Melt the Nutella and white chocolate in a bain-marie and mix together.
2. Stir in the cornflakes.
3. Empty on to a flat baking tray lined with a sheet of greaseproof paper, cover with a second sheet and roll flat so it is about 3 mm (⅛ inch) thick. Allow to set in the fridge.
4. Melt a little more white chocolate in a bain-marie, remove the top layer of greaseproof paper and drizzle with the chocolate to decorate. Return to the fridge to set.
5. Peel off the greaseproof paper and cut into diamond shapes, or squares if you prefer.

Chocolate & Pecan Fudge

INGREDIENTS ££

75g (2¾ oz) pecans
175g (6 oz) high cocoa chocolate (60% minimum), *roughly chopped*
½ a 397g tin condensed milk
15g (½ oz) butter
Pinch of salt

METHOD

1. Roast the pecans in the oven for about 5 minutes. Allow to cool slightly.
2. Warm the chocolate, condensed milk, butter and salt in a saucepan until combined.
3. Put the nuts into a freezer bag and bash with a rolling pin to break them up. Then stir into the chocolate.
4. Pour into a small baking tray lined with cling film and smooth over the top with a pallet knife *(warm the knife in hot water to make it easier)*.
5. Refrigerate until set then cut into squares.

It will keep in the freezer and can be served from frozen.

Variations: raisins / rum / glacé cherries / pistachios / walnuts etc.

Peppermint Creams

INGREDIENTS £

450g (1 lb) icing sugar, *sieved*
1 tsp lemon juice
1 **egg white**, *lightly whisked*
3-4 drops of peppermint flavouring
Green food colouring or dark **chocolate**, *to decorate*

METHOD

1. Mix the icing sugar and lemon juice together.
2. Fold in the egg white and add a few drops of peppermint to taste.
3. Gently knead on a surface dusted with icing sugar until smooth.
4. Roll out to a thickness of about 6 mm (¼ inch) and cut out circles using a smooth edged pastry cutter about 2½ cm (1 inch) in diameter.
5. Place on a sheet of greaseproof paper and allow to dry out for a few hours.
6. To decorate, either dip a pastry brush in green colouring and draw your finger along the bristles to spray the mints, or melt some dark chocolate in a bain-marie and drizzle chocolate over them.

Sugared Nuts

INGREDIENTS ££

85g (3 oz) caster sugar
55ml (2 fl oz) water
55g (2 oz) **almonds** or **hazelnuts**, *flaked or roughly chopped and toasted*

METHOD

1. Heat the sugar and water in a saucepan over a low heat until the sugar dissolves, swirling the pan occasionally.
2. Increase the heat and cook until it turns golden.
3. Stir in the nuts and cook for a couple of minutes.
4. Spoon out on to a baking tray lined with greased baking paper, *(place a heat mat underneath the tray)* either in small clumps, or in one large piece and then break up when cooled.

This will keep in the fridge for up to three weeks.

White Chocolate Discs

INGREDIENTS £

100g (3½ oz) white chocolate
Dark chocolate, *to decorate*
30g (1 oz) walnuts, *chopped (optional)*

METHOD

1. Melt the white chocolate in a bain-marie.
2. Spoon drops of white chocolate on to a lined baking tray and use the back of the spoon to shape into circular, bite size discs, about 3 cm (1¼ inch) in diameter.
3. To decorate, melt the dark chocolate in a bain-marie and drizzle thin lines of chocolate over the white discs *(you can use a cocktail stick to draw patterns in the chocolate)* or grate dark chocolate over them.
4. Sprinkle over the chopped walnuts and refrigerate to set.

Half Moon Truffles

INGREDIENTS ££

Centre:
Peppermint Cream
Icing Sugar, *sieved*
Water
Peppermint essence
Green food colouring *(optional)*

or

White Chocolate
140g (5 oz) white chocolate, *chopped*
55ml (2 fl oz) double cream
2 tsp liquid glucose

Coating:
55g (2 oz) unsalted butter
200g (7 oz) plain chocolate, *chopped*
3 tbsp double cream
2 tbsp Grand Marnier
Icing sugar, *sieved*

METHOD

1. **To make the peppermint centre**, add a couple of drops of peppermint essence, food colouring and a drop of water to the icing sugar and combine. Taste and adjust consistency so that you have a firm mixture which you can handle.
2. **To make the white chocolate centre**, bring the cream and glucose to the boil in a saucepan, remove from the heat and add the white chocolate. Cover and let it stand to allow the chocolate to melt and then stir until smooth *(you may need to return it to the heat).* Pour the mixture into a bowl lined with foil and chill until firm.
3. Roll the peppermint / white chocolate mixture into thin, sausage shapes and freeze if using white chocolate, or chill if using the peppermint creams.
4. **To make the chocolate coating**, melt the butter in a saucepan, add the chocolate and remove from the heat.
5. Stir until smooth, add the cream, Grand Marnier and chill.
6. To make the truffles, flatten the dark chocolate and wrap it around the peppermint / white chocolate sausage. Roll to secure in place.
7. Roll in icing sugar and freeze until firm.

To serve, slice and arrange individually on a plate. Chill until served.

They can be stored in the freezer for up to 8 weeks.

CAKES

CAKES

CAKES

Cakes - General Information

If making a cake in a food processor, blend for 10 seconds.

Cakes must go in to a preheated oven.

Do not open the over door for at least 20 minutes after the cake has gone into the oven as it will affect the rising of the cake.

How you know when your cake is cooked:

Avoid opening the oven during the first 20 minutes of cooking.

There are several ways to tell if a cake is cooked:

a) *The cake is just coming away from the sides of the tin.*

b) *The centre feels springy when lightly touched and no imprint remains.*

c) *There is no cake mixture on a skewer when it is inserted into the middle of the cake and removed.*

d) *If you can smell cake in the kitchen.*

How to ice your cake:

a) *When the cake is cool, choose the best looking cake for the top, turn the other cake over and gently spread the icing over the top to completely cover the flat surface.*

b) *Place on to the plate that you want to serve the cake on.*

c) *Gently place the top of the cake onto the base and ice the top, making sure you take the icing right to the edge.*

d) *You can decorate your cake by creating a pattern in the icing using a fork, or by topping with nuts, grated chocolate etc.*

Lemon Drizzle Cake

INGREDIENTS £

85g (3 oz) caster sugar
110g (4 oz) margarine
140g (5 oz) self raising flour
2 eggs
1 tsp baking powder
4 tbsp milk
1 lemon, *grated zest*
(juice is used for the topping)

Topping
110g (4 oz) caster sugar
1 lemon, *juiced*

METHOD

Preheat the oven to 170°C / 340°F / gas mark 3

1. Blend all the cake ingredients in a food processor.
2. Turn out into a loaf tin lined with baking paper and bake for 50 minutes until cooked *(see beginning of cakes section to see how you know when your cake is cooked).*
3. **To make the topping**, heat the sugar and lemon juice in a saucepan until the sugar has dissolved *(do not allow it to boil).*
4. Pierce the top of the hot cake with a skewer *(so the topping will seep through)* and pour over the topping.

Allow to cool in the tin.

Victoria Sandwich

INGREDIENTS ££

Cake Mixture - cooking at home
170g (6 oz) caster sugar
170g (6 oz) self raising flour
170g (6 oz) margarine
3 large eggs
1 tsp baking powder
1 tbsp hot water *(if needed)*
Vanilla essence

Cake Mixture - cooking at altitude
1 pot (150ml / 5 fl oz / 1/4 pt) natural yoghurt
1 pot (150ml / 5 fl oz / 1/4 pt) sugar *(use yoghurt pot to measure)*
3 pots (450ml / 16 fl oz) self raising flour
1 pot (150ml / 5 fl oz / 1/4 pt) vegetable or sunflower oil
4 eggs
¾ sachet (1 tsp) baking powder

Filling
Strawberry jam
150ml (5 fl oz / ¼ pt) double cream, *whipped*

Topping
Icing sugar
Fresh strawberries, *for garnish*

METHOD

Preheat the oven to 180°C / 350°F / gas mark 4

1. Line the base of two 18 cm (7 inch) cake tins using greaseproof paper cut to size. Grease the sides with butter.
2. Blend the cake mixture ingredients and a few drops of vanilla essence in a food processor *(add a little hot water if the mixture is too thick). (If cooking at altitude beat the ingredients together in a large bowl).*
3. Divide the mixture between the cake tins and spread evenly.
4. Bake in the oven for 25-35 minutes *(35-40 minutes at altitude)* until cooked *(see beginning of cakes section to see how you know when your cake is cooked).*
5. When the cake has cooled slightly, slide a spatula around the cake to loosen it from the tin and turn out on a cooling rack.
6. Carefully peel off the paper from the base of the cake and allow to cool before icing.
7. Place one of the sponges upside down on the plate on which you wish to serve the cake. Spread a generous layer of strawberry jam on the sponge, followed by a layer of cream.
8. Gently lower the top sponge, so that the cream is not squeezed out.
9. Sift a little icing sugar over the top and decorate with fresh strawberries.

Scones

INGREDIENTS £

225g (8 oz) self raising **flour**
1 tsp **baking powder**
30g (1 oz) caster sugar
¼ tsp salt
55g (2 oz) **butter**
150ml (5 fl oz / ¼ pt) **milk** *(approx)*
Milk, *for glazing*
Clotted cream
Strawberry jam

METHOD

Preheat the oven to 220°C / 425°F / gas mark 7

1. Put the flour, baking powder, sugar and salt into a bowl. Using your hands rub in the butter until the mixture resembles fine breadcrumbs.
2. Add the milk and mix into a soft dough *(you may not need all of the milk).*
3. Turn out onto a lightly floured board and knead into shape.
4. Roll out to about 1¼ cm (½ inch) thick and use a cutter 6½ cm (2½ inch) in diameter to cut out the scones.
5. Glaze with milk and bake on a lined baking tray for 8-10 minutes until golden brown.
6. Allow to cool on a cooling rack and serve with clotted cream and strawberry jam.

If making scones for a diabetic you can leave out the sugar.

Chocolate Fudge Icing

INGREDIENTS ££

75g (2¾ oz) caster sugar
5 tbsp (75ml) **evaporated milk**
110g (4 oz) plain **chocolate**
40g (1½ oz) unsalted **butter**
Vanilla essence, *a few drops*

METHOD

1. Slowly heat the sugar and evaporated milk in a saucepan until the sugar dissolves.
2. Bring to the boil and simmer for 6 minutes, stirring continuously *(It should thicken slightly).*
3. Add the chocolate, butter and vanilla essence and stir off the heat until the chocolate and butter have melted.

Immediately pour over the cake *(do not try to spread it).*

Banana & Walnut Cake

INGREDIENTS ££

Cake Mixture - cooking at home
170g (6 oz) caster sugar
170g (6 oz) self raising flour
170g (6 oz) margarine
3 large eggs
1 tsp baking powder
1 tbsp hot water *(if needed)*

Cake Mixture - cooking at altitude
1 pot (150ml / 5 fl oz / ¼ pt) natural yoghurt
1 pot (150ml / 5 fl oz / ¼ pt) sugar *(use yoghurt pot to measure)*
3 pots (450ml / 16 fl oz) self raising flour
1 pot (150ml / 5 fl oz / ¼ pt) vegetable or sunflower oil
4 eggs
¾ sachet (1 tsp) baking powder

1 banana, *chopped (save a little for the icing)*
30g (1 oz) walnuts, *chopped*
6 walnut halves, *for decoration*

Butter Icing
125g (4½ oz) unsalted butter
255g (9 oz) icing sugar
Vanilla essence
2 tsp hot water *(approx)*

METHOD

Preheat the oven to 180°C / 350°F / gas mark 4

1. Line the base of two 18 cm (7 inch) cake tins using greaseproof paper cut to size. Grease the sides with butter.
2. Blend the cake mixture ingredients in a food processor *(add a little hot water if the mixture is too thick). (If cooking at altitude beat the ingredients together in a large bowl)* and stir in the banana and walnuts.
3. Divide the mixture between the cake tins and spread evenly.
4. Bake in the oven for 25-35 minutes (35-40 minutes at altitude) until cooked *(see beginning of cakes section to see how you know when your cake is cooked).*
5. When the cake has cooled slightly, slide a spatula around the cake to loosen it from the tin and turn out on a cooling rack.
6. Carefully peel off the paper from the base of the cake and allow to cool before icing.
7. To make the butter icing, put all ingredients into the food processor with the remaining banana and blend until smooth. Be careful not to over blend the mixture. *(To change the consistency of the icing add a little water to make it runnier or a little icing sugar to make it thicker).*
8. Ice *(see beginning of cakes section to see how to ice your cake)* and decorate with walnuts.

Apple & Cinnamon Cake

INGREDIENTS ££

Cake Mixture - cooking at home
170g (6 oz) caster sugar
170g (6 oz) self raising flour
170g (6 oz) margarine
3 large eggs
1 tsp baking powder
1 tbsp hot water *(if needed)*

Cake Mixture - cooking at altitude
1 pot (150ml / 5 fl oz / 1/4 pt) natural yoghurt
1 pot (150ml / 5 fl oz / 1/4 pt) sugar *(use yoghurt pot to measure)*
3 pots (450ml / 16 fl oz) self raising flour
1 pot (150ml / 5 fl oz / 1/4 pt) vegetable or sunflower oil
4 eggs
¾ sachet (1 tsp) baking powder

¼ tsp ground cinnamon
1-2 apples, *peeled, cored and chopped*
1 tbsp Demerara sugar
Clear honey

Jono's Crumble Topping
(to add on top of cake mix)
or 1 tbsp flaked almonds
50g (1¾ oz) unsalted butter, *soft*
75g (2¾ oz) wholemeal flour
75g (2¾ oz) Demerara sugar
1 tsp ground cinnamon

Butter Icing Filling
55g (2 oz) unsalted butter
125g (4½ oz) icing sugar
Pinch of ground cinnamon
1 tsp hot water *(approx)*

METHOD

Preheat the oven to 180°C / 350°F / gas mark 4

1. Line the base of two 18 cm (7 inch) cake tins using greaseproof paper cut to size. Grease the sides with butter.
2. Blend the cake mixture ingredients and the cinnamon in a food processor *(add a little hot water if the mixture is too thick). (If cooking at altitude beat the ingredients together in a large bowl)* and stir in the apple.
3. Divide the mixture between the cake tins and spread evenly. Then sprinkle the almonds or Jono's cinnamon crumble over the top. *(To make Jono's crumble, mix the ingredients together, rubbing the butter into the flour and sugar using your fingertips, so that you end up with a breadcrumb consistency).*
4. Bake in the oven until cooked *(see beginning of cakes section to see how you know when your cake is cooked - 25-*35 minutes at home, *35-40 minutes at altitude)*
5. When it has cooled slightly, slide a spatula around the cake to loosen it from the tin and turn out on a cooling rack.
6. Carefully peel the paper from the base of the cake and allow to cool before icing.
7. **To make the butter icing filling**, put all ingredients into the food processor and blend until smooth. Be careful not to over blend the mixture. *(To change the consistency of the icing add a little water or juice to make more runny or a little icing sugar to make it thicker).*
8. When the cake is cool, place one of the sponges upside down on a serving plate and cover with the butter icing. Place the other sponge on top, drizzle with honey and sprinkle Demerara sugar over the top.

CAKES

Chocolate Cake

INGREDIENTS £

Cake Mixture - cooking at home
170g (6 oz) caster sugar
170g (6 oz) self raising flour
170g (6 oz) margarine
3 large eggs
1 tsp baking powder
1 tbsp hot water *(if needed)*

Cake Mixture - cooking at altitude
1 pot (150ml / 5 fl oz / 1/4 pt) natural yoghurt
1 pot (150ml / 5 fl oz / 1/4 pt) sugar *(use yoghurt pot to measure)*
3 pots (450ml / 16 fl oz) self raising flour
1 pot (150ml / 5 fl oz / 1/4 pt) vegetable or sunflower oil
4 eggs
¾ sachet (1 tsp) baking powder

2 tbsp cocoa
Chocolate buttons, *to decorate*

Butter Icing
125g (4½ oz) unsalted butter
255g (9 oz) icing sugar
Cocoa to taste
2 tsp hot water *(approx)*

METHOD

Preheat the oven to 180°C / 350°F / gas mark 4

1. Line the base of two 18 cm (7 inch) cake tins using greaseproof paper cut to size. Grease the sides with butter.
2. Blend the cake mixture ingredients and the cocoa in a food processor *(add a little hot water if the mixture is too thick). (If cooking at altitude beat the ingredients together in a large bowl).*
3. Divide the mixture between the cake tins and spread evenly.
4. Bake in the oven for 25-35 minutes *(35-40 minutes at altitude)* until cooked *(see beginning of cakes section to see how you know when your cake is cooked).*
5. When the cake has cooled slightly, slide a spatula around the cake to loosen it from the tin and turn out on a cooling rack.
6. Carefully peel off the paper from the base of the cake and allow to cool before icing.
7. **To make the butter icing**, put all ingredients into the food processor and blend until smooth. Be careful not to over blend the mixture. *(To change the consistency of the icing add a little water to make it runnier or a little icing sugar to make it thicker).*
8. Ice the cake and decorate. Chocolate buttons, walnuts or glacé cherries can be used.

Carrot Cake

INGREDIENTS ££

2 cups caster sugar
2 cups plain flour
1 cup vegetable oil
4 eggs
1 tsp baking powder
1 tsp salt
1 tsp vanilla essence
1 tsp ground cinnamon
3 cups grated carrot
1 cup walnuts, *chopped*

Icing
45g (1½ oz) unsalted butter
85g (3 oz) cream cheese
125g (4½ oz) icing sugar, *sieved*

METHOD

Preheat the oven to 180°C / 350°F / gas mark 4

1. Line the base of two 18-20 cm (7-8 inch) cake tins using greaseproof paper cut to size. Grease the sides with butter.
2. Beat all ingredients *(except for the carrot and walnuts)* in a large bowl, then stir in the carrot and walnuts.
3. Bake in the oven for 25-35 minutes until cooked *(see beginning of cakes section to see how you know when your cake is cooked).*
4. When the cake has cooled slightly slide a spatula around the cake to loosen it from the tin and turn out on a cooling rack. Carefully peel off the paper from the base of the cake and allow to cool.
5. To make the icing, simply mix together all the ingredients.
6. Ice *(see beginning of cakes section to see how to ice your cake)* and decorate with walnuts.

Cherry Cake

INGREDIENTS ££

Cake Mixture - cooking at home
170g (6 oz) caster sugar
170g (6 oz) self raising flour
170g (6 oz) margarine
3 large eggs
1 tsp baking powder
1 tbsp hot water *(if needed)*

Cake Mixture - cooking at altitude
1 pot (150ml / 5 fl oz / ¼ pt) natural yoghurt
1 pot (150ml / 5 fl oz / ¼ pt) sugar *(use yoghurt pot to measure)*
3 pots (450ml / 16 fl oz) self raising flour
1 pot (150ml / 5 fl oz / ¼ pt) vegetable or sunflower oil
4 eggs
¾ sachet (1 tsp) baking powder

55g (2 oz) glacé cherries, *chopped*
4 glacé cherries, *to decorate*

Butter Icing
125g (4½ oz) unsalted butter
255g (9 oz) icing sugar
2 tsp hot water *(approx)*
Vanilla essence to taste

METHOD

Preheat the oven to 180°C / 350°F / gas mark 4

1. Line the base of two 18 cm (7 inch) cake tins using greaseproof paper cut to size. Grease the sides with butter.
2. Blend the cake mixture ingredients in a food processor *(add a little hot water if the mixture is too thick). (If cooking at altitude beat the ingredients together in a large bowl)* then stir in the cherries.
3. Divide the mixture between the cake tins and spread evenly.
4. Bake in the oven for 25-35 minutes *(35-40 minutes at altitude)* until cooked. *(see beginning of cakes section to see how you know when your cake is cooked).*
5. When the cake has cooled slightly, slide a spatula around the cake to loosen it from the tin and turn out on a cooling rack.
6. Carefully peel off the paper from the base of the cake and allow to cool before icing.
7. **To make the butter icing**, put all ingredients into the food processor and blend until smooth. Be careful not to over blend the mixture. (To change the consistency of the icing add a little water to make it runnier or a little icing sugar to make it thicker).
8. Ice *(see beginning of cakes section to see how to ice your cake)* and decorate with halved cherries.

Orange or Lemon Cake

INGREDIENTS £

Cake Mixture - cooking at home
170g (6 oz) caster sugar
170g (6 oz) self raising flour
170g (6 oz) margarine
3 large eggs
1 tsp baking powder
1 tbsp hot water *(if needed)*

Cake Mixture - cooking at altitude
1 pot (150ml / 5 fl oz / 1/4 pt) natural yoghurt
1 pot (150ml / 5 fl oz / 1/4 pt) sugar *(use yoghurt pot to measure)*
3 pots (450ml / 16 fl oz) self raising flour
1 pot (150ml / 5 fl oz / 1/4 pt) vegetable or sunflower oil
4 eggs
3/4 sachet (1 tsp) baking powder

1-2 oranges or lemons, *grated zest*
Chocolate, *grated (for decoration)*
1-2 tbsp poppy seeds, *(optional)*

Butter Icing
125g (4½ oz) unsalted butter
255g (9 oz) icing sugar
A little juice from the orange or lemon

METHOD

Preheat the oven to 180°C / 350°F / gas mark 4

1. Line the base of two 18 cm (7 inch) cake tins using greaseproof paper cut to size. Grease the sides with butter.
2. Blend the cake mixture ingredients, the zest and the poppy seeds in a food processor *(add a little hot water if the mixture is too thick)*. *(If cooking at altitude beat the ingredients together in a large bowl).*
3. Divide the mixture between the cake tins and spread evenly.
4. Bake in the oven for 25-35 minutes *(35-40 minutes at altitude)* until cooked *(see beginning of cakes section to see how you know when your cake is cooked).*
5. When the cake has cooled slightly, slide a spatula around the cake to loosen it from the tin and turn out on a cooling rack.
6. Carefully peel off the paper from the base of the cake and allow to cool before icing.
7. **To make the butter icing**, put all ingredients into the food processor and blend until smooth. Be careful not to over blend the mixture. *(To change the consistency of the icing add a little juice to make it runnier or a little icing sugar to make it thicker).*
8. Ice *(see beginning of cakes section to see how to ice your cake)* and decorate with grated chocolate.

Lemon Polenta Cake (Gluten free)

INGREDIENTS £

Cake
200g (7 oz) unsalted **butter**
200g (7 oz) caster sugar
1½ lemons, *juice and grated zest*
200g (7 oz) ground **almonds**
2 **eggs**
1 tsp vanilla essence
100g (3½ oz) polenta
1 tsp gluten free **baking powder**
Pinch of salt

Icing
100g (3½ oz) icing sugar
1½ tbsp lemon juice

METHOD

Preheat the oven to 160°C / 315°F / gas mark 2½

1. Line the base of two 18 cm (7 inch) cake tins using greaseproof paper cut to size. Grease the sides with butter.
2. Blend the butter, sugar and lemon zest in a food processor until light and fluffy.
3. Add the almonds, eggs and vanilla essence and blend for a further 10 seconds.
4. Remove the blade and stir in the rest of the ingredients *(except for 1½ tbsp lemon juice which you need for the icing).*
5. Bake in the oven for 25-35 minutes until cooked *(see beginning of cakes section to see how you know when your cake is cooked).*
6. When the cake has cooled slightly, slide a spatula around the cake to loosen it from the tin and turn out on to a cooling rack *(be very careful handling the cake because it will break up very easily).*
7. To make the icing, mix the icing sugar and the lemon juice, adding a little juice at a time until you have the right consistency. Drizzle over each cake and allow to set *(do not sandwich together).*

The cake is best served the following day as it does not break up so much.

Mars Bar Cake

INGREDIENTS ££

3 **Mars bars**, *chopped*
85g (3 oz) unsalted **butter**
3 cups of **Rice Krispies**
Plain **chocolate** for decoration, *grated*

METHOD

1. Gently melt the butter with the Mars bars, beat until smooth *(be very careful not to over cook as it will turn to toffee).*
2. Remove from the heat and gently stir in the Rice Krispies.
3. Transfer the mixture to a baking tray lined with cling film, level and press firmly into place.
4. While the mixture is still warm sprinkle over the chocolate and refrigerate to set.
5. Peel off the cling film before serving.

Cherry & Chocolate Cake

INGREDIENTS ££

Cake Mixture - cooking at home
170g (6 oz) caster sugar
170g (6 oz) self raising flour
170g (6 oz) margarine
3 large eggs
1 tsp baking powder
1 tbsp hot water *(if needed)*

Cake Mixture - cooking at altitude
1 pot (150ml / 5 fl oz / ¼ pt) natural yoghurt
1 pot (150ml / 5 fl oz / ¼ pt) sugar *(use yoghurt pot to measure)*
3 pots (450ml / 16 fl oz) self raising flour
1 pot (150ml / 5 fl oz / ¼ pt) vegetable or sunflower oil
4 eggs
¾ sachet (1 tsp) baking powder

100g (3½ oz) plain chocolate and a little extra, *to decorate*
Milk
225g (8 oz) black cherry jam

Butter Icing
55 g (2 oz) unsalted butter
110g (4 oz) icing sugar
½ tbsp hot water *(approx)*

METHOD

Preheat the oven to 180°C / 350°F / gas mark 4

1. Melt the chocolate with a few drops of milk and allow to cool slightly
2. Line the base of two 18 cm (7 inch) cake tins using greaseproof paper cut to size. Grease the sides with butter.
3. Blend the cake mixture ingredients and the jam in a food processor *(if cooking at altitude beat the ingredients together in a large bowl)* and stir in the chocolate mixture.
4. Divide the mixture between the cake tins and spread evenly.
5. Bake in the oven for 25-35 minutes *(35-40 minutes at altitude)* until cooked *(see beginning of cakes section to see how you know when your cake is cooked).*
6. When the cake has cooled slightly, slide a spatula around the cake to loosen it from the tin and turn out on a cooling rack.
7. Carefully peel off the paper from the base of the cake and whilst still hot grate chocolate over the top of one, which will end up being the top of the cake.
8. **To make the butter icing**, put all ingredients into the food processor and blend until smooth. Be careful not to over blend the mixture. (To change the consistency of the icing, add a little water to make it runnier or a little icing sugar to make it thicker).
9. When the cake is cool ice the base, sandwich together and dust with icing sugar.

Dundee Cake

INGREDIENTS £££

85g (3 oz) glacé cherries
170g (6 oz) margarine
170g (6 oz) plain flour
30g (1 oz) soft brown sugar
140g (5 oz) caster sugar
3 eggs
¼ tsp baking powder
Pinch of salt
450g (1 lb) sultanas
30g (1 oz) ground almonds

METHOD

Preheat the oven to 150°C / 300°F / Gas Mark 2

1. Line an 18-20 cm (7-8 inch) high sided cake tin with greaseproof paper.
2. Rinse the cherries in boiling water to remove the syrup *(this stops the cherries sinking to the bottom of the cake)*. Dry them and roughly chop.
3. Beat together the margarine, flour, brown and white sugar, eggs, baking powder and salt.
4. Fold in the sultanas, cherries and almonds and pour the mixture into the cake tin.
5. Bake in the oven for 1 hour, then turn the oven down to 130°C / 250°C / Gas Mark 1 and cook for a further 2 hours.

Allow to cool slightly then remove from the tin.

Banana Bread

INGREDIENTS £

130g (4¾ oz) butter
170g (6 oz) wholegrain spelt flour
2 tsp baking powder
2 bananas
30g (1 oz) clear honey
2 eggs
130g (4¾ oz) dark soft brown sugar

METHOD

Preheat the oven to 180ºC, 350ºF, gas mark 4

1. Melt the butter in a saucepan and allow to cool slightly.
2. Mash together the bananas, honey and melted butter.
3. Put the flour and baking powder into a bowl, make a well in the centre and stir in the banana mixture.
4. Whisk the eggs and brown sugar together until slightly fluffy and then add to the flour mixture
5. Pour the mixture into a greased and floured loaf tin and bake for 40-50 minutes until cooked *(see beginning of cakes section to see how you know when your cake is cooked)*.
6. Rest for a few minutes before turning out.

Serve sliced with butter.

Coffee & Walnut Cake

INGREDIENTS £

Cake Mixture - cooking at home
170g (6 oz) caster sugar
170g (6 oz) self raising **flour**
170g (6 oz) **margarine**
3 large **eggs**
1 tsp **baking powder**
1 tbsp hot water *(if needed)*

Cake Mixture - cooking at altitude
1 pot (150ml / 5 fl oz / ¼ pt) natural **yoghurt**
1 pot (150ml / 5 fl oz / ¼ pt) sugar *(use yoghurt pot to measure)*
3 pots (450ml / 16 fl oz) self raising **flour**
1 pot (150ml / 5 fl oz / ¼ pt) vegetable or sunflower oil
4 **eggs**
¾ sachet (1 tsp) **baking powder**

1 tbsp instant coffee
30g (1 oz) **walnuts**, *chopped* & 6 halves, *for decoration*

Butter Icing
125g (4½ oz) unsalted **butter**
255g (9 oz) icing sugar
2 tsp hot water *(approx)*
1 tbsp instant coffee

METHOD

Preheat the oven to 180°C / 350°F / gas mark 4

1. Line the base of two 18 cm (7 inch) cake tins using greaseproof paper cut to size. Grease the sides with butter.
2. Add a few drops of water to the instant coffee and stir until it dissolves.
3. Blend the cake mixture ingredients and the coffee mixture in a food processor *(add a little hot water if the mixture is too thick). (If cooking at altitude beat the ingredients together in a large bowl)* then stir in the chopped nuts.
4. Divide the mixture between the cake tins and spread evenly.
5. Bake in the oven for 25-35 minutes (35-40 minutes at altitude) until cooked *(see beginning of cakes section to see how you know when your cake is cooked).*
6. When the cake has cooled slightly, slide a spatula around the cake to loosen it from the tin and turn out on a cooling rack.
7. Carefully peel off the paper from the base of the cake and allow to cool before icing.
8. **To make the butter icing**, dissolve the coffee in the hot water then put all ingredients into the food processor and blend until smooth. Be careful not to over blend the mixture. *(To change the consistency of the icing, add a little water to make it runnier or a little icing sugar to make it thicker).*
9. Ice *(see beginning of cakes section to see how to ice your cake)* and decorate with walnuts.

Chocolate & Nut Fridge Cake

INGREDIENTS £

110g (4 oz) unsalted butter
200g (7 oz) Bournville chocolate
4 tbsp golden syrup
285g (10 oz) digestive biscuits, *crushed*
110g (4 oz) pecans, *roughly chopped*
55g (2 oz) pistachio nuts, *roughly chopped*
10 glacé cherries, *roughly chopped*

Variations: add marshmallows / sultanas / other nuts…

METHOD

Preheat the oven to 180°C / 350°F / gas mark 4

1. Melt the butter, chocolate and golden syrup together in a large saucepan.
2. Stir in the rest of the ingredients.
3. Press the mixture into a loaf tin lined with tin foil and refrigerate to set.

To serve, remove from the fridge and slice after about 20 minutes.

Fairy Cakes

INGREDIENTS £

This is a plain cake recipe. Additional ingredients can be used to make a variety of different cakes eg. chocolate chips, coffee essence, cocoa powder, lemon or orange zest, walnuts etc.

170g (6 oz) caster sugar
170g (6 oz) self raising flour
170g (6 oz) margarine
3 large eggs
1 tsp baking powder
1 tbsp hot water *(if needed)*

Butter Icing
190g (6½ oz) unsalted butter
385g (12½ oz) icing sugar
3 tsp hot water *(approx)*

METHOD

MAKES 12

Preheat the oven to 180°C / 350°F / gas mark 4

1. Blend the ingredients in the large bowl of the food processer *(add a little hot water if the mixture is too thick).*
2. Divide the mixture evenly between 12 prepared cupcake cases *(they should be just over half full of cake mixture)* and bake in the oven for 15 minutes until golden *(avoid opening the oven door during the first 10 minutes of cooking as it will affect the rising of the cakes)*
3. Transfer on to a cooling rack and allow to cool before icing.
4. **To make the butter icing**, put all ingredients into the food processor and blend until smooth. *Be careful not to over blend the mixture. (To change the consistency of the icing add a little water to make it runnier or a little icing sugar to make it thicker).*

Vanilla Cupcakes

INGREDIENTS ££

Cake
120g (4¼ oz) plain **flour**, *sieved*
140g (5 oz) caster sugar, *sieved*
1½ tsp **baking powder**
Pinch of salt
40g (1¼ oz) unsalted **butter**, *cubed*
120ml (2½ fl oz) whole **milk**
1 large **egg**
½ tsp vanilla extract *(good quality)*

Icing
120g (4¼ oz) unsalted **butter**
250g (8 oz) icing sugar, *sieved*
½ tsp vanilla extract *(good quality)*
1-4 tsp boiling water *(depending on room temperature)*
Colour of your choice

METHOD

MAKES 12

Preheat the oven to 170°C / 325°F / gas mark 3

1. Place 12 paper cases in a muffin tin.
2. Put the sieved flour, sugar, baking powder, salt and butter in a food processor, pulse to combine until you get a sandy consistency.
3. Put the egg, vanilla extract and milk in a bowl and roughly beat together with a fork.
4. Turn on the food processor, pour the egg mixture through the feeding tube and blend until smooth *(do not over blend)*.
5. Put the cake mixture into a jug and pour into the paper cases, so they are half full.
6. Bake for 18–22 minutes until lightly golden and the sponge bounces back when touched *(a skewer inserted in the centre should come out clean, with no cake mixture on it)*.
7. Remove from the oven and leave in the tin for 3-5 minutes, then transfer the cupcakes to a cooling rack and allow to cool.
8. **To make the icing,** whisk the butter *(using a mixer or hand whisk)* until smooth and pale in colour.
9. Add the sieved icing sugar and vanilla extract and beat slowly to combine. Once combined turn up to full speed and beat for 5 minutes.
10. Gradually add some boiling water, a teaspoon at a time, to get a really light and fluffy consistency.
11. **To ice the cakes,** put a blob of icing on the centre of each cake and spread to cover the whole top using a palette knife *(rotating the cake as you go and working from middle out)*.
12. Using a piping bag decorate each one with a walnut whip shape on top. Sprinkle with edible glitter or sprinkles.

With thanks to Helen Jackson from The Cutnall Green Cake Company.

Chocolate Cupcakes

INGREDIENTS ££

Cake
100g (3¼ oz) plain flour, *sieved*
20g (¾ oz) cocoa powder
140g (5 oz) caster sugar, *sieved*
1½ tsp baking powder
Pinch of salt
40g (1¼ oz) unsalted butter, *cubed*
120ml (2½ fl oz) whole milk
1 large egg
½ tsp vanilla extract *(good quality)*

Icing
120g (4¼ oz) unsalted butter
250g (8 oz) icing sugar, *sieved*
½ tsp vanilla extract *(good quality)*
1-4 tsp boiling water *(depending on room temperature)*
2 tbsp cocoa powder

With thanks to Helen Jackson from The Cutnall Green Cake Company

METHOD

MAKES 12

Preheat the oven to 170ºC / 325ºF / gas mark 3

1. Place 12 paper cases in a muffin tin.
2. Put the sieved flour, cocoa, sugar, baking powder, salt and butter in a food processor, pulse to combine until you get a sandy consistency.
3. Put the egg, vanilla extract and milk in a bowl and roughly beat together with a fork.
4. Turn on the food processor, pour the egg mixture through the feeding tube and blend until smooth *(do not over blend)*.
5. Put the cake mixture into a jug and pour into the paper cases, so they are half full.
6. Bake for 18–22 minutes until lightly golden and the sponge bounces back when touched *(a skewer inserted in the centre should come out clean, with no cake mixture on it)*.
7. Remove from the oven and leave in the tin for 3-5 minutes, then transfer the cupcakes to a cooling rack and allow to cool.
8. **To make the icing**, whisk the butter *(using a mixer or hand whisk)* until smooth and pale in colour.
9. Add the sieved icing sugar, cocoa and vanilla extract and beat slowly to combine. Once combined turn up to full speed and beat for 5 minutes.
10. Gradually add some boiling water, a teaspoon at a time, to get a really light and fluffy consistency.
11. **To ice the cakes**, put a blob of icing on the centre of each cake and spread to cover the whole top using a palette knife *(rotating the cake as you go and working from middle out)*.
12. Using a piping bag decorate each one with a walnut whip shape on top. Sprinkle with edible glitter or sprinkles.

Lemon Cupcakes

INGREDIENTS £

Cake

120g (4¼ oz) plain flour, *sieved*
150g (5¼ oz) caster sugar, *sieved*
1½ tsp baking powder
40g (1¼ oz) unsalted butter, *cubed*
120ml (2½ fl oz) whole milk
1 large egg
1 tbsp lemon zest, *grated*

Icing

120g (4¼ oz) unsalted butter
250g (8 oz) icing sugar, *sieved*
½ tsp vanilla extract *(good quality)*
1-4 tsp boiling water *(depending on room temperature)*
1 tbsp lemon zest, *grated*

With thanks to Helen Jackson from The Cutnall Green Cake Company

METHOD

MAKES 12

Preheat the oven to 170°C / 325°F / gas mark 3

1. Place 12 paper cases in a muffin tin.
2. Put the sieved flour, sugar, baking powder, salt and butter in a food processor, pulse to combine until you get a sandy consistency.
3. Put the egg, lemon zest and milk in a bowl and roughly beat together with a fork.
4. Turn on the food processor, pour the egg mixture through the feeding tube and blend until smooth *(do not over blend)*.
5. Put the cake mixture into a jug and pour into the paper cases, so they are half full.
6. Bake for 18–22 minutes until lightly golden and the sponge bounces back when touched *(a skewer inserted in the centre should come out clean, with no cake mixture on it)*.
7. Remove from the oven and leave in the tin for 3-5 minutes, then transfer the cupcakes to a cooling rack and allow to cool.
8. **To make the icing**, whisk the butter *(using a mixer or hand whisk)* until smooth and pale in colour.
9. Add the sieved icing sugar, vanilla extract and lemon zest and beat slowly to combine. Once combined turn up to full speed and beat for 5 minutes.
10. Gradually add some boiling water, a teaspoon at a time, to get a really light and fluffy consistency.
11. **To ice the cakes**, put a blob of icing on the centre of each cake and spread to cover the whole top using a palette knife *(rotating the cake as you go and working from middle out)*.
12. Using a piping bag decorate each one with a walnut whip shape on top. Sprinkle with edible glitter or sprinkles.

Carrot Cupcakes

INGREDIENTS £

Cake

225g (8 oz) carrots, *peeled*
2 **eggs**
130g (4¾ oz) golden caster sugar, *sieved*
120ml sunflower oil
½ tsp vanilla extract *(good quality)*
2 tbsp orange zest
120g (4¼ oz) plain **flour**, *sieved*
1 tsp bicarbonate of soda
Pinch of salt
1 tsp ground cinnamon
130g (4¾ oz) **raisins**

Icing

90g (3¼ oz) **cream cheese**
225g (8 oz) icing sugar
65g (2¼ oz) unsalted **butter**
½ orange, *grated zest*

With thanks to Helen Jackson from The Cutnall Green Cake Company

METHOD

MAKES 12

Preheat the oven to 170°C / 325°F / gas mark 3

1. Place 12 paper cases in a muffin tin.
2. Finely grate the carrots and squeeze out the liquid. Sandwich the carrots between a double layer of kitchen paper and press thoroughly to dry.
3. Beat the eggs and sugar together in a large bowl until light and fluffy.
4. Add the oil, vanilla and orange zest and beat well.
5. Sieve the flour, bicarbonate of soda, salt and cinnamon into another bowl and gradually add it to the egg mixture, beating well each time you add a little.
6. Stir in the carrots and raisins then spoon into the paper cases and fill them so they are two thirds full.
7. Bake for about 25 minutes until the sponge bounces back when touched *(a skewer inserted in the centre should come out clean, with no cake mixture on it).*
8. Remove from the oven and leave in the tin for 10 minutes, then transfer the cupcakes to a cooling rack and allow to cool.
9. **To make the icing,** put all the ingredients into a bowl and beat using an electric whisk until smooth and pale in colour.
10. **To ice the cakes**, put a blob of icing on the centre of each cake and spread to cover the whole top using a palette knife *(rotating the cake as you go and working from the middle out).*
11. Using a piping bag top each one with a walnut whip shape and sprinkle with decorations of your choice, eg chopped **walnuts**.

BISCUITS & COOKIES

BISCUITS & COOKIES

BISCUITS & COOKIES

Shortbread Biscuits

INGREDIENTS £

55g (2 oz) cornflour
225g (8 oz) plain **flour**
55g (2 oz) icing sugar
225g (8 oz) unsalted **butter**
Caster sugar, *to decorate*

METHOD

1. Blend all ingredients in a food processor. Bring the mixture together using your hands and mould into a large sausage shape.
2. Wrap in cling film and refrigerate for about 30 minutes.
3. Preheat the oven to 170°C / 325°F / gas mark 3. When the mixture is firm, slice and place on a lined baking tray *(allow enough space between the biscuits as they will expand in the oven).*
4. Using a fork, prick each biscuit several times *(to prevent them from rising)* and bake in the oven for 10-12 minutes.
5. On removing from the oven immediately dust the biscuits with caster sugar. Allow the biscuits to cool slightly before transferring to a cooling rack *(as they will be too soft to move).*

Shortbread Biscuits (Gluten Free)

INGREDIENTS £

50g (1¾ oz) caster sugar
80g (2¾ oz) white rice flour
50g (1¾ oz) cornflour
65g (2½ oz) unsalted **butter**

METHOD

Preheat the oven to 170°C / 325°F / Gas mark 3

1. Blend all the ingredients in a food processor and gather into a ball.
2. Make into small evenly sized balls, flatten slightly with a fork and place on a lined baking tray *(allow enough space between the biscuits as they will expand in the oven).*
3. Bake for 10-15 minutes until lightly golden.
4. Remove from the oven and immediately dust the biscuits with caster sugar. Allow to cool slightly before transferring on to a cooling rack *(as they will be too soft to move).*

Butter Biscuits (& other variations)

INGREDIENTS £

40 biscuits:
225g (8 oz) unsalted butter
110g (4 oz) caster sugar
340g (12 oz) self raising flour

20 biscuits:
110g (4 oz) unsalted butter
55g (2 oz) caster sugar
170g (6 oz) self raising flour

10 biscuits:
55g (2 oz) unsalted butter
30g (1 oz) caster sugar
85g (3 oz) self raising flour

Variations:
Chocolate chips / raisins / chopped nuts / coconut / ground cinnamon / golden syrup / cocoa / ground ginger / grated lemon or orange zest / chopped glacé cherries / oats etc.

METHOD

Preheat the oven to 180°C / 350°F / gas mark 4

1. Blend all the ingredients in a food processor and gather into a ball *(they are delicious plain but if you want to add chocolate chips or chopped nuts etc. add your chosen ingredients to the mixture and mix in by hand).*
2. Make into evenly sized small balls *(like a large walnut),* flatten slightly with a fork and place on a lined baking tray *(allow enough space between the biscuits as they will expand in the oven).*
3. Bake for 7-10 minutes until golden brown.
4. On removing from the oven, immediately dust the biscuits with caster sugar. Allow the biscuits to cool slightly before transferring to a cooling rack *(as they will be too soft to move).*

Oatcakes

INGREDIENTS £

55g (2 oz) medium **oatmeal**
55g (2 oz) plain **flour**
30g (1 oz) salted **butter** or lard
¼ tsp salt
2 tbsp water
1 tbsp **Parmesan** *(optional)*
½ tbsp **milk**, *to glaze*

Variations: **Cranberries** / thyme / rosemary / roasted garlic / fennel or poppy seeds etc.

METHOD

Preheat the oven to 180°C / 350°F / gas mark 4

1. Blend all the ingredients *(except for the milk)* in a food processor.
2. Knead the mixture on a floured surface *(add a little more water or flour if necessary)* and add a flavour of your choice, or leave plain.
3. Roll out thinly and cut to required size. To make 12 large oatcakes to serve with cheese use a 7 cm (2¾ inch) plain cutter, to make 30-35 small oatcakes for a canapé, use a 3½ cm (1⅜ inch) plain cutter.
4. Glaze with milk and bake on a lined baking tray until slightly golden: 8-10 minutes for small oatcakes and approx 15 minutes for the large oatcakes. Allow to cool on a cooling rack.

Chocolate & Orange Biscuits

INGREDIENTS ££

30g (1 oz) margarine
45g (1½ oz) lard
85g (3 oz) caster sugar
110g (4 oz) plain flour
1 tsp baking powder
45g (1½ oz) plain chocolate, *chopped*
1 orange, *grated zest*
½ tbsp orange juice
Caster sugar, *to decorate*

METHOD

MAKES 18

Preheat the oven to 180°C / 350°F / gas mark 4

1. Mix all ingredients, except the chocolate, in the food processor and then stir in the chocolate.
2. Roll out on a floured board and cut out the biscuits using a pastry cutter *(7 cm / 2½ inch in diameter)*. Place on a lined baking tray, sprinkle with caster sugar and bake for about 10-15 minutes until golden *(allow enough space between the biscuits as they will expand in the oven)*.

Chocolate Krispies

INGREDIENTS £

55g (2 oz) caster sugar
55g (2 oz) unsalted butter
2 level tbsp golden syrup
1 tbsp cocoa
55g (2 oz) Rice Krispies

METHOD

1. Gently melt the sugar, butter, golden syrup and cocoa in a large saucepan.
2. Remove from the heat and carefully fold in the Rice Krispies.
3. Divide the mixture into individual paper cases and allow to cool.

Peanut Butter Cookies

INGREDIENTS £

85g (3 oz) unsalted butter
55g (2 oz) peanut butter
110g (4 oz) caster sugar
85g (3 oz) wholemeal flour
55g (2 oz) plain flour

METHOD

Preheat the oven to 180°C / 350°F / gas mark 4

1. Blend all the ingredients in a food processor and gather into a ball *(the mixture should be quite dry).*
2. Roll into small balls and place on a lined baking tray *(allow enough space between the biscuits as they will expand in the oven),* flatten with a fork and bake for 10-15 minutes.
3. Allow to cool for 10 minutes before placing on a cooling rack.

Marshmallow Krispies

INGREDIENTS ££

110g (4 oz) marshmallows
150g (5½ oz) toffee
110g (4 oz) margarine
170g (6 oz) Rice Krispies

METHOD

1. Melt the margarine, toffee and marshmallows in a large saucepan over a low heat.
2. Remove from the heat and gently stir in the Rice Krispies.
3. Transfer the mixture to a square tin lined with cling film, level and press firmly into place.
4. Allow to cool and then cut into squares.

Chocolate Brownies

INGREDIENTS ££

250g (9 oz) plain **chocolate**
250g (9 oz) unsalted **butter**
500g (1 lb 2 oz) caster sugar
250g (9 oz) plain **flour**
100g (3½ oz) **walnuts**, *chopped*
1 tsp **baking powder**
Pinch of salt
4 **eggs**

METHOD

Preheat the oven to 160°C / 315°F / gas mark 3

1. Gently melt the chocolate and butter in a large saucepan and then remove from the heat.
2. Stir in the other ingredients except for the eggs.
3. When the ingredients are combined stir in the eggs, then pour into a 30 x 20 cm *(12 x 8 inch)* tin lined with greased baking paper and bake for 40 minutes. *(The perfect brownie should be crunchy on the outside and gooey on the inside).*
4. Leave to cool in the tin, then peel off the baking paper and cut into squares.

Twisted Langues de Chat

To be served as an accompaniment to a pudding

INGREDIENTS £

50g (2 oz) unsalted butter
50g (2 oz) caster sugar
1 egg white
50g (2 oz) plain flour
3 drops vanilla essence

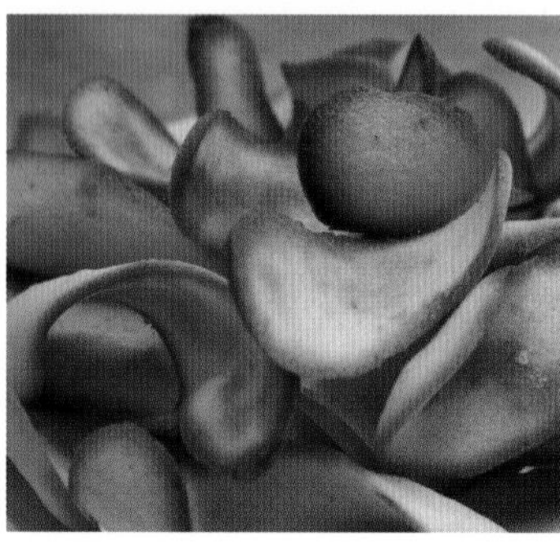

METHOD

MAKES 12

Preheat the oven to 220°C / 425°F / gas mark 7

1. Blend the butter and sugar in the mini food processor, add the egg white and mix until light and fluffy.
2. Add the flour and vanilla essence and blend for a further 10 seconds.
3. Line a baking tray and place the mixture into a piping bag with a 1 cm (3/8 inch) plain nozzle.
4. Pipe pencil thickness lines, approximately 6 cm (2 1/2 inch) long, leaving plenty of space between each one because they expand in the oven.
5. Bake for 4-5 minutes until the edges turn brown and the centre is still white.
6. Remove from the tray while hot and shape around a rolling pin or the handle of a wooden spoon, then leave to cool on a cooling rack.

They keep in an airtight container for a few weeks.

Sticky Almond Shortbread

INGREDIENTS ££

Shortbread Base
170g (6 oz) plain flour
55g (2 oz) caster sugar
110g (4 oz) unsalted butter

Topping
6 tbsp jam
85g (3 oz) flaked almonds
30g (1 oz) caster sugar
30g (1 oz) unsalted butter
1 tbsp milk

METHOD

Preheat the oven to 180°C / 350°F / gas mark 4

1. Blend the shortbread ingredients in the food processor until just combined.
2. Press the shortbread mix into a tin approximately 18 x 28 cm (7 x 11 inch) in size, lined with greased baking paper.
3. Stir the jam in a small bowl to soften then spread it evenly over the shortbread.
4. Place the rest of the topping ingredients into a small saucepan and warm until the butter has melted.
5. Spread the mixture evenly over the jam and bake for 20-25 minutes.
6. Leave to cool for 5 minutes. Take out of the tin and cut into pieces while still warm.

Chocolate Cookies (Gluten Free)

INGREDIENTS ££

15g (½oz) butter
140g (5 oz) Bournville chocolate or low cocoa chocolate
112g (4 oz) sugar
1 egg
½ tsp vanilla essence
50g (1¾ oz) gluten-free white flour
⅛ tsp gluten free baking powder
45g (1½ oz) chocolate chips
Pinch of salt

Variations: Milk or white chocolate chips / cranberries / nuts etc

METHOD

Preheat the oven to 180°C / 350°F / Gas mark 4

1. Melt the butter and chocolate in a saucepan on a very low heat *(do not allow to boil)*.
2. Whisk the sugar and egg together in a bowl until light and fluffy.
3. Stir in the chocolate mixture, then the vanilla essence, flour, baking powder, chocolate chips and salt.
4. Spoon the mixture on to a lined baking tray, so that each biscuit is a little bigger in size than a walnut. *(Allow lots of space between the biscuits as they will really spread in the oven)*.
5. Bake for approximately 10 minutes until the biscuits are cooked around the edges but still slightly shiny in the middle.
6. Allow the biscuits to cool slightly before transferring to a cooling rack *(they will be too soft to move)*.
7. Dust with icing sugar before serving.

Flapjacks

INGREDIENTS £

200g (7 oz) butter
200g (7 oz) sugar
4 tbsp golden syrup or honey
400g (14 oz) rolled oats
85g (3 oz) chocolate chips
(optional)

Variations:
Pumpkin seeds / sunflower seeds / apricots / cranberries / raisins / dates / white chocolate / nuts.

METHOD

Preheat the oven to 180°C / 350°F / gas mark 4

1. Line a 20 cm (8 inch) square baking tray with greased baking paper.
2. Melt the butter, sugar and golden syrup / honey in a large saucepan over a low heat.
3. Stir in the oats and chocolate chips, transfer the mixture to the baking tray, level and press firmly into place.
4. Bake for 20-25 minutes until pale golden in colour.
5. Leave in the tin to cool slightly and cut into squares while still warm.

Oat Biscuits

INGREDIENTS £

Makes 8 biscuits

60g (2¼ oz) unsalted butter
½ tbsp golden syrup
60g (2¼ oz) self raising flour
60g (2¼ oz) porridge oats
60g (2¼ oz) soft brown sugar
¼ tsp bicarbonate of soda
25g (1 oz) chocolate, *to decorate (optional)*

Makes 16 biscuits

125g (4½ oz) unsalted butter
1 tbsp golden syrup
125g (4½ oz) self raising flour
125g (4½ oz) porridge oats
125g (4½ oz) soft brown sugar
½ tsp bicarbonate of soda
55g (2 oz) chocolate, *to decorate (optional)*

METHOD

Preheat the oven to 160°C / 320°F / gas mark 2-3

1. Melt the butter and syrup in a saucepan, remove from the heat and allow to cool slightly.
2. Add the rest of the ingredients and mix together into a dough.
3. Divide the mixture into even sized small balls, place on a lined baking tray and flatten slightly with a fork *(allow enough space between each biscuit as they will expand in the oven).*
4. Bake for approximately 15 minutes until golden brown.
5. Allow the biscuits to cool slightly before transferring onto a cooling rack *(as they will be too soft to move).*
6. Melt the chocolate in a bain-marie and drizzle chocolate across the biscuits.

Millionaire's Shortbread

INGREDIENTS ££

Shortbread
55g (2 oz) cornflour
225g (8 oz) plain flour
55g (2 oz) icing sugar
225g (8 oz) unsalted butter

Caramel
110g (4 oz) margarine
110g (4 oz) sugar
2 tbsp golden syrup
170g tin condensed milk

110g (4 oz) plain chocolate, *for the topping*

METHOD

Preheat the oven to 180°C / 350°F / gas mark 4

1. Blend the shortbread ingredients in a food processor.
2. Bring the mixture together using your hands and press into a tin approximately 18 x 28 cm (7 x 11 inch) in size, lined with greased baking paper.
3. Using a fork, prick the base *(to prevent it from rising)* and bake for about 20-25 minutes.
4. To make the caramel, place all the caramel ingredients in a saucepan and heat slowly until the margarine has melted.
5. Bring to the boil and simmer, stirring continuously. After about 8 minutes test to see if it has reached the 'soft ball' stage *(when a small amount of the caramel mixture is dropped into cold water it forms a soft ball).*
6. Cook for a couple more minutes then pour over the shortbread and leave to set.
7. Melt the chocolate in a bain-marie and spread over the top. When the chocolate has set cut into slices.

BREAKFASTS

BREAKFASTS

BREAKFASTS

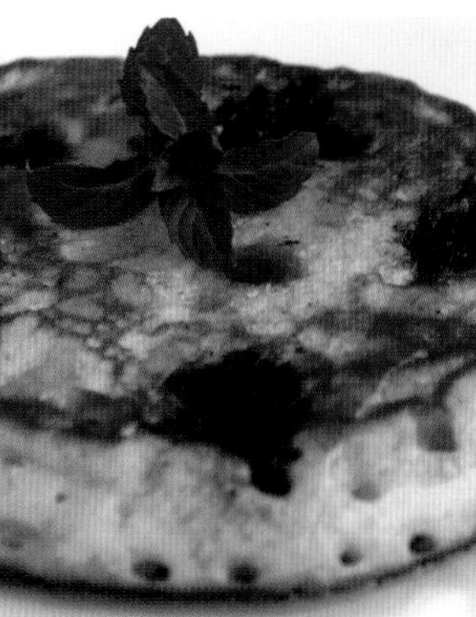

American Pancakes

INGREDIENTS ££

Pancake Batter Mix
1 egg
200ml (7 fl oz) milk
180g (6¼ oz) self raising flour
40g (1¼ oz) sugar
½ tsp baking powder

Knob of butter
Blueberries
Maple syrup

METHOD

SERVES 10

1. **To make the batter**, blend all the ingredients in a food processor.
2. Melt the butter in a frying pan, spoon about 2 tbsp of the batter into the pan to make a pancake. *(The pancake should be about 9-10 cm / 3½ - 4 inch in diameter).*
3. Gently push 5 blueberries into the batter.
4. When large bubbles start to appear, turn and cook the other side until golden.

Serve with maple syrup.

Poached Egg with Black Pudding

INGREDIENTS ££

1 slice of brown bread
Vegetable oil
3 baby tomatoes
Olive oil
Fresh chives, *chopped, keep two whole chives for presentation*
1 slice of black pudding *(about 1 cm / ⅜ inch thick)*
1 egg
Dash of malt vinegar

METHOD

SERVES 1

1. Use a smooth edged pastry cutter to cut out a circle of bread, slightly larger than the diameter of the black pudding and fry on both sides in a little vegetable oil.
2. Cut the tomatoes in half across the core and cook in a little olive oil for a few minutes. Season and stir in the chives.
3. Slice the black pudding and fry in a little vegetable oil for about 5 minutes on each side *(keep warm while you poach the egg).*
4. **To poach the egg**, break 1 egg into a ramekin. Bring a medium sized saucepan of water up to the boil, then turn down the heat so that it is just off the boil. Add a dash of vinegar *(to help keep the white together).*
5. Stir the water vigorously to create a vortex and carefully, but quickly, pour the egg into the vortex *(the swirling water helps keep the egg together).* Leave to cook for about 3 minutes.
6. Use a slotted spoon to remove the egg from the water and drain well.

To serve, place the black pudding on the fried bread. Top first with the poached egg *(turn the egg over to serve as the other side looks nicer)* and then the tomatoes, garnish with chives and serve immediately.

Breakfast Pancetta / Bacon Baskets

INGREDIENTS ££

Butter, *for greasing*
1 slice of white **bread**, *crust removed*
1 rasher of pancetta / streaky bacon, *cut in half*
1 cherry tomato, *sliced*
15g (½ oz) **cheese**, *grated*
1 **egg**

METHOD

SERVES 1

Preheat the oven to 180°C / 350°F / Gas mark 4

1. Grease a muffin tin with butter and line with greaseproof paper.
2. Press the bread into the tin, pushing it down well so that it holds the shape of the tin.
3. Place the bacon on top, creating a basket and bake in the oven for 8 minutes.
4. Remove from the oven and top with the slices of tomato. Sprinkle over the cheese and crack and egg over the top.
5. Season and bake for about 10 minutes until the white of the egg is firm.

Serve immediately.

Eggy Bread

INGREDIENTS £

1-2 eggs
Fresh bread, *sliced*
Butter

METHOD

SERVES 1

1. Break an egg or two into a shallow dish, season and beat with a fork.
2. Place the bread *(preferably French bread)* in the bowl for 5 minutes so that it soaks up the egg.
3. Melt a generous knob of butter in a non-stick frying pan, when it starts to bubble add the slices of bread and brown each side.

Boiled Egg

INGREDIENTS £

1 egg
Butter
1 slice of bread, *toasted*

METHOD

SERVES 1

1. Fill a pan with water from the kettle so it will just cover the egg, gently lower the egg into the water and simmer for 4 minutes *(6 minutes if cooking at altitude)* for a runny yolk. *(Eggs crack when used straight from the fridge, so place into warm water, bring to the boil and simmer for less time).*
2. Serve immediately with hot, buttered toast.

Baked Eggs

INGREDIENTS ££

2 eggs
2 tsp double cream
Butter
Cheese, *grated*

METHOD

SERVES 1

Preheat the oven to 180°C / 350°F / Gas mark 4

1. Butter the inside of a ramekin.
2. Add a generous teaspoon of cream and then break two eggs into it.
3. Season with salt and pepper and spoon over a second teaspoon of cream.
4. Top with grated cheese and bake in the oven until set.

Eggs Benedict & Other Variations

INGREDIENTS ££

½ **muffin**, *toasted and buttered*
1 slice of ham or cooked bacon
1 **egg**, *poached (page 391)*
Fresh chives, *chopped*
Hollandaise sauce *(page 122)*

METHOD

SERVES 1

1. Put a slice of ham or bacon on the muffin, top with a poached egg and hot hollandaise sauce and sprinkle with chives and black pepper. Serve immediately.

Variations:

Black Pudding Benedict
Substitute ham or bacon with black pudding *(to cook the black pudding, fry for about 5 minutes on each side).*

Egg Florentine
Substitute ham or bacon with spinach *(to cook the spinach sauté in butter for a few minutes).*

Eggs Benedict with Smoked Salmon and Rocket
Substitute the ham or bacon with smoked salmon and rocket.

Eggs Atlantic or Eggs Hemingway *(also known as Eggs Royale, Eggs Montreal, Eggs Benjamin)* Substitute ham or bacon with smoked salmon.

Eggs Blackstone
Substitute ham or bacon with a slice of tomato.

Eggs Mornay
Substitute Hollandaise with Mornay sauce *(which is a Béchamel sauce* with grated *Gruyère and Parmesan cheese added).*

Portobello Benedict
Substitute the ham or bacon with a cooked Portobello mushroom.

Eggs John Scott
Substitute the Hollandaise sauce with brown sauce.

Oscar Benedict *(also known as Eggs Oscar)*
Substitute the ham or bacon with asparagus and lump crab meat.

Eggs Provençal
Substitute the Hollandaise sauce with Béarnaise sauce.

Russian Easter Benedict
Substitute the Hollandaise sauce with a Béchamel sauce flavoured with lemon juice and mustard and top with black caviar.

Eggs Chesapeake
Substitute the ham or bacon with crab cake.

Fried Egg

INGREDIENTS £

Vegetable oil
1 **egg**
1 slice of **bread**, *toasted*
Butter

METHOD

SERVES 1

1. Warm some vegetable oil in a non-stick frying pan.
2. Break an egg into the pan and cook over a medium to high heat until all the white has set. Spoon the oil over the yolk.
3. Serve on a piece of buttered toast. Season with black pepper and serve immediately.

Poached Eggs

INGREDIENTS £

Water
Malt vinegar
1 **egg** *(very fresh)*

METHOD

SERVES 1

1. Break the egg in to a ramekin.
2. Bring a medium sized saucepan of water up to the boil and turn down the heat so that it is just off the boil. Add a dash of vinegar *(to help keep the white together)*.
3. Stir the water vigorously to create a whirlpool and carefully but quickly, pour the egg into the vortex *(the swirling water helps keep the egg together)*. Leave to cook for about 3 minutes.
4. Using a slotted spoon, remove the egg from the water, drain well and serve *(turn the egg over to serve as the other side looks better)*.

French Toast (Pain Perdu)

INGREDIENTS £

1-2 **eggs**
1-2 tbsp sugar
½ tsp ground cinnamon *(optional)*
Brioche, *sliced*
Butter

METHOD

SERVES 1

1. Break an egg or two into a shallow dish, add the sugar, cinnamon and beat with a fork.
2. Place the brioche in the bowl for 5 minutes so that it soaks up the egg.
3. Melt a generous knob of butter in a non-stick frying pan. When it starts to bubble add the brioche and brown each side.

English Breakfast on the Run!

INGREDIENTS £££

1 cocktail **sausage**
2 slices of streaky bacon, *halved*
1 mushroom, *sliced*
1 **egg**, *beaten*
Butter
1 slice of **bread**, *crusts removed*
½ cherry tomato

METHOD

SERVES 1

Preheat the oven to 180°C / 350°F / Gas mark 4

1. Prick the sausage with a fork and cook in the oven for 15 minutes.
2. Fry the bacon in a hot frying pan until it just starts to brown.
3. Add the mushrooms to the beaten egg and season.
4. Butter the bread on both sides and press it into the base of a muffin tin *(to make a basket)* and bake for 10 minutes.
5. Arrange the bacon slices around the edge of the bread basket. Place the sausage and tomato in the opposite corners and pour the egg mixture into the centre.
6. Bake for 12-15 minutes until just firm.
7. Top with chopped chives and black pepper and serve immediately.

Scrambled Eggs

INGREDIENTS £

2 **eggs**
Butter
1 slice of **bread**, *toasted*

METHOD

SERVES 1

1. Break two eggs into a small bowl, season and beat with a fork.
2. Melt a generous knob of butter in a non-stick pan.
3. Add the eggs and cook over a medium heat. Stir continuously, scraping the egg from the base of the pan as it cooks. *(It is easy to overcook as it will continue to cook once the pan is taken off the heat. It needs to look wet, if you over cook the eggs it will look dry).*
4. Serve on a piece of buttered toast. Season with black pepper and serve immediately.

Chef's Omelette

INGREDIENTS £

3 **eggs**
15g (½ oz) **butter**
30g (1 oz) **cheese**, *grated*

Filling suggestions; ham and **cheese**, left over vegetables, bacon, cooked vegetables such as onion, sliced potato and mushrooms

METHOD

SERVES 1

1. Break the eggs into a small bowl, season and beat with a fork.
2. Melt the butter in a small non-stick frying pan, add the eggs and tilt the pan to spread evenly. Cook over a medium heat.
3. As the egg cooks, bring the edges to the middle so that the uncooked egg runs to the bottom of the pan. Continue to do this until the egg is just starting to set.
4. Sprinkle with your chosen filling, top with cheese and fold over the omelette. Leave to cook for a few minutes to warm the filling and to finish cooking the egg.

Serve immediately.

Blueberry & Apple Compote with Greek Yoghurt

INGREDIENTS ££

30g (1 oz) **butter**
4-6 eating apples, *peeled, cored and sliced*
⅛ tsp mixed spice
1 tbsp golden syrup
200g (7 oz) blueberries
Greek **yoghurt**
Soft brown sugar

METHOD

SERVES 6

1. Melt the butter in a non-stick frying pan and gently fry the apples for about 5 minutes.
2. Add the mixed spice and golden syrup and continue to cook for a few minutes until the apples are almost cooked.
3. Add the blueberries and cook for about 2 minutes to warm through.
4. Divide the fruit between 6 presentation glasses.
5. Spoon over the yoghurt and top with a sprinkling of brown sugar.

INFORMATION

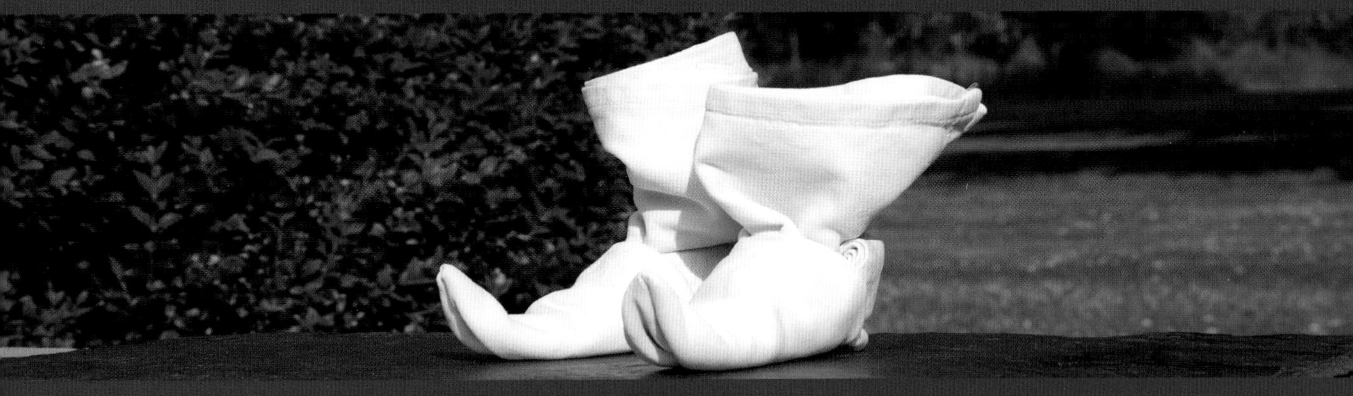

INFORMATION

INFORMATION

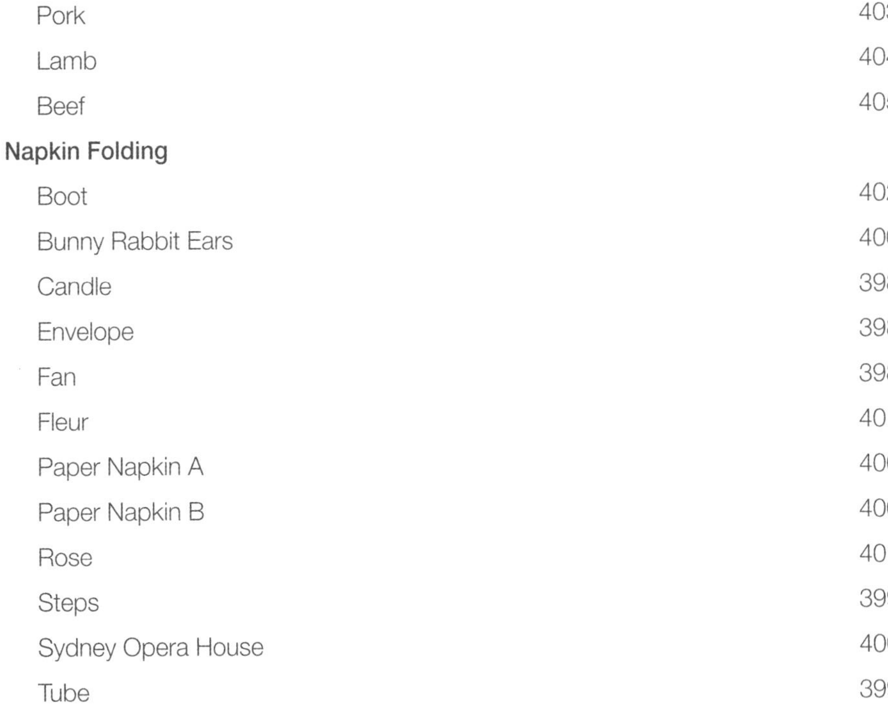

INFORMATION

Napkin Folding

FAN

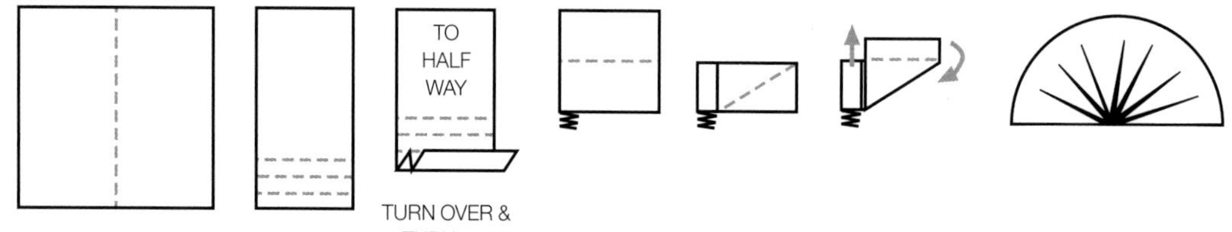

CANDLE

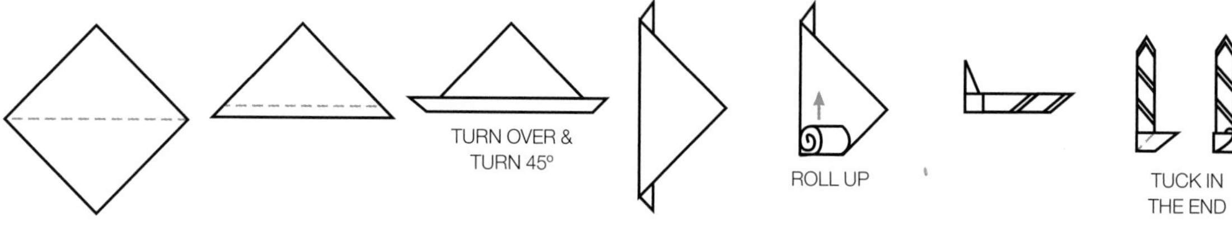

ENVELOPE

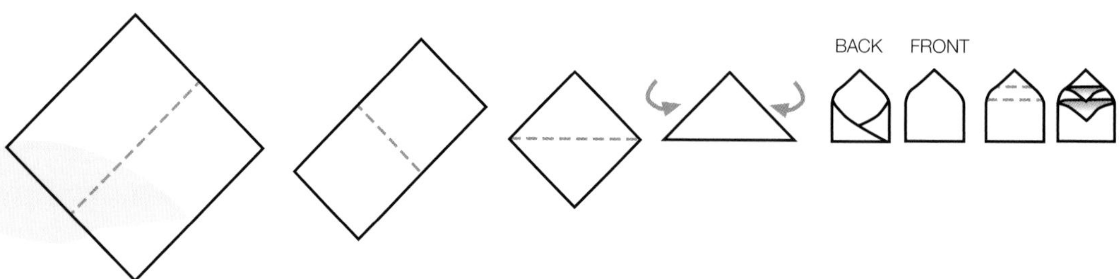

INFORMATION

Napkin Folding

STEPS

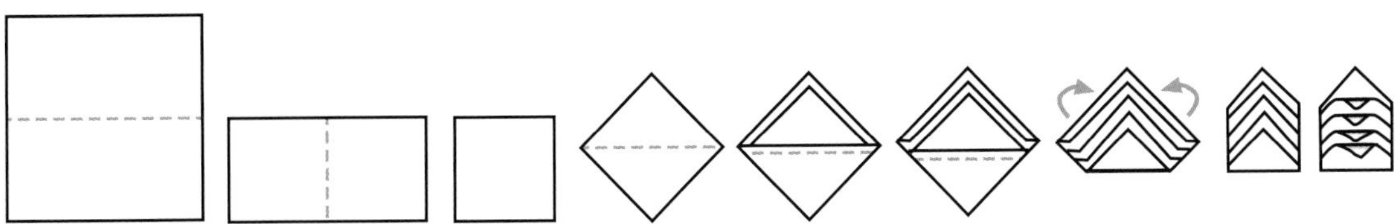

TUBE

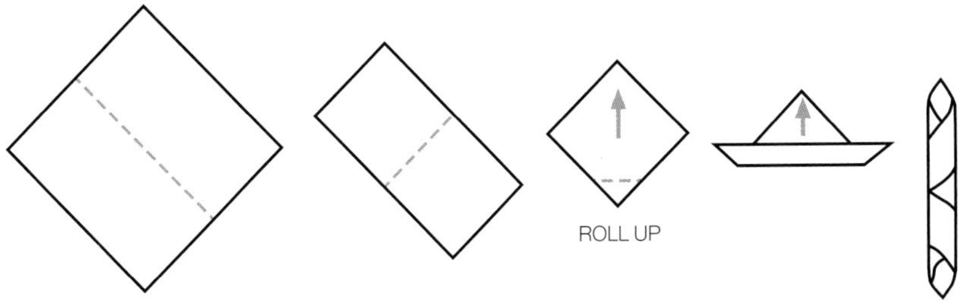
ROLL UP

WATERLILY

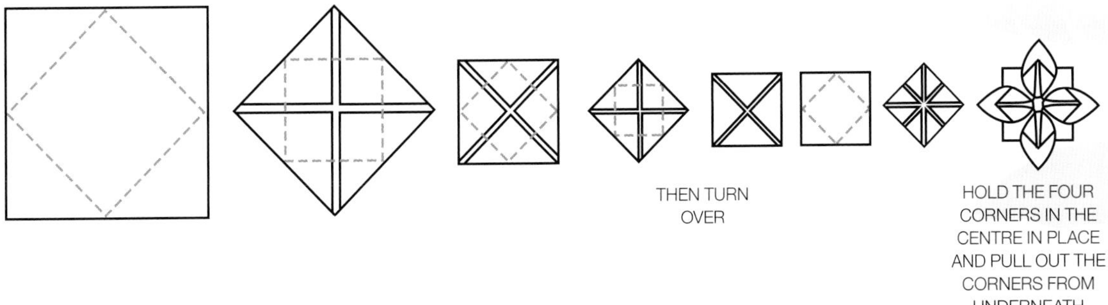
THEN TURN
OVER
HOLD THE FOUR
CORNERS IN THE
CENTRE IN PLACE
AND PULL OUT THE
CORNERS FROM
UNDERNEATH

Napkin Folding

SYDNEY OPERA HOUSE

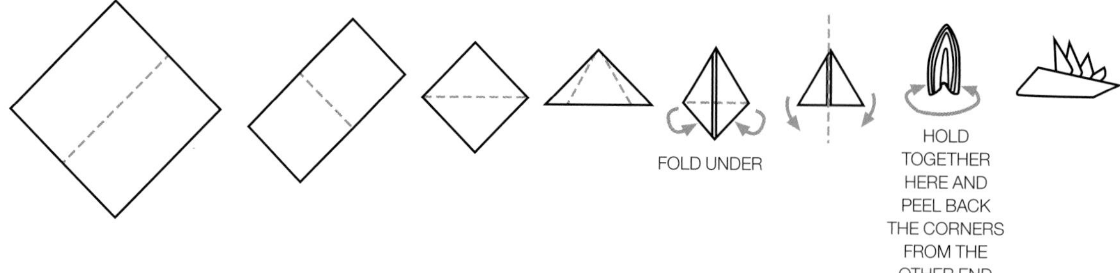
FOLD UNDER
HOLD TOGETHER HERE AND PEEL BACK THE CORNERS FROM THE OTHER END

BUNNY RABBIT EARS

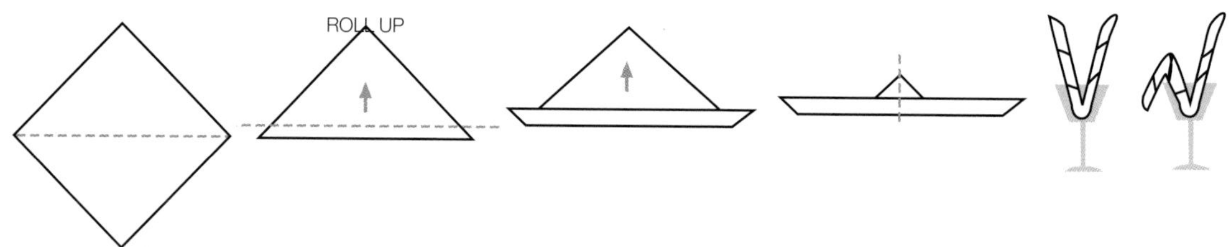
ROLL UP

PAPER A

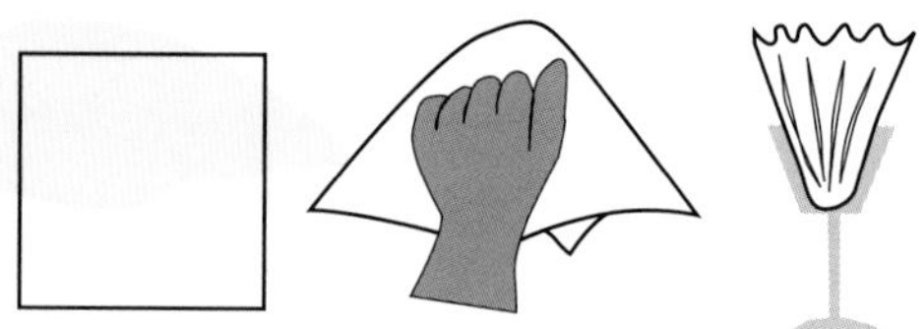

PAPER B

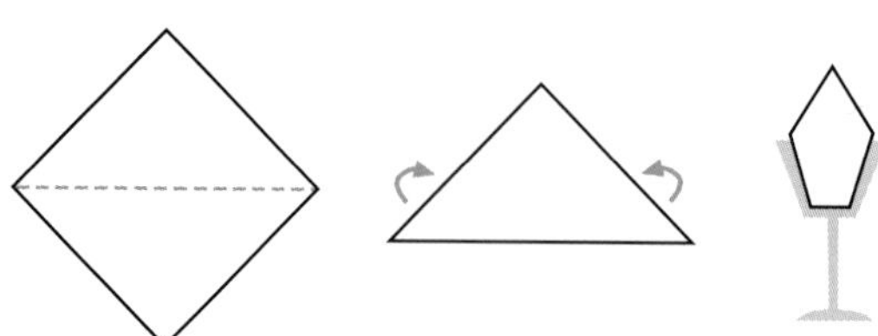

Napkin Folding

ROSE

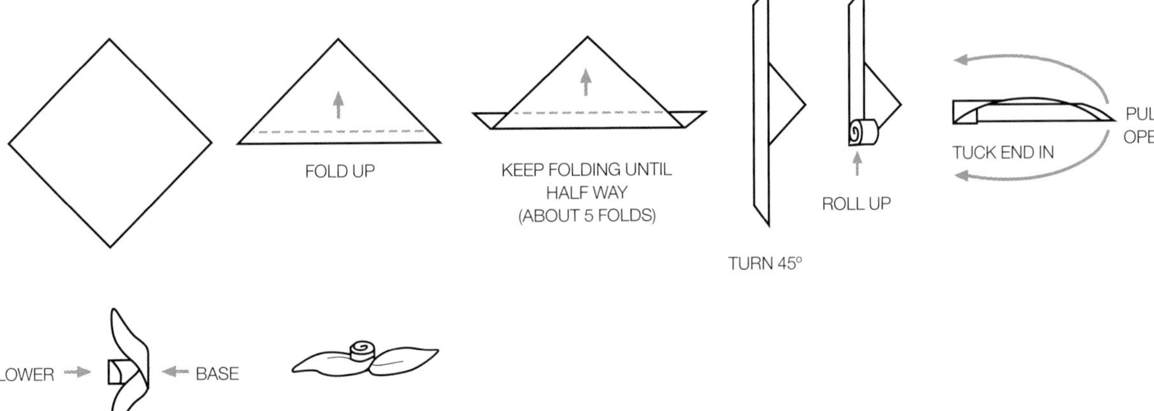

FLEUR

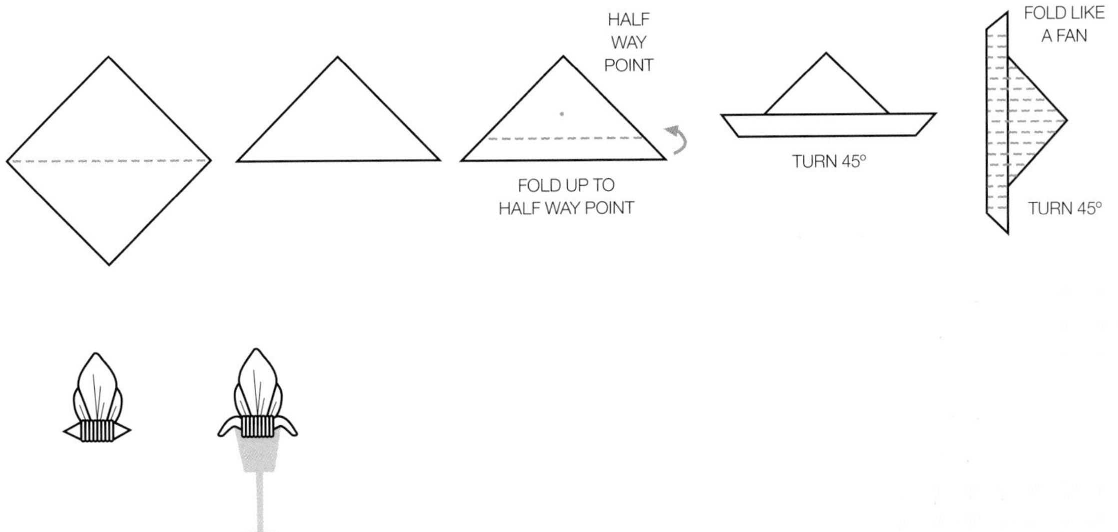

Napkin Folding

BOOT

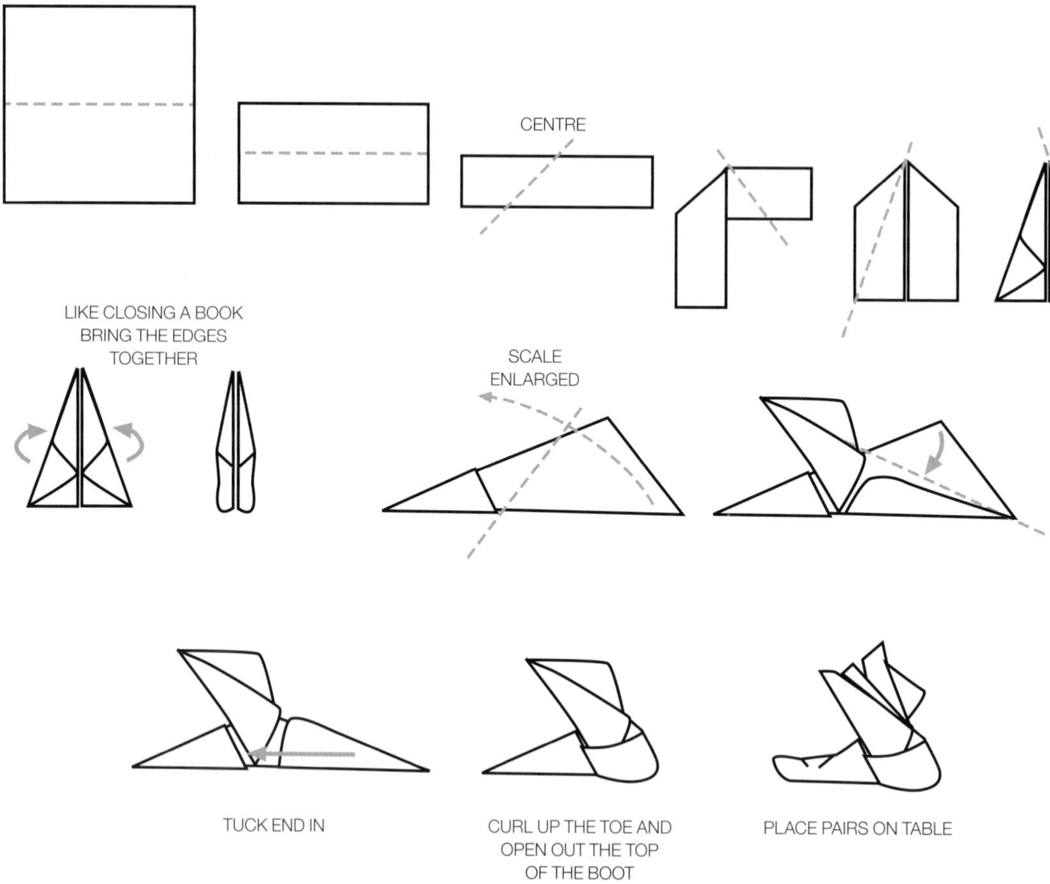

CENTRE

LIKE CLOSING A BOOK BRING THE EDGES TOGETHER

SCALE ENLARGED

TUCK END IN

CURL UP THE TOE AND OPEN OUT THE TOP OF THE BOOT

PLACE PAIRS ON TABLE

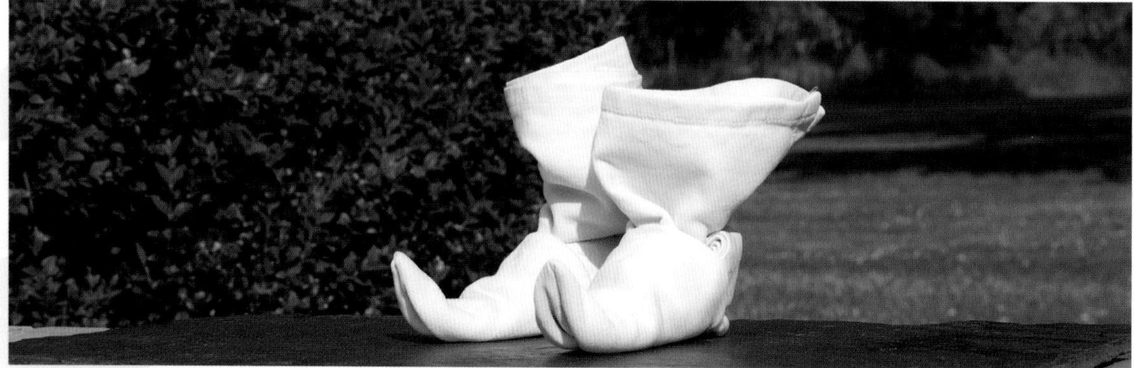

Pork

ENGLISH CUTS

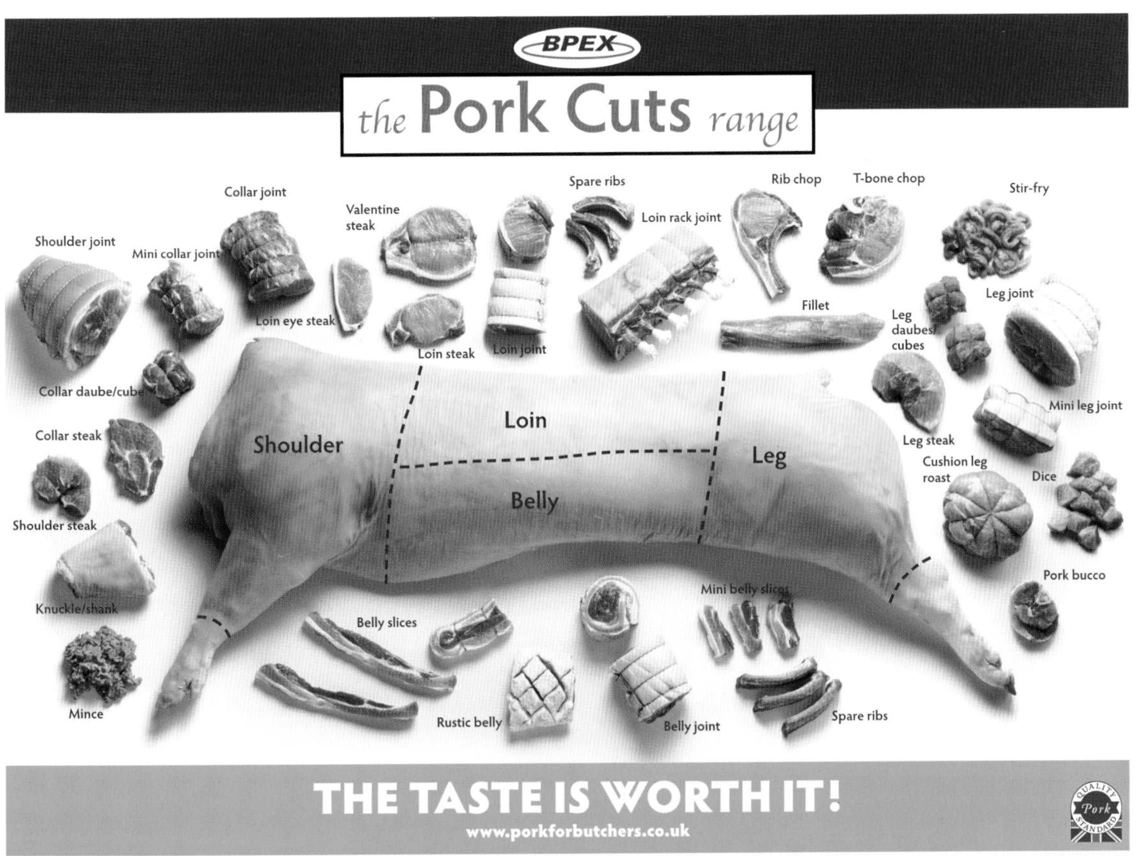

Orchards Cookery thanks EBLEX and BPEX for permission to print the meat images.

Lamb

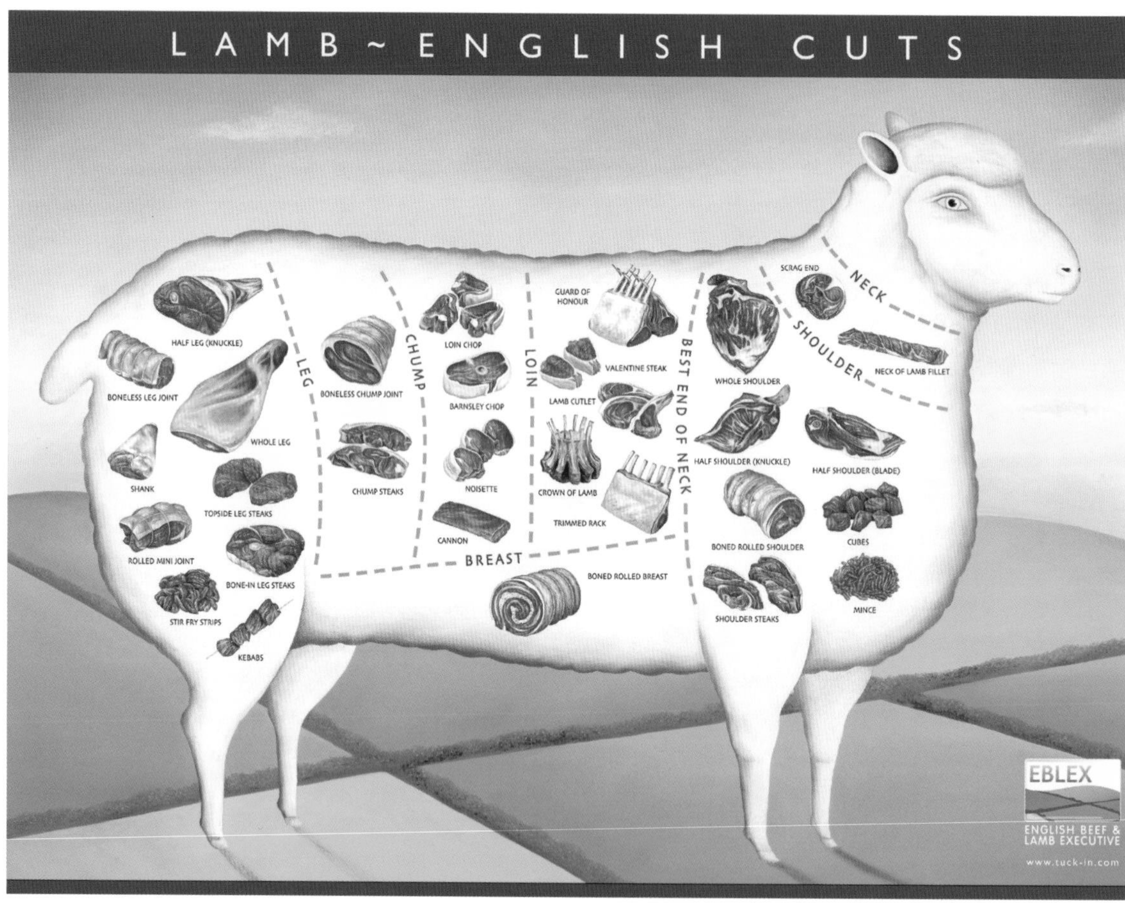

Orchards Cookery thanks EBLEX and BPEX for permission to print the meat images.

Beef

Orchards Cookery thanks EBLEX and BPEX for permission to print the meat images.

Quantities to Cook

PRODUCE	AMOUNT TO COOK *METRIC*	*IMPERIAL*	SERVES
Beef			
Roasting (on the bone)	340g	12 oz	Per person
Roasting (off the bone)	170–225g	6-8 oz	Per person
Diced, for casseroles	170–225g	6-8 oz	Per person
Fillet (Beef Wellington)	1.8 kg	4 lb	10 people
Mince, for spaghetti bolognese	55g	2 oz	Per person
Mince, for lasagne	85g	3 oz	Per person
Mince, for sheperds pie, hamburgers	170g	6 oz	Per person
Steak	170–225g	6-8 oz	Per person
Lamb			
Diced, for casseroles	285g	10 oz	Per person
Leg, for roasting	1.35kg	3 lb	3-4 people
Leg, for roasting	1.8kg	4 lb	4-5 people
Leg, for roasting	2.7kg	6 lb	7-8 people
Pork			
Cutlet (medallions)	170g	6 oz	Per person
Diced, for casseroles	170g	6 oz	Per person
Roast leg or loin (on the bone)	340g	12 oz	Per person
Roast leg or loin (off the bone) for stuffing	200g	7 oz	Per person
Chicken			
Whole bird, medium size	1	1	4-6 people
Breast	1	1	Per person
Turkey			
Breast	175-200g	6-7 oz	Per person
Duck			
Breast (French are larger in size)	1	1	2 people
Fish			
Fillet, boned	170g	5-6 oz	Per person
Vegetables			
Most vegetables	110g	4 oz	Per person
French beans, peas	50-60g	2 oz	Per person
Leafy vegetables, eg. cabbage	75-100g	3-4 oz	Per person
Potatoes, new	75-100g	3-4 oz	Per person
Potatoes, old	175-225g	6-8 oz	Per person
Soup	290ml	10 fl oz / ½ pt	Per person

Conversion Tables

WEIGHT

METRIC	IMPERIAL
7 g	1/4 oz
15 g	1/2 oz
30 g	1 oz
55 g	2 oz
85 g	3 oz
110 g	4 oz (1/4 lb)
140 g	5 oz
170 g	6 oz
200 g	7 oz
225 g	8 oz (1/2 lb)
255 g	9 oz
285 g	10 oz
310 g	11 oz
340 g	12 oz (3/4 lb)
370 g	13 oz
400 g	14 oz
425 g	15 oz
450 g	16 oz (1 lb)
560 g	1 1/4 lb
675 g	1 1/2 lb
900 g	2 lb
1.35 kg	3 lb
1.8 kg	4 lb
2.3 kg	5 lb
2.7 kg	6 lb
3.2 kg	7 lb
3.6 kg	8 lb
4.0 kg	9 lb
4.5 kg	10 lb

LIQUIDS

Imperial	ml	fl oz
1 tsp	5 ml	
1 tbsp	15 ml	1/2 fl oz
	30 ml	1 fl oz
	55 ml	2 fl oz
1/4 pint	150 ml	5 fl oz
	200 ml	7 fl oz
1/2 pint	290 ml	10 fl oz
	400 ml	14 fl oz
3/4 pint	425 ml	15 fl oz
	500 ml	17.5 fl oz
1 pt	570 ml	20 fl oz
1 1/2 pts	900 ml	30 fl oz
1 3/4 pts	1 L	35 fl oz
2 pts	1.1 L	40 fl oz
3 pts	1.7 L	60 fl oz
8 pts	4.5 L	160 fl oz

OVEN TEMPERATURES

°C	°F	Gas Mark	Terms used
80	175	–	
100	200	–	COOL
110	225	–	
130	250	1	
140	275	1	VERY SLOW
150	300	2	SLOW
170	325	3	SLOW
180	350	4	MODERATE
190	375	5	MODERATELY HOT
200	400	6	FAIRLY HOT
220	425	7	HOT
230	450	8	
240	475	8	VERY HOT

KEY

tbsp	tablespoon
tsp	teaspoon
g	grams
kg	kilograms
oz	ounces
lb / lbs	pounds
ml	millilitres
pt / pts	pints
fl oz	fluid ounces
cm	centimetres
£	is cheap to make
££	
£££	is expensive to make

* Can be left at this stage and continued later.

USEFUL MEASUREMENTS

1 egg white	28 ml	1 fl oz
1 rounded tbsp (flour or sugar)	30 g	1 oz
1 cup of flour	140 g	5 oz
1 cup of sugar	225 g	8 oz

The weights, measures and temperatures used in this book are simplified for cookery purposes and are not precise.

ALLERGENS

Pink text in the list of ingredients highlights food allergens, see page 2

Cadbury
DAIRY MILK
AGA

INDEX

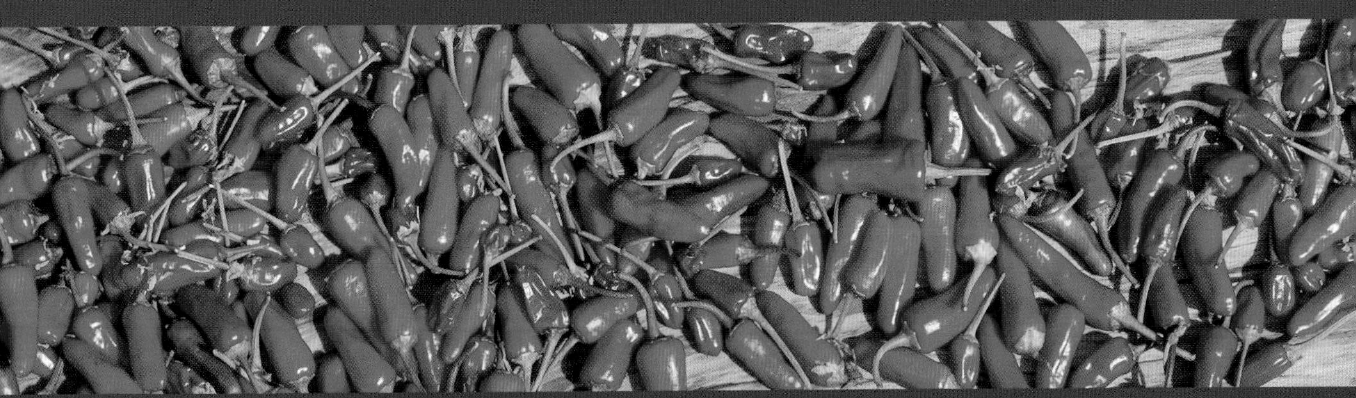

INDEX

INDEX

INDEX

INDEX

INDEX

INDEX

INDEX

INDEX

INDEX

INDEX

INDEX

INDEX

INDEX

INDEX

INDEX

INDEX

INDEX

INDEX

INDEX

INDEX

INDEX